PRACTICAL
MAGICK

Also by Mitch Horowitz

Modern Occultism

Occult America

One Simple Idea

The Miracle Club

Uncertain Places

Daydream Believer

The Seeker's Guide to the Secret Teachings of All Ages

The Miracle Habits

The Miracle Month

Secrets of Self-Mastery

The Miracle of a Definite Chief Aim

The Power of the Master Mind

Magician of the Beautiful

Mind As Builder

Cosmic Habit Force

Happy Warriors

MITCH HOROWITZ

PRACTICAL MAGICK

ANCIENT TRADITION
AND
MODERN PRACTICE

Published 2025 by Gildan Media LLC
aka G&D Media
www.GandDmedia.com

PRACTICAL MAGICK. Copyright © 2025 Mitch Horowitz. All rights reserved.

No part of this book may be used, reproduced or transmitted in any manner whatsoever, by any means (electronic, photocopying, recording, or otherwise), without the prior written permission of the author, except in the case of brief quotations embodied in critical articles and reviews. No liability is assumed with respect to the use of the information contained within. Although every precaution has been taken, the author and publisher assume no liability for errors or omissions. Neither is any liability assumed for damages resulting from the use of the information contained herein.

Front cover design by Tom McKeveny

Interior design by Meghan Day Healey of Story Horse, LLC.

Library of Congress Cataloging-in-Publication Data is available upon request

ISBN: 978-1-7225-0654-4

10 9 8 7 6 5 4 3 2 1

Look at my King all dressed in red
Iko Iko unday
I bet you five dollars he kill you dead
Jockamo fee nané
 — "Iko Iko," New Orleans traditional

"I despise people who don't get their hands dirty."
 — Arturo Pérez-Reverte, *The Club Dumas*

CONTENTS

CHAPTER ONE 11
A Return to Magick

CHAPTER TWO 21
A Brief History of Magick

CHAPTER THREE 55
Magick, Ethics, and Risks

CHAPTER FOUR 81
Sex Transmutation

CHAPTER FIVE 91
Sigil Work and "Established Lines"

CHAPTER SIX 99

Cut-Up Magick

CHAPTER SEVEN 107

Walking the Lefthand Path

CHAPTER EIGHT 125

Spontaneous Deity Petition

CHAPTER NINE 137

The Logic of Tarot

CHAPTER TEN 149

Backwards Causation

CHAPTER ELEVEN 171

Total Environment

CHAPTER TWELVE 189

Silence

CHAPTER THIRTEEN 197

Tipping the Scales of Luck

CHAPTER FOURTEEN 209

Is the Wish Enough?

EPILOGUE 237

Letter to a Prisoner

APPENDIX A 241

Wild Talents: Why ESP Is Real

APPENDIX B 265

30-Day Mental Challenge

APPENDIX C 269

The Kybalion Without Tears

INDEX 277

ABOUT THE AUTHOR 301

CHAPTER ONE

A Return to Magick

My aim in writing this book is to attempt, to the degree I am capable, to fulfill or at least take a step toward fulfilling, a wish expressed by visionary occultist and rocket scientist Jack Parsons before his tragically early death at age thirty-seven in 1952.

In the years leading up to a fatal explosion at his Pasadena garage-laboratory, which Jack's widow Marjorie Cameron considered murder, the scientist-seeker experienced betrayal by pretended friends, including Scientology founder L. Ron Hubbard, and fissure with his once-venerated mentor Aleister Crowley. As a seeker, Jack was largely on his own. He believed that *something* was missing from modern ceremonial magick. I use Crowley's spelling, derived from early modern English, to distinguish occult magick from stagecraft. The term magick itself is rooted in the Greek-Persian *magus*, meaning hereditary priest.

"Simplicity," Jack wrote Cameron, "has been the key to victory in all the idea wars and, at present, Magick does not have it. There is a skeleton in the Rights of Man [Crowley's brief Thelemic credo

Liber Oz], and the coverings in the main literature. But the true body has never been shown forth."*

This theme emerges in nascence through writing Jack produced near his death, much of it published posthumously. In his essay "On Magick," Jack noted: "Magick is not created by man, it is a part of man, having its basis in the structure of his brain, his body and his nervous system in their relationships to his conceptual universe, the matrix of thought, and of speech, the mother of thought."**

If the individual is innately magickal—if perception and emotional conviction form the basis, or are at least co-creators, of reality—could not magick itself be unmoored from rite, ritual, and liturgy, areas to which Crowley and Jack himself had dedicated immense effort?

"In its absolute basis," Jack continued, "magick is a passion and a discipline which relates to the mystery of love . . . In its relative and applied basis, which is the root of all secret traditions of mankind, magick relates to the sacrament of sex and the mystery of the creative will."

Jack's statement is my guiding light in this book. It moves me to ask: Is magick as near as the psyche itself—as near as the compact of thought and emotion, as near as the passion of a defined and deeply felt wish?

It is not that I want to whisk away ceremonial and liturgical complexities of our near and distant past, such as magickal circles, languages, passion plays, elemental and astrological correspondences and the symbols and talismans they produce; rather I aim, as a personal objective, to reform such practices in an era when many of us embrace *warranted belief* in the extraphysical capacities of the

---

* Undated correspondence from *Sex and Rockets: The Occult World of Jack Parsons* by the pseudonymous John Carter (Feral House, 1999).

** *Freedom is a Two-Edged Sword and Other Essays* by Jack Parsons, edited by Cameron and Hymenaeus Beta (New Falcon Publications, 1989)

psyche and humanity's correspondence to the paces and patterns of nature. Because I frequently reference verity of the extraphysical, it forms the subject of Appendix A: Wild Talents, a pocket history of psi-research findings.

Let me clarify terms, as every historical writer must. Without defining premises, all arguments, for or against something, are, as twentieth-century spiritual teacher G.I. Gurdjieff (1866–1949) said, "pouring from the empty into the void." In my usage, magick is *causative ritual*. Magick may also be considered ritual that heightens psychological aptitude or inclination—or, very possibly, an amalgam of psychology and extra-physicality, a topic considered throughout this journey. In any case, magick is results based—or it is nothing but a museum piece.

I take seriously immaterial aspects of existence, including the presence of what might be considered non-human intelligences or entities with whom petitionary relationships may be formed. Returning to Jack Parsons' concerns, I also believe—and this might be a matter of taste as much as an intellectually sound choice—that ceremonial magick possesses layers of complexity that prove unnecessary the more one comes to appreciate the inherently metaphysical dimensions of the psyche. I consider psyche a compound of thought and emotion.

Does a bridge exist between ceremony and psyche? Recent to this writing, a thoughtful reader from South America, who asked to be identified only as Miguel, helped clarify the matter for me. He wrote:

> Thanks to Joseph Murphy, I now understand how ceremonial magic works. If you evoke a demon from the *Goetia* [an anony-

mous mid-seventeenth century grimoire or spell book sometimes called *The Lesser Key of Solomon*] and do the lengthy preparations including fasting and prayer, you will get your results because you are preparing the subconscious mind to believe in it . . . If you read a grimoire, the descriptions of the demons are fantastic and the powers they promise are incredible. It drives the imagination wild and, according to Murphy, this is an important ingredient for impressing the subconscious mind. Also when you get into the magic circle and are wearing robes, you are isolating yourself from your familiar surroundings and identity and so it's easier to become someone else or convince yourself something is true.

My correspondent raises an important and insightful point; though I am not necessarily in total agreement. Unlike twentieth-century New Thought minister Joseph Murphy (1898–1981) and his contemporary Neville Goddard (1905–1972), the latter a great source of insight to me, I do, in fact, place stock in the actuality of disincarnate entities and events beyond the immediate nature of the psyche, or rather coexistent with it. I see no necessary barrier between New Thought's mind-is-all ethos and the existence of deific or spiritual beings.

Throughout history, from our earliest ancestors across myriad global cultures, deity worship has proven fundamental to spirituality. Our forebearers, venturing beyond needs of immediate survival, sought to connect with and petition personified energies. Is there danger that such contact is self-generated fantasy? Yes. But *not knowing* the ultimate basis of reality, all of us, at a certain point, abide *maybes*. William James observed in his 1895 essay, "Is Life Worth Living?":

> Not a victory is gained, not a deed of faithfulness or courage is done, except upon a maybe . . . It is only by risking our persons

from one hour to another that we live at all. And often enough our faith beforehand in an uncertified result is the only thing that makes the result come true. Suppose, for instance, that you are climbing a mountain and have worked yourself into a position from which the only escape is by a terrible leap. Have faith that you can successfully make it, and your feet are nerved to its accomplishment. But mistrust yourself, and think of all the sweet things you have heard the scientists say of maybes, and you will hesitate so that, at last, all unstrung and trembling, and launching yourself in a moment of despair, you roll in the abyss. In such a case . . . the part of wisdom as well as of courage is to believe what is in the line of your needs, for only by the belief is the need fulfilled.

The spiritual seeker does not know; the physicalist skeptic does not know. We may have only a fragment of truth on our side. But a fragment, in matters of search, may suffice.* I reckon that appealing to a deity transcends spiritual or religious custom; it becomes an emotionally charged interaction. This approach exceeds orthodoxy and liturgy, focusing instead on resonance and sincerity of relationship. The ancients often negotiated and bargained with their gods, displaying dynamics of veneration, affinity, and, at times, contention.

I believe that seeking communion with a deific intelligence forms a *natural complement* to your psyche's latent capacities. The spiritual search, as I pursue it, welcomes *enigmatic interplay of paradoxes* and *harmonization of seemingly discordant practices*. Venturing into the realm of deity relationship might prove a pivotal chapter in

---

* Critics sometimes dismiss self-experiment as hopelessly clouded by *confirmation bias*—a clinical term for prejudice. We all suffer from it (including those who wield it, scalpel-like). But to submit all self-insight to this compact yet brutal judgment requires conscripting the independent drive to know oneself to the category of delusion. Our knowledge of cognitive biases must function as guardrails not tethers. A short guide from which further reading can be ventured appears at: https://www.britannica.com/science/cognitive-bias.

your search. And if it is, finally, *self* that you are experiencing, well, how much greater, bolder, and efficacious might that self be?

If I have any inviolate rule in magickal work, it is a clarified wish. I encourage unprejudiced and even uncomfortable acknowledgment of your innermost aspirations. I suggest revisiting your earliest memories, around ages three or four, to uncover authentic desires that predate full-on social conditioning. This period is critical, marking the genesis of long-term memories and galvanized dreams and wishes. Ask yourself, *with unadulterated honesty*, what you truly want from life, free from shackles of embarrassment or moral judgment, which is often little more than internalized peer pressure. This effort of introspection must remain untainted by societal labels or expectations. Writing your wish on paper provides a particulate yet tangible nascency of realized desires. Something is present that was not there before.

Looking back on my search, I find that deeply felt wishes I harbored as a child have appeared, albeit over a considerable span of time, such as speaking and communicating in public—including the words you are now reading. This aligns with Goethe's insight, explored later, that wishes of youth, for good or ill, emerge unexpectedly as we mature. Recognizing and honoring these wishes, shielded from external influence, is paramount. The path to self-discovery and activation of inner power often commences with this simple yet profound act: internally acknowledging a radically honest, unabashed wish. Clarity of intent, in my experience, concentrates power and catalyzes change, whether immediately or over time.

Frequent references to disincarnate entities appear in this book. Hence, I must clarify today's overused term "demon." As translated from Latin into English, Renaissance-era occultists, including the tireless and pioneering Cornelius Agrippa (1486–1535), not infrequently used the term demon or daemon. Scholar Eric Purdue made a clarifying note in volume one of his 2021 translation of Agrippa's 1533 *Three Books of Occult Philosophy*:

> The modern usage of "demon" typically implies an evil spirit. The Greek root, *daimon*, is more complex. Sometimes it could mean a deity or sometimes a spirit. By the Renaissance, the Latin *daemon* often referred to a lower-level spirit, one that was more terrestrial. Some daemons were good, some evil. Later in book three, Agrippa quotes Iamblichus at length, showing that daemons could be attending spirits for people, places, and various activities of life. Some support life and happiness, others do not.

This highlights how occultic terms are sometimes reprocessed in a uniformly negative light due to centuries of cultural conditioning. In the Middle Ages, the Latin *daemon* or Arabic *jinn* (genie) referred to worker-bee spirits, neither intrinsically good nor bad. At root, such terms are neutral.

Deity or spirit summoning, worship, or petitioning is an area where grimoires can provide some guidance. (I strongly disfavor the practice of "spirit binding," more on which later.) It is also an area that I personally believe is invested with too much fear. Our era has witnessed an uptick in reportage of claimed "possessions" and "exorcisms." In the years recent to this writing, the Vatican has more than quadrupled the number of church-sanctioned exorcists in the United States. On last known count, the number has risen from twelve to fifty, and probably surpasses that today.* Church authorities generally blame this wave of demand on New Age culture, popularized

---

* "Leading U.S. exorcists explain huge increase in demand for the Rite—and priests to carry them out" by Rachel Ray, *The Telegraph*, September 26, 2016

occultism, Ouija boards, and so on. Another, likelier facet is entertainment. Horror is among the few movie genres that coincide with belief due to congruency between many of its themes and spiritual or religious concepts, ranging from ghosts to after-death survival to demon possession. Hence, the 1973 movie version of *The Exorcist*—one of the most talked-about films ever made and without which I doubt most people would know the term exorcism—produced myriad spinoffs. How an idea goes viral remains mysterious but coinciding of perception and screen is a near given.

It is not that I dismiss the topic—by no means. A groundbreaking scholarly paper published in the Winter 2023 *Journal of Scientific Exploration*, "Interdisciplinary Review of Demonic Possession Between 1890 and 2023: A Compendium of Scientific Cases" by Álex Escolà-Gascón, María Alejandra Ovalle, and Luke J. Matthews, notes: "'Demonic possession' cases published in the academic literature over the last 130 years indicate that about 5% lack a scientific explanation and thus require further study." To these figures I can only add a personal observation: in thirty-plus years as a publisher, writer, and seeker in the fields of occultism, esotericism, and both alternative and traditional spirituality, I have not encountered a colleague *on the magickal or occult path* who experienced possession or like-invasion or harassment.* Historian Massimo Introvigne observes that in general "the possessed claim they have been 'found'" by an entity that "they had not consciously sought."

I personally believe that we—and our kids (I have two adolescent sons)—face far greater risks daily when interacting on social media, often with anonymous account holders whose interests and good will may diverge from our own, than in any presumed occult realm.

---

* I distinguish between occultism and esotericism, although they overlap. Occultism references ancient, often pre-Abrahamic spiritual forms and outlooks adapted or reconstructed in modernity (sometimes from fragmentary retentions). Esotericism is the inner or mystical core of religious traditions, Western or Eastern, which retain perennial (and sometimes occultic) insights.

Indeed, problems of everyday life—including in ethics, relationships (personal or digital), plain dealing, keeping of one's word—are sometimes projected by critics onto magickal or alternative-spiritual practices, whereas they are most commonly and devastatingly felt in the fluorescent environs of domestic existence. Put another way, demonstrate your own capacity for husbandry, broadly defined, before laying guardrails for another's search.

This book grew from an online class of the same title that I delivered in 2022 for the Theosophical Society in America. Founded in New York City in 1875, the Theosophical Society, chartered to explore the world's faiths including supernatural traditions, has an uneasy relationship with magick. In fact, an executive told me that this six-part class was the first exploration of magick he knew of under the society's auspices. The reasons for this are complex but relate to cofounder Madame H.P. Blavatsky's (1831–1891) rising interest in Vedic ideas following relocation of the society's nucleus in late 1878 to India, where, among other ventures, it played a decisive role in the nation's nascent independence movement. India today is the largest electoral democracy in the world. Moreover—and as critics overlook—Theosophy embraced universalistic religious ethics and, in principle at least, evinced unease over what might be considered self-seeking methods. Hence, I dedicate a chapter to the question of magick and ethics, which touches upon what some frame as the white-black magick divide, if such exists.

The class was especially rewarding because it included participants from around the world, including China, Norway, Canada, the U.S., and Australia. (I would also like to add that a surprising number of American inmates are reading works of Theosophy which, it must be admitted, shows how outdated our prison libraries are, but in my experience correspondents are engaging with the literature meaningfully and ethically.) I began by putting to my classmates a series of questions. Why should magick be relevant to twenty-first-century people? Is it a museum piece or relic of a bygone world? Is it leftover detritus from primeval and early religion? What *solutions*, if any, does it hold for contemporary seekers?

Human nature is constant. To understand our present, we must know our past. Before entering the hands-on material to which this book is dedicated, I consider the history of magick, less in terms of names, dates, and personas than in ideas, concepts, and practices. The historic or enduring faiths share certain ancient antecedents, sometimes a great deal more ancient than conventional thinking notes. Hence, the purpose of exploring esoteric ideas is not just a will to know but to be a more wholly developed person, to understand more of who we are, what we are, and how we are connected.

I have referenced human will. British occultist Aleister Crowley (1875–1947) famously defined magick as "the Science and Art of causing Change to occur in conformity with Will."* But what *is* human will? Is it just a subjective term for whatever I like or dislike? Or whatever I desire, consequences be damned? Or does there exist behind it some greater sense of reciprocity, of transcendent or karmic interrelation? Is refinement necessary before the individual can be said to have actual will, to have actual destiny, to have actual intelligent *being*? The path of our distant ancestors, to which we now turn, may hold insights.

---

* *Magick in Theory and Practice, Book 3* (1929)

CHAPTER TWO

A Brief History of Magick

The things associated with magick—operations, ceremonies, rites, rituals, liturgy—are intended to grant access to extraphysical forces and, with that, ability to influence events within your framework. What I describe has been foundational to religious practice since its earliest forms. In strictest terms, this even includes Neanderthal or *pre-Sapiens* expression.

Spirituality is said to be as old as humanity—and that is self-evidently true. But, and I mean this literally, the spiritual search is *older than humanity* and in that sense prehistoric. One of the extraordinary pillars of both the human and pre-human story is the spiritual appeal or petition, which existed among Neanderthals, not Homo Sapiens but Homo Neanderthalensis, and we have known of their existence only since the mid-nineteenth century. These beings, of course, bore great similarity to us with notable differences in height, gait, and cranium. They dwelled from about 400,000 years ago, the best-known about 150,000 years, to their probable point of extinction about 40,000 years ago.

Since the mid-to-late nineteenth century, a wide range of museums and universities have verified surviving talismans and statuettes used by our Neanderthal ancestors. They practiced what we might call arts, crafts, and sciences even the making of tools such as hatchets, spears, and hammers. In addition to hunting apparatus, they fashioned talismans, necklaces, and little statuary. Their talismanic jewelry or charms include eagle talons and bear claws, which may have been injunctions for help with the hunt, upon which life and death pivoted. These ornaments were almost certainly more than decorative because everything had to be useful or multi-useful in a primeval society.

More remarkably, we possess hundreds of little statues that our Neanderthal and early human ancestors crafted in hominid form.* Victorian-age archeologists termed them "Venus figurines," for the Roman goddess of beauty—a being that would not, of course, exist culturally for tens of millennia. Venus figurines are considered fertility talismans or appeals to "mother goddesses," although their uses were possibly myriad. In physical appearance, these feminine figures are round and bulbous with pendulous breasts, almost resembling the grinning "chubby Buddha" statues or Budai, a depiction beginning in eleventh-century China. Usually about four inches high, these presumably pregnant figurines could be carried around, an important feature in a nomadic, hunter-gather society.

Neanderthal beings—so like and unlike us—*practiced spirituality*, a belief in the existence of an extraphysical world. Such findings counter materialist tropes that spirituality is an epiphenomenon of social conditioning or a serotonin hit or dopamine-infused delusion.** Primeval spirituality, rather than culture or chemistry, is, I believe, *realization*.

---

* E.g., see "Why Prehistoric Venus Figurines Still Mystify Experts" by Alexxa Gotthardt, Artsy.com, July 3, 2019, and The "Venus" Figurines by O. Soffer, J. M. Adovasio, and D. C. Hyland, *Current Anthropology*, Volume 41, Number 4, August–October 2000.

** E.g., see "Neanderthals Turned to Faith When Confronting Death, New Evidence Suggests" by Ruth Schuster, *Haaretz*, December 15, 2016.

Hominids, historically and prehistorically, have practiced magick through petitionary relationships with greater intelligences or forces. Among our earliest ancestors across myriad global cultures, deity worship and petition has proven a central facet—maybe *the* central facet—of spirituality, or engagement with the extra-physical.

In a bow to early antiquity or prehistory and to personal proclivity, I encourage seekers to embrace a *magickal primitivism* and seek relations with forces or energies—under whatever name—rendered into hominid or human form. As alluded, I suggest a porous perspective, where personal energy and external deities coexist, blurring the lines between the material and immaterial, between psyche and numinosity.

In a conversation with psychical researcher Dean Radin, I once mentioned my love for a series of graphic novels depicting the death of Superman. In one of the works, the Man of Steel loses his powers, I told Dean—but nonetheless continues attempting acts of justice. "Does he have super-emotions?" Dean asked. "He has super-ethics," I replied. "Ethics," Dean observed, "come from the emotions." It was an epiphanic moment.

If our primeval ancestors' perceptions of external energies as intelligent and emotionally capable beings—who can be honored, learned from, and appealed to—are correct, it opens the door to forming empathic relationships with such deities. The ancients, from Celtic to African to Egyptian cultures, portrayed their gods with deeply human traits including rage, jealousy, and envy. The humanization of gods suggests that if these extra-physical intellects exist, they may crave interaction and veneration. As I often venture: *the old gods may be lonely.*

This understanding suggests a remarkable possibility to establish relations with a deity. Is it a "maybe" you are willing to try? By aligning with a deity from ancient pantheons that resonates with you emotionally—emotions being the seat of ethics—you can, perhaps, foster significant exchange. The depth and complexity of these deities, as portrayed in myth and parable, reflects your own human experience.

In terms of the post-primeval era, probably every religion, whether continuous or fixed to a historical epoch, commenced with some kind of miraculous claim. That is true whether it is Muhammad ascending to the heavens on a winged steed, Moses parting the waters of the Red Sea, Christ turning water into wine, or different gurus within Vedic tradition practicing *siddhis*, or occult powers, where they are said to withstand pain, forego food or water, or demonstrate "impossible" physical acts like levitation or bilocation.

Many religions still venture miraculous claims, such as divine healings in Catholicism, Christian Science, and Pentecostal and Charismatic Christianity; Messianic claims within some branches of Judaism; the contemporary practice of siddhis in Buddhism and Hinduism, such as "yogic flying" in Transcendental Meditation. Those who practice the Catholic faith and receive communion are engaged in what could be called a kind of alchemical operation during mass in which sacraments of wine and wafer are literally said to be blood and flesh of Christ.

Such practices endure domestically. As I write these words, I am wearing around my neck, in plainest terms, a Jewish magickal amulet of luck called a *mezuzah*. It contains two verses from Deuteronomy (6:4–9, 11:13–21) and the Hebrew word *Shaddai* (שדי) for "Almighty" on the back of the parchment. The character shin ש often appears on the mezuzah casing, standing for *Shaddai*. Shin also stands for *Shadad* (שדד) meaning "Destroyer." Observant Jews fix it on the entry to their homes. I have seen it in Mormon households. A more recent practice is wearing the mezuzah as a personal talisman, although such uses also have ancient roots.

We tend to think of magick and the occult as beyond the framework of traditional faith. But as suggested, magick occurs within traditional faiths often by different names and under auspices of conditional validation from authorities within those faiths. Only a priest within Catholicism or some of the Protestant denominations (remember magick is rooted in magus) is endorsed to perform certain rituals, such as mass or last rites. Imams within Islam are granted to lead prayers and provide religious guidance. Within traditional Judaism, elements of Kabbalah are considered off limits unless you have reached a mature age (typically forty) or certain level of study. Such strictures appear in all faiths.

An ancient case of magick within Abrahamic tradition appears in Genesis 41:43, where the patriarch Joseph, after being sold into slavery by his brothers, is named viceroy by the Pharaoh, who rewards the former captive for his dream interpretations. We read that Pharaoh, sometimes identified as Senusret I (ruling c. 1,971 B.C. to 1,926 B.C.) places Joseph in a chariot second only to his; when Joseph rides his chariot, subjects run before it shouting, *"Abrech, Abrech!"* Here is one of the enduring mysteries of Scripture: *we do not know what the term means*. It reaches us transmuted from Ancient Egyptian to Aramaic to Hebrew to Greek. In Hebrew, a knee is *berech*. Some scholars connect the word *berech* to *beracha* or blessing, suggesting a knee bended in supplication. Phonetically, the term bears some similarity to Arabic for blessed, *mabruk* or the proper name *Mubarak*. In Hebrew, it appears as *baruch*, sometimes amalgamated with Arabic into the proper name *Barack*, as in Barack Obama or Israeli statesman Ehud Barak. In any case, we can surmise that *abrech*, or perhaps *abrak*, formed an Ancient Egyptian incantation.

While a matter of debate, the word may share etymological root with the Hellenic *abraxas* found in Gnostic tradition. Mediterranean Gnostic sects often combined elements of Christianity and Judaism with retentive practices from paganism, hence assembling a syncretic faith that honored the Christian salvific message but maintained initiatory and esoteric practices of pre-Christian antiquity. Some branches of Gnostic practice included Persian gods, such as the sun deity Abraxas, who alternatively appeared as an *archon* or governor of a malicious demiurge or false God, associated with Hebraic Scriptural concepts of a punitive and "jealous God." The term *abraxas* also appeared in late antiquity as a magickal incantation inscribed on stones and amulets.

The syncretic terms I have noted travel a strange and fascinating road, persisting as bywords for magick into modernity. According to historian D. Michael Quinn in his monumental 1997 study *Early Mormonism and the Magic World View*, the family of Mormon prophet Joseph Smith (1805–1844) possessed magickal charms, divining rods, amulets, a ceremonial dagger inscribed with astrological symbols of Scorpio and seals of Mars, and parchments marked with occult signs and cryptograms popular in eighteenth- and nineteenth-century English and American folklore. In her 1845 oral memoir, family matriarch Lucy Mack Smith recalled the Smiths' interest in "the faculty of *Abrac*" [emphasis mine].

In addition to these permutations, the biblical term *abrech* and its travels may form the root of a magic word known today throughout the world: *abracadabra*, the etymology of which is widely debated. A Latin rendering—and possibly its first use—appears in *Liber Medicinalis*, a verse grimoire by Roman sorcerer-healer Serenus Sammonicus (d. 212 A.D.), which reappeared in a thirteenth-century reproduction housed in the British Museum. Abracadabra was also fixed on talismans in the sixth and seventh centuries A.D. and returned to use during the years of bubonic plague, about 1346 to 1353, when based on its original Latin usage it was deployed as a magickal charm to ward off disease. During the Enlightenment, the incantation was famously remade into a stage term, like *hocus-pocus*—itself a source of debate, possibly a Latin parody of Eucharist prayers.

The familiar term *alchemy* is likewise shrouded in etymological mystery. Although the word alchemy appeared in Arabic in the centuries following Christ, we cannot pinpoint its origin. It is tantalizing and important to understand the word's probable background and what it means for our enduring connection to Ancient Egypt. Alchemy was practiced in Persia, North Africa, and later different parts of the Mediterranean and Western world; it was an effort by ancient and early modern seekers and proto-scientists to transform gross into fine matter. Or, as is typically heard, lead into gold. There existed physical, psychological, and mystical dimensions to alchemy. In antiquity, every thought form intermingled. There existed no difference between so-called science (not yet extant) and spirituality. Astrology and astronomy were adjoined; art, mathematics, and sacred geometry or use of numbers to unlock the code of creation were adjoined; architecture and worship were adjoined; chemistry and mysticism, in alchemy, were adjoined.

Alchemy is the acknowledged root of our modern term chemistry but, as noted, its etymology is unsettled. The likelihood is that alchemy is a Latin-Anglicized version of Ancient Egypt's name for itself. The term *Egypt* is Hellenic in nature. Ancient Egyptians referred to themselves by the hieroglyphic characters K M T or *Kemet*. The term means Black Land. Egypt called itself the Black Land to connote the rich soil and fertility that the Nile River brought to Central Egypt. The desert, the outlying regions, were called the Red Land, where life was harsher and less fertile. *Al* is Arabic for "the," hence alchemy may be an Arabic and later Hellenic version of Ancient Egypt's name for itself. We are uncertain what phonetic pronunciation Ancient Egyptians used. In Hebrew, one of several neighboring languages, the sounds for S and T are sometimes transliterated—in similar vein an early Greek phonetic pronunciation of Kemet is *Chemi*. Hence, *Al-Chemi* or alchemy.

Modern people speak of black magic or black arts with sinister connotation. But if the etymology I am attempting is correct, the sinister connotation is culturally conditioned. Black arts or black magic—used as a persecutory epithet in the West starting in the fifteenth century—would, in its purest form, reference the origin of alchemy: the Black Land and its arts of transformation.

The spoken word itself has magickal connotations and roots. In Scripture, we read in John 1:1, "In the beginning was the Word" or as sometimes translated, "In the beginning the Word already existed." In a sense, this reflects the development and socialization of humanity itself. A newborn's only means of communication, generally to signal hunger, tiredness, or any state of physical distress, is crying, i.e., "word" or sound. Developmentally, after the infant gains some degree of motor skill, his or her capacity for sound develops more fully to include laughing, cooing, and so on. Speech soon develops—only long after followed by writing. Writing is a phonetic representation of conversant speech. (This, incidentally, is why I believe that almost anyone can learn to write well.) Linguistically, a system of written communication without a verbal adjunct or antecedent is not considered a language or alphabet. Likewise, across the arc of human history, spoken word and sound *predates written language* by tens of millennia. To record their outlook, early civilizations used symbol, song, parable, passion play, initiation, architecture, and only later wrote things down.

One of humanity's earliest written alphabets still extant consists of the sixty-four hexagrams of the ancient Chinese oracle called the I Ching or *Book of Changes*. The six-lined characters or pictograms of this complex oracular device signify states of nature: an upper or lower or trigram, as each hexagram is divided, might stand for a mountain or rushing water; another trigram for clouds or a field, and so on, picturizing fundamentals of landscape, livestock, humans, and weather.

These pictograms, stacked in vertical lines that are either "broken" (yin) or "solid" (yang), form an ancient antecedent to binary computer code. They may possess a phonetic adjunct, making the I Ching an actual alphabet, but pronunciation is lost to history. The first known written edition of the I Ching dates to the late-ninth century B.C. Notable English translations include Richard Wilhelm's in 1950 and John Blofeld's in 1968. If you take the time to peruse a book of the I Ching, you may well be encountering iterations of some of humanity's earliest linguistic efforts, surpassed in antiquity by Persian cuneiform. But the I Ching holds special interest for our purposes insofar as it was not only a pictographic alphabet but also a divinatory device, calendric system (more on which ahead), and wisdom book in itself.

The querent seeking oracular insight may use various methods—usually six tosses of three coins but sometimes, more traditionally, fifty yarrow stalks (often employed by a sage)—to reach a hexagram intended to reveal a given situation. Since the I Ching implicitly teaches that the image of a random moment of time captures, in effect, all of time, I likewise consider randomly computerized "coin throws" and even bibliomancy—i.e., opening an interpretive book of the I Ching to an arbitrary page—valid methods. Each hexagram holds a dramatic meaning, like a Tarot card, hieroglyph, or Hebrew character. Each meaning is also inherently changing and in motion; depending on your throw and method, your hexagram may include one or more "changing" lines, morphing into an adjunct hexagram.

The I Ching may be understood as an esoteric calendric device, both in antiquity and modernity. In 1987, consciousness theorist Terrence McKenna (1946–2000) mapped the I Ching into a calendar called Timewave Zero. Collaborating with programmer Peter J. Meyer, McKenna discovered that the ancient Chinese oracle resulted in a calendar "ending" in 2012, coinciding with the cyclical end date (or restarting) of the Mayan Long Count calendar. McKenna's innovation, coupled with the contemporaneous work of spiritual explorer José Argüelles (1939–2011), ignited the New Age millennialist movement focused on 2012.

Astrology is another system of deep antiquity that has not only persisted into the current age but has given us the science of astronomy. Astrology as we know it had its earliest beginnings around 2,000 B.C. in Mesopotamia. It passed through many permutations across centuries until the Western system was more or less codified in the Roman Empire around 150 A.D. by astrologer-mathematician Claudius Ptolemy in a series of tracts called *Tetrabiblos* ("Four Books"). In that era, what came to be regarded as Western or tropical (i.e., seasonal) astrology and what came to be regarded as Eastern, Vedic, or sidereal (i.e., star-based) astrology informally broke from one another because Ptolemy's Western system, in short, was *keyed to the seasons* versus the *actual positioning of celestial bodies.*

Western astrology does not reflect the actual map of the solar system and its coordinates as seen from earth. The position of the constellations has not changed, of course; but the heavenly bodies *shift* from our terrestrial perspective due to earth's wobble on its axis. Ptolemy and other Western observers argued that the coordinates of astrology should nonetheless remain fixed, as permanent windows on the seasons, so to speak. Many Vedic astrologers disagreed and thereafter adjusted coordinates to reflect *accurate positioning* of the stars. Both camps correctly observed the mechanics of the solar system but dealt differently with changes resulting from earth's vantage point.

Whichever system one follows—both are defensible, though experience has led me to favor the Western model—the remarkable aspect of astrology for modern people is its endurance. Virtually everyone, almost everywhere in the world, can tell you his or her sun sign, or constellation the sun occupied at the moment of first breath outside the womb, and something about its traits. Although many changes, interruptions, and permutations have occurred, this analysis extends back millennia to the Babylonian empire.

Whether one believes, disbelieves, or is indifferent toward astrology, its practice and historicism connect us to humanity's earliest systems of self-study as well as efforts to map the solar system and provide a sense of cosmic causation, at least in the Ptolemaic view. And that highlights the gambit of magick: *as above, so below*, as goes the ancient Hermetic principle.

Hermeticism itself was an esoteric philosophy of self-development and cosmology recorded by Greek-Egyptian scribes in the city of Alexandria in the generations following the death of Christ. Written in expository Greek, with ideas adapted from earlier Egyptian oral tradition and symbol, the Hermetic tracts—the most widely known dubbed the *Corpus Hermeticum* during the Renaissance—contain fragments of Ancient Egyptian philosophy that, most scholars agree, are conceptually centuries or millennia older than the late-ancient environs in which the works were recorded. Hermeticism is a sprawling, piecemeal philosophy of varying tracts, including so-called philosophical Hermetica, represented in the *Corpus,* and technical Hermetica, which focus more narrowly on prescriptive spells, prayers, and oblations. Virtually all surviving Hermetic writings (we possess few of the originals) enunciate the core principle that the individual is an extension of the greater cosmos and can advance in scale through the cosmic order, progressing closer to the source of creation, *Nous,* sometimes seen as a great Overmind. Scholar of esotericism Wouter J. Hanegraaff disputes this interpretation and posits *Nous* more as a *great light* or life force.

The key concept I referenced—*as above, so below*—appears in different iterations throughout Hermetic literature but most directly in the late-ancient work called *The Emerald Tablet*. The tract was first translated from Latin to English by Sir Isaac Newton (1643–1727), in whose papers the seminal translation was posthumously discovered.* As Newton rendered it: "Tis true without lying, certain and most true. That which is below is like that which is above." I believe this Greek-Egyptian principle mirrors the Western Scriptural precept, "God created man in his own image." (Genesis 1:27)

Like most Hermetic literature, *The Emerald Tablet* traveled a jagged path to modernity. Until the 1920s, the work was widely deemed a medieval fakery composed in Latin. Since then, however, scholars have discovered progressively earlier fragments and translations. Our oldest extant source is from the eighth century A.D. in Arabic. German scholar of alchemical texts Julius Ruska (1867–1949) estimated the composition of *The Emerald Tablet* sometime between 600 and 750 A.D., with the lost original possibly in Greek. I venture this detail to demonstrate the difficulty of locating a thread of connection between our world and antiquity. The thread is there—but it is not easy to find or trace, and it meets with frequent corruptions, permutations, and interruptions.

Another theme of Hermetic philosophy is that you, the individual, are a microcosm of all that is, and that you were created by an Overmind or source of light (possibly one and the same): *Nous*. As such, you are a projection of infinite intelligence—and you can, in your own realm, albeit limited by the physical framework that we occupy including the experience of mortality and mass—likewise create not only via cognition and motor skill but through psyche.

---

* Newton's Hermetic and alchemical interests were revealed by seminal economist John Maynard Keynes (1883–1946), whose analysis of boom-and-bust cycles did much to stabilize market economies in the twentieth century. In 1936, Keynes purchased Newton's dust-gathering papers and discovered, to his surprise, "Newton was not the first of the age of reason. He was the last of the magicians..."

As alluded, I consider psyche a compact of intellect and emotion. I believe that is what the ancients were driving at when they referenced the creative powers of mind or imagination, which were also considered dispensation by spirits or genii. Psyche in the ancient mind—as well, I believe, in the dawning awareness of our century—is both personal and nonlocal.

Although limited by earthly laws, the individual can expand through concentric circles of creation where these limits slacken. In Book I of the *Corpus Hermeticum*, often called "Poimandres" (a Greek-Egyptian term of unknown origin, possibly meaning man-shepherd), the individual rises through the seven-known planetary spheres shedding vices picked up earlier when descending: Moon (appetite), Mercury (scheming), Venus (longing), Sun (arrogance), Mars (recklessness), Jupiter (coveting), and Saturn (deceit). Each of the seven spheres has its own ruling deity, angel, or *archon*—a maleficent governor who keeps humanity from knowing itself—depending on the querent's point of view. The numeral seven repeats throughout Western and Eastern culture—seven deadly sins, seven chakras, seven seals, seven days, lucky seven—echoing the original planetary schema. Due to this process, Hermeticism sees the individual as greater than the gods because the gods are fixed in immortality whereas the seeking individual is ever in the process of *becoming*.

From technical Hermetica arises one of the key philosophical tenets of magic, which is: *like attracts like*, related to *as above, so below*. Hence within Hermetic magick if you create or employ the image of something, that image or form possesses a kind of power and hidden tendril or occult bond with the original; the image fuses with the animating or projective powers of your imagination, or what idealist philosopher Arthur Schopenhauer (1788–1860) called "the light of speculative thought." As we were created by higher mind, so can our minds or psyches create in like form, albeit on a lesser but progressing scale. This outlook jibes with a principle that Japanese essayist and novelist Yukio Mishima (1925–1970) voiced in his 1968 manifesto *Sun and Steel*: "Anything that comes into our minds for even the briefest of moments, exists."

Among the final great philosophers of Hellenic antiquity was Proclus (412–485 A.D.). Proclus, who died in 485 A.D., was one of the last deans of the Platonic academy in Athens. Not all of Proclus's writings have reached us. Some are fragmentary. But Proclus occupied an important if elegiac role in the twilight of pagan or magickal antiquity. In his zeal to hasten the spread of Christianity, Roman Emperor Justinian, ruling from Constantinople, ordered closure of the Platonic academy in Athens in 529 A.D., which for centuries sustained Pythagoreanism, Hermeticism, and Neoplatonism. The edict silenced formalized study and promulgation of esoteric and pagan philosophy. Some historians consider it the end of classical antiquity.

I use the term *pagan* for purposes of generality but dislike the word. Historically, it has a derogatory quality. As used in the Roman Empire, pagan meant a rural or vulgar villager—someone from the boondocks to whom news of Christianity had not yet arrived or arrived slowly; hence, pagans retained the old ways. Christianity had been making fitful advent throughout the Roman Empire since the Emperor Constantine converted to the faith, or a variant of it, around 312 or 313 A.D. Those who perpetuated polytheistic and magickal traditions, who clung to worship of Jupiter, Mercury, Pan, Minerva, and countless local and household gods, were considered outside the understanding of the new, often state-sanctioned faith.

Many of our religious traditions, as alluded, have at their core formulas intended to expand the individual's creative power, albeit sometimes beyond mainstream parameters and requiring significant, even exhaustive, effort. One example is the tradition of Kabbalah within Judaism, a thought school that, similar to many Ancient Egyptian teachings, existed for centuries in oral form before being written down. This claim is often made about the Kabbalistic *Sefer Yetzirah* or *Book of Formation*, believed to be written in Mesopotamia in Hebrew sometime in the third to sixth centuries A.D. Or the *Zohar*, or *Book of Splendor*, written down in Spain in Aramaic around 1275, possibly by Rabbi Moses de Leon (c. 1240–1305).

A popularly known Jewish supernatural tradition allows an individual to breathe life into an animated being of clay called the Golem. This is, of course, at the heart of the Frankenstein mythos. There exist many historical and folkloric permutations of the Golem story. The most popular involves Rabbi Loew of Prague (c. 1512/1526–1609) creating a Golem to protect his people in the late-sixteenth century. In some iterations, a magickal word animates the Golem. This must be spoken or written on the creature's chest or forehead, or alternately stuffed into its mouth. The word is *emet* (אמת), Hebrew for truth, composed of three Hebrew characters (read right to left): *aleph, mem,* and *tav*. In order to put down the Golem—which, to great tragedy, Rabbi Loew forgets or fails to do one sabbath—the maker must wipe out the first letter, *aleph*, leaving the word *met* (מת), for dead or death, after which the being reverts to a lifeless hulk.

For those with ambition, the Kabbalistic *Sefer Yetzirah* contains elliptical instructions on how to animate a Golem. The explanatory commentary is complex, probably purposefully obfuscatory, and the operation requires two to three Jewish scholars—it is forbidden to attempt alone (a warning lost on Victor Frankenstein). The sages who set down the instructions were intentionally obtuse, as I see it, so that some degree of oral tradition remains necessary in order to raise the creature. Again, the magickal past is never as distant from our traditions as we think.

In a comparable note, beings called *egregores* appear within both Western and Eastern traditions—they are loosely considered personifications of thought by a group or individual. The concept of an egregore, by etymology, emerges from ancient Hellenic spirituality. A similar concept of *tulpas*, an animated form produced via psychical energies, appears in Tibetan Buddhism. Relatedly, *Thought Forms* is the title of a revolutionary 1905 book by Annie Besant and Charles Leadbeater, second-generation Theosophical Society leaders. The authors describe using clairvoyance to witness material forms emanating from matter and emotion, which they convey to artists who paint them. The resulting images, unprecedented for the era and yet timeless, form the germination of abstractionism, spiritual expressionism, and psychedelia. *Thought Forms* was a widely acknowledged influence on pioneering abstractionist Wassily Kandinsky (1866–1944), a Theosophical Society member who owned a copy of the 1908 German edition, which he referenced into the 1920s. Besant and Leadbeater considered thought an *actual presence*, a reality that can be physically represented and transferred. Kandinsky wrote as much in his 1911 book, *Concerning the Spiritual in Art*: "Thought is matter, but of a fine and not coarse substance."

The anonymous author of the esoteric classic *Meditations on the Tarot* (who addresses the reader as "Unknown Friend"), Traditionalist Catholic scholar Valentin Tomberg (1900–1973), writes compellingly that *all religious congregations are egregores*: material forms of group awareness and intention, burdened with the same flaws and limits: "The egregore of Catholicism, for example, is its parasitic double (the existence of which it would be futile to deny), which manifests itself as fanaticism, cruelty, 'diplomatic wisdom,' and excessive pretensions."

Seen in a certain light—Tomberg speaks directly to this—there exists no contradiction between Hermeticism and Catholicism: "You see therefore, dear Unknown Friend, that we are able, you and

I, to declare openly our faith in analogy [i.e., *as above, so below*] and proclaim aloud the formula of the *Emerald Table*, consecrated by tradition, without appearing thereby to be infidels to philosophy, science, and the official doctrines of the Church. We are able to use it in good conscience as a philosophers, as scientists and as Catholics. There is nothing to be said against it according to these three points of view."

I consider Tomberg's statement one of the most radical—and authoritative—declarations of correspondence ever made of secular and sacred, Neoplatonic and Christian, outlooks. At Penguin Random House, I issued a 2002 edition of *Meditations on the Tarot*—thought to date to 1967 with its first publication in French in 1980 and its English publication five years later—with the translator's corrections and for the first time in the U.S. an afterword by Traditionalist theologian Cardinal Hans Urs von Balthasar, who was nominated cardinal by Pope John Paul II in 1988 but died in June of that year, two days before his inauguration.

Upon Balthasar's death, the Pope called him, "One of the most extraordinary theologians and social scientists, who deserves a special place of honor in the cultural life of today." Cardinal Ratzinger—later Pope Benedict XVI—said in his 1988 funeral oration for Balthasar that "he is right in what he teaches of the faith." And further as Pope in 2005, "I am convinced that his theological reflections preserve their freshness and profound relevance undiminished to this day and that they incite many others to penetrate ever further into the depths of the mystery of the faith . . ." This tribute—for an exponent of an ostensibly occult book. More still, Pope John Paul II was photographed in 1988 with a copy of the two-volume 1983 German edition of *Meditations on the Tarot* on his desk.*

---

* For a helpful commentary see: https://www.alpheus.org/html/articles/esoteric_history/Wojtyla&Tarot.htm.

One of the facets of Church culture sometimes missed is that figures generally considered "conservative," theologically or socially, often prove among the Church's most mystically oriented exponents and scholars. Hence, one cannot always or wholesale export today's (rapidly realigning) political coordinates onto religious cultures.

An important and influential grimoire that survived late-antiquity and the early Middle Ages is an Arabic-Latin work popularly called the *Picatrix*. The volume seems to have been written in the mid-eleventh century in Arabic, although some scholars argue for earlier vintage. In their 2019 translation of the Latin for Penn State University Press, scholars Dan Attrell and David Porreca date the original to circa 954–959 A.D. Most agree that it is based on myriad earlier works reflecting syncretic Hellenic, Kabbalistic, and alchemical Arabic ideas. The *Picatrix*, whose original Arabic title was roughly *The Goal of the Sage*, is of unknown authorship but the work is sometimes attributed to Arab scholar Maslama ibn Ahmad al-Majriti (d. 1005–1008). It was translated into Latin and Spanish in the mid-thirteenth century, with its Latinate name perhaps a mangling of the earlier Arabic title. In any case, its meaning is unknown.

In broad terms, the *Picatrix* might be considered the most influential work of "technical Hermetica," dedicated to specific operations and experiments. In Latin, the *Picatrix* wielded formative guidance over the dawning occult Renaissance. Among the book's concepts are decans, a method of dividing astrological signs in degrees of ten. This likely influenced Cornelius Agrippa, making the *Picatrix* an important building block in modern astrology. The *Picatrix* is also a key surviving record of late-ancient spells for divination, creating of talismans, and summoning of planetary energies and corresponding deities, such as Saturn and Mercury.

Concepts with Near- or Far-Eastern origin sometimes reach us in a Western manner through Latinized volumes or those of more recent vintage. This is the case with a Sanskrit term appearing in esoteric yoga or Tantric practice: *vamachara*, which means *lefthanded path of attainment*. It references practitioners who seek virtuosity in traditional Tantric practice: they pursue magickal rites said to grant extra-normal or superhuman power, including acts of strength, longtime holding of breath, abstention from food or water, withstanding pain, levitating, and gifts of virility, seduction, and sexuality. These practices, as noted, are sometimes dubbed *siddhis* (*attainments* in Sanskrit) and are still pursued, such as ultra-marathon running within the Sri Chinmoy (1931–2007) movement.

But the term Lefthand Path has adopted a life of its own within Western occultism. Its widespread use in the West originated with world-traveled occultist and seeker Madame H.P. Blavatsky in volume I of her 1888 arcanum of esoteric history and philosophy, *The Secret Doctrine*. Blavatsky did not originate but popularized the upside-down pentagram in connection with lefthand philosophy. We explore this Westernized concept and its implications in chapter seven.

Today's occult seeker may be surprised by the extent to which certain historical texts, including the work of Cornelius Agrippa, who provided a Latinized curation of magickal practices from antiquity (many rooted in Ancient Egypt and Mesopotamia), reprocess magick in Christian vernacular and Abrahamic hierarchy. For needs of politics, personal safety, and publication, Agrippa and other Renaissance-era occultists sought, and for a time received, the imprimatur of ecclesiastical authorities. Agrippa diplomatically framed his *Three Books of Occult Philosophy* with prayers and prefatory material of a devoutly Christian nature. The scholar diplomatically opened his volumes with an admiring letter from 1510 by Johannes Trithemius (1462–1516), a German Benedictine abbot with his own deep and carefully framed interests in alchemy and occultism. Even still, Agrippa, in an act of great fortitude, bided decades with his controversial material, waiting until 1531 for his first volume to appear. All three volumes did not see print until 1533, two years before the scholar's death.

Such political necessities colored the surviving work of many Renaissance occultists, alchemists, and Kabbalists, who infused Western grimoires with Christian tones, a legacy that continues today. The practice of "spirit binding" featured in some grimoires descends largely (though not exclusively) from works of biblical apocrypha and contemporaneous non-canonical works called pseudepigrapha ("false writings"), i.e., late-ancient books of dubious authorship that often feature biblical figures. Among the most influential is the "Testament of Solomon" (c. first century A.D.), a Greek text in which archangel Michael gives Solomon a magickal ring with a pentagram on it that allows the king to command demons and enlist their aid in building the temple. Some pseudepigraphic works share commonalities with biblical and rabbinic texts. I do not consider the contemporary seeker bound by this paradigm.

Even stringent diplomacy and ecclesiastical liberalism could not finally forestall a religious, judicial, and military backlash against Renaissance occultism. The dawn of the 1600s saw a rollback of religious liberties and rising tensions between Protestant and old-regime Catholic forces. This occurred even as new expressions of esotericism appeared, including aboveground emergence of three anonymously written so-called Rosicrucian manuscripts between 1614 and 1616. Seen in a certain light, these mysterious tracts, which began circulating in the German-speaking region of Central Europe, reflected the coda of Renaissance religious experiment and esotericism. The works proclaimed existence of a secret, initiatory brotherhood, sometimes dubbed an "invisible college," dedicated to ecumenism, protection of the search, and acts of common polity, such as public hospitals and education. These inspiring and noble allegories, though they would remerge, proved insufficient to stem rising tides of reaction. The death of relatively liberal Queen Elizabeth in 1603 brought a chill to magickal arts in England and resulted in impoverishment and exile of the monarch's titular court magician: scholar and scientist John Dee who died in poverty in 1609. In 1614, the year that the first of the Rosicrucian manifestos appeared (it had probably circulated privately since 1610), there occurred a decisive and peculiar revelation, which shook and eventually dashed the ideal of Renaissance Hermeticists. This episode, although critically important, indirectly contributed to an intellectual error in the Western mind from which I personally believe we are only beginning to recover.

The incident was a groundbreaking textual analysis of the *Corpus Hermeticum*—the chief body of Hermetic writings valued by esotericists and occultists—by linguist Isaac Casaubon (1559–1614). Renaissance seekers believed that these tracts extended to primeval antiquity. But in a study published in 1614, Casaubon determined through vernacular and historical references that the Hermetic works were written in *late antiquity*, specifically the generations following Christ. The voice of Hermes, at least in these hallowed volumes, did not share vintage with Abraham and Moses or belong to the mists of deepest antiquity. Casaubon's revelation, which had appeared fragmentarily in the work of earlier linguists, gradually deflated the ideals of many spiritual iconoclasts and religious scholars of the era and in decades ahead.

Along with these withered hopes, however, an odd and persistent thought-habit calcified over the Western cultural scene. This viewpoint held that because the wished-for vintage of the Hermetic tracts was dispelled, something was compromised, fraudulent, and corrupt about the literature itself. (In one of the ironies of thought history, similar judgment is today directed online against a modern novelty of Hermeticism, the 1908 occult-New Thought work, *The Kybalion*. As Karl Marx wrote in 1852, "first time as tragedy, the second time as farce."*) Other theological statements of questionable vintage, both Abrahamic and Eastern, were spared this verdict.

Summary judgment of the Hermetica's "illegitimacy" grew from an ingrained malady of the Western intellect, which is "either/or" or "take it or leave it" thinking based, in part, on the absolutist formulas of Aristotle. In the Gurdjieff work it is called "formatory thinking." This binary thought habit colors nearly every aspect of contemporary life—and contributed to neglect of Hermetic writings, which were, until recently, scant in translation. For centuries, English speakers had to rely upon a not wholly accurate translation produced in 1650 by John Everard. Another full-scale publication was not ventured until 1906 by scholar and one-time secretary to Madame H.P. Blavatsky, G.R.S. Mead. The *Corpus* itself has received quality English translations and scholarly analysis only over the past several decades.**

Intellectual crises represented only one facet of the backlash against occultism. In 1618, counter-Reformist and Vatican-allied Habsburg monarch Ferdinand II (1578–1637) revoked religious freedom for Protestants in Bohemia. In so doing, Ferdinand ignited tensions across the German-speaking region of Central Europe, which

---

* *The Eighteenth Brumaire of Louis Bonaparte*, chapter one. For my assessment of this modern occult work, see Appendix C: *The Kybalion* without Tears.

** Our generation possesses the first truly serviceable English translations of Hermetic literature especially Brian P. Copenhaver's 1992 *Hermetica* from Cambridge University Press. Another important effort is from Clement Salaman, who with a team of collaborators issued *The Way of Hermes* in 2000 with Inner Traditions. There exist other recent translations, including of technical Hermetica, such as *Greek Magical Papyri in Translation* (Volume 1) by Hans Dieter Betz published in 1996 with University of Chicago Press. This scholarly and highly readable material opens doors closed to previous generations. Also important—particularly in its attention to paucity of primary source material and the problem of translator prejudice—is *Hermetic Spirituality and the Historical Imagination* by Wouter J. Hanegraaff (Cambridge University Press, 2022).

triggered the Thirty Years' War. Extending from 1618 to 1648, the war essentially pitted Habsburg Catholic armies against Protestant forces—and decimated not only the region but all hopes of broadening religious freedom within it. In nascence, the Thirty Years' War began as a Church-based tug of the leash against occult and esoteric religious experimentation of the Renaissance and general religious toleration. The war's aftermath, including famine, fires, agricultural and economic devastation, destruction of villages and cultural centers, and marauding bandits (often former soldiers), was suffered for decades. At its end, with the 1648 Peace of Westphalia, resurgent Church powers clamped down on religious life.

The late-Renaissance backlash was also felt within aristocratic environs. This is typified by the fate of Italian philosopher and scientist Giordano Bruno (1548–1600), burned at the stake in Rome in 1600. After seven years of Bruno's trial and imprisonment, the Vatican's court of inquisition convicted the philosopher-scientist of multiple heresies, including practice of magick, teaching reincarnation or transmigration of souls, and endorsing "cosmic pluralism," or existence of other worlds and beings.

Other forms of violence included the centuries-long Witch Craze. The numbers are difficult to track but historical consensus holds that from 1450 to 1750, roughly 40,000 people, and possibly more, were killed, with tens of thousands more subjected to brutal and terrifying trials. Although difficult to believe, the last modern witch trial occurred in Switzerland, a relatively wealthy country in 1782, deep into the Age of Enlightenment. Its victim was a rural housemaid, Anna Goldi, who was tortured and beheaded. In 1790, Italian magician, self-styled Freemason, and occult adventurer Alessandro Cagliostro (1743–1795) was lured under false pretenses to Rome, where he was arrested by the Vatican's Office of the Inquisition. Sentenced to death in 1791, he received a stay of execution but died of disease four years later in the dungeons of the Inquisition at the Fortress of San Leo. His crimes were heresy and Freemasonry. This gives a sense of why certain groups opted for secrecy.

Freemasonry, the esoteric initiatory brotherhood with a mysterious past, emerged aboveground in 1717 with establishment of the Grand Lodge of England. Masonry's earliest origins probably stem from the medieval stonemason guilds of the cathedral-building era, orders dedicated to sacred architecture and steeped in the art of mnemonics. The brotherhood is an expression of Rosicrucian social polity, ecumenical values, and use of esoteric symbols as codes for ethical development. Masonry is, I believe, the final outpost of the occult Renaissance. In 1738, Pope Clement XII issued a papal bull—the most solemn form of announcement and considered infallible—against Freemasonry. The edict prohibited church members from participating in Masonry (there still exist many Catholic Masons) and named it a heretical order antithetical to church doctrine. Several reaffirming bulls and encyclicals appeared in generations following, most recently in 1983.

Those outside England, where such orders were of limited reach, had more to fear than denunciation. The renegade Masonic order the Illuminati, formed in 1776 in Bavaria, suffered crushing monarchal edicts between 1784 and 1790. These laws outlawed the clandestine and politically reformist fraternity—which promoted church-state separation and legal rights for citizens—stipulating banishment, property seizure, and even death for members. Conspiracies and speculations aside, there exist no records or documentable trails of the lodge and its 600-650 members surviving the crackdown in any organized capacity.

Remarkable figures endured. As Benjamin Franklin was capturing lightening, other icons sought to harness forces both natural and supernatural. Swedish mystic-scientist Emanuel Swedenborg (1688–1772) reported out-of-body journeys into other ethereal, dimensional, and planetary realms, describing parallel worlds that mirror ours—and a "Divine influx" emanating from cosmic environs into the individual. Swedenborg's writings appeared in Latin from 1749 to 1771, the year preceding his death. In 1778, Swiss-Viennese occult healer Franz Anton Mesmer (1734–1815) entered Paris, where Franklin was then serving as American ambassador. Mesmer brought his own theory of vital, invisible forces traversing the individual. He contended that all life is animated by etheric fluid called *animal magnetism*, which, if properly manipulated during sittings or *séances* could result in alleviated physical or emotional ailments. While Mesmer backed his theories until this death in 1815, his students took the next leap of innovation. They theorized that the master may have been mistaken about vitalist fluids but had nonetheless detected an unseen force, which moved his protégés to formulate the earliest modern notions of the subconscious mind.

Magick proved resilient in conditions of tragedy and deprivation. In America, embondaged people crafted the syncretic magickal system of hoodoo, not to be confused with the proper Afro-Caribbean faith of Vodou. Hoodoo was (and remains) an extraordinary admixture of West African retentions and a porous range of spells and practices relying on domestic and agricultural objects, such as soaps, pins, candles, roots, and perfumes. Hoodoo practitioners integrated folk and religious beliefs from the Americas, traversing from threads of Kabbalah to Catholic saint veneration to Pennsylvania-Dutch folklore, creating the New World's first truly combinative spirituality.

In America, it was not uncommon for occultism to flourish among working or poor people. In winter of 1848, two adolescent girls, Kate and Margaret Fox, shocked their Methodist parents—and much of the nation—with claims that the bangs and knocks ringing throughout the family's small cabin outside Rochester, New York, were *spirit raps*: part of a code the girls devised to communicate with the afterworld (including a creepily named Mr. Splitfoot). A contemporaneous medium living in the Hudson Valley, New York, town of Poughkeepsie, Andrew Jackson Davis, was recording his own astral journeys to the spirit realm. Davis, a onetime cobbler's apprentice whom the press dubbed the Poughkeepsie Seer, offered eager Americans instructions on how to form séance circles, remaking Mesmer's term and spawning the do-it-yourself occultism of the Spiritualist era. In the years immediately ahead, everyone from farmhands to President Abraham and First Lady Mary Todd Lincoln tried their hands at talking to the dead. Most spirit mediums, as it happened, were women, providing an opening in religious and civic life that fortified the nascent suffragist movement.

In Europe, occultism found dramatic new voice in 1854 with publication of the first of a two-volume work by a French socialist and ex-seminarian who used the pseudonym *Eliphas Lévi*. He was born Alphonse-Louis Constant but adopted the magickal name Eliphas Lévi Zahed, which Constant, as a Christian Kabbalist, considered Hebraic phonetization of his birth name. That year, Lévi published *The Doctrine of High Magic*, which he followed up in 1855 with *The Ritual of High Magic*. In 1856, both were combined as *The Doctrine and Ritual of High Magic*.

Lévi was an extraordinary figure who ignited a new magickal renaissance, which reverberates to this day. He boldly announced his intention in his first volume: "Beyond the veil of all hieratic and mystical allegories of the ancient doctrines, beyond the shadows and strange rituals of all initiations, under the seal of all sacred writings . . . we find the traces of a doctrine which is the same everywhere and everywhere is carefully hidden."*

Lévi began to revive aspects of Kabbalah and astrology, and proffer an ambitious, occult interpretation of Tarot, which he and others remade from an intriguing game of the early Renaissance to an alchemical-zodiacal-Kabbalistic tool. I return to Tarot in chapter nine but for now wish to venture some historical clarifications about the deck's emergence as an occult device. In 1773, speculative historian, Freemason, and French nobleman Antoine Court de Gébelin (c. 1725–1784) began issuing a nine-volume series called *Le Monde Primitif* or *The Primeval World*. In volume eight, publishing in 1781, Court de Gébelin deemed Tarot an arcane work of wisdom emanating from Ancient Egypt. It was the first time since Tarot's inception as an archetypally illustrated gaming deck in the early 1400s that it was publicly designated a codex of Ancient Egyptian wisdom.

Court de Gébelin invited a co-author, Comte de Mellet, to contribute a short essay on Tarot to the work. In homage to Hermeticism, Comte de Mellet called Tarot the "Book of Thoth," pairing it to divinatory meanings and instructions for a spread. Comte de Mellet also made the first connections between Tarot and Hebrew characters, associating the 22 trumps with the like-numbered Hebrew alphabet, another previously unknown device. Still another Frenchman adopted and expanded this innovation: Jean-Baptiste Alliette (1738–1791), an occultist who used the reverse spelling of his surname: *Etteilla*. (Another aficionado of Christian Kabbalah, the cartomancer elected to read his name from right to left in the style of Hebrew.) In 1789, Etteilla produced the *Grand Etteilla Tarot*—the first Tarot deck explicitly designed for divination.

---

* I am quoting from *The Doctrine and Ritual of High Magic* translated by John Michael Greer and Anthony Mikituk, which I published at Penguin Random House in 2017. Greer and Mikituk's translation is the first full English rendering of Lévi's work since Arthur Edward Waite's 1896 *Transcendental Magic*; I consider it the flagship edition.

From these precedents, Eliphas Lévi created a complex and remarkable pastiche of Kabbalistic interpretations and correspondences—albeit "brilliant misunderstandings," wrote German-Israeli historian Gershom Scholem (1897–1982), whose seminal 1946 *Major Trends In Jewish Mysticism* revived study of traditional Kabbalah in the twentieth century. The classicist grudgingly but explicitly credited Lévi and Aleister Crowley with keeping Kabbalah before the public eye, albeit in *sui generis* form, during a period when most Jewish scholars allowed the body of mystical insight to languish in neglect.

Lévi did a great deal in the mid-nineteenth century to instigate an occult revival that was, in many respects, completed by the influence of world-traveled Russian seeker Madame H. P. Blavatsky. She and retired Civil War colonel Henry Steel Olcott (1832–1907) collaborated in founding the Theosophical Society in 1875 in New York City. So much can be said of Madame Blavatsky's indefinable career. This book would not exist without her. As a matter of thought history, Blavatsky was probably the first person, around 1876, to use the term *occultism*, which was quickly embraced in vocabulary and concept by artists, seekers, intellectuals, and scientists. This is one of many reasons one cannot overstate the degree to which Blavatsky completed and fortified the occult revival that Lévi helped instigate. But it is also important to note that Madame Blavatsky and Colonel Olcott left the United States just a few years after founding the Theosophical Society to venture to India in 1878, where they and colleagues played a decisive role instigating the early independence movement. As she and Colonel Olcott, William Quan Judge, A.P. Sinnett, Annie Besant, Charles Leadbeater, and other first and second-generation Theosophists grew dedicated—not exclusively but deeply—to Vedic and Buddhist thought, as noted in chapter one, the Western tradition of ceremonial magick, rite, and ritual faded from their outlook.

In response to the wish for training in magickal tradition, other organizations began to appear. Most were offshoots from Theosophy and Freemasonry, often founded by iconic, inventive, dramatic individuals who endeavored to provide explicit exercises in magick. They not infrequently accomplished their aims through historical adaptions and modern inventions of complex liturgy and strict initiatory hierarchy. The most influential was Hermetic Order of the Golden Dawn, founded around 1888. Its originators, in a leaf from Theosophy, claimed tutelage to living masters known as "Secret Chiefs" whose insights they first encountered via mysterious folios of encrypted occult instruction called the "Cypher Manuscripts." This echoes Madame Blavatsky's report of unseen Masters or Mahatmas dispatching phenomenally produced or "precipitated" letters to her and key Theosophists. Also like Theosophy—and probably a general reflection of human nature—the Golden Dawn grew riven by faction fights over who had access to the Chiefs and their mysteries.

For a time, however, the Golden Dawn proved an extraordinary womb of activity for a wide range of both male and female artists, intellectuals, and seekers eager to revive the mythical and magickal. Luminaries included poet W.B. Yeats (1865–1939), magickian Aleister Crowley (1875–1947), historian Evelyn Underhill (1875–1941), actress Florence Farr (1860–1917), and occultists and artists S.L. MacGregor Mathers (1854–1918) and wife Moina Mathers (1865–1928)—both in leadership roles—as well as A.E. Waite (1857–1942), Dion Fortune (1890–1946), and Israel Regardie (1907–1985). Crowley hastened the fraying and demise of the Golden Dawn as one of several fiercely ambitious, powerful, and charismatic figures who yearned to seize leadership. Faction fights led the group to splinter and fade out in the years following World War I.

Although the Golden Dawn was short lived, it proved enormously influential, especially in terms of aesthetics and symbol. The ideals of Eliphas Lévi and of seekers from different (and sometimes renegade) Masonic or self-styled Rosicrucian groups centered on rediscovering and reconstituting ancient magickal methods, ceremonies, rites and rituals, which mostly survived in fragmentary form. The Golden Dawn, with some brilliance, produced a good deal of (often self-invented) pageantry and truly alluring aesthetics. Its leading lights also produced complex and thickly rendered liturgies, correspondences, and rites and ranks of initiation that contributed, I believe, to an excessively complex culture of magick. The beauty and intrepidness of the Golden Dawn's efforts, however, cannot be denied.

Crowley branched off to his own calicoed career, which included the extraordinary and controversial work *The Book of the Law*, channeled across three days in Cairo in 1904. Among much else, the work gave the world the oft-quoted but rarely understood line, "Do what thou wilt shall be the whole of the law." Rather than a paean to moral whimsy or rampant libertinism—although the artist displayed both in his life—the text, which Crowley reported receiving from an ethereal intelligence called Aiwass, describes a new epoch of human relations and strivings, spiritual insights and modes of being, in the self-determinative philosophy called Thelema, Greek for *will*. As Crowley saw it, form had smothered meaning—but, more so, meaning had been divorced from True Self. This is the basis of his jeremiad against the spirituality of the old and heralding of the cosmic new.

Some twentieth-century seekers ventured beyond magickal formalism or ethereal messages. These artists rejected searching for fragmentary threads of antiquity and weaving layers over what they found. They accepted the magickal premises of antiquity—but only as springboards for unknown journeys. One such figure was English magickian, author, and graphic artist Austin Osman Spare (1886–1956). Rumor held that Spare once told a rising Adolf Hitler to go to hell when the Fuhrer offered the impoverished painter desperately needed cash for a personal portrait. The visionary left behind an extraordinary body of writings and images that pioneered what came to be called sigil or chaos magick, which we put to work in chapter five.

A model of simplicity, sigil magick requires writing a short sentence or phrase of your desire, eliminating repeating letters (this method can vary), and turning the remaining letters into an abstract symbol or sigil, Latinate for "little symbol." You then reach a state of ecstasy over the image, usually through sexual climax. For Spare, the bridge from wish to magick requires bypassing rational, conscious thought to fuse your intentions with *Kia*, the energy of life. In Spare's view, *Zos*—the physical man or energy manifest—functions as a receptor for Kia. Spare's Kia parallels earlier philosophies. For Hermetic-Egyptian Greeks, such a concept meant the light of *Nous*. For Eliphas Lévi, it was *astral light*. For Mesmer, *animal magnetism*. For Paracelsus, *light of nature*. For Schopenhauer, *light of speculative thought*. For novelist and occultist Edward Bulwer-Lytton, *Vril*. And for the much abused though underrated twentieth-century self-help author Napoleon Hill, sexual energy or *sex transmutation*, applied in chapter four. As it happens, Hill's interpretation was closest to both Lévi's and Spare's, a vitality recognized by artists William S. Burroughs and Brion Gysin who coauthored a 1977 book inspired by Hill's ideas, *The Third Mind*. This, too, is revisited.

Spare, as noted, planted seeds of what became broadly known as chaos magick. Chaos magick differs from the ceremonial magick of figures like Crowley or the Golden Dawn insofar as it is more ascetic and less steeped in liturgy, ceremony, costume, and vestment. Chaos offers glorious ease: in essence, chaos magick, like chaos theory (to which it has no direct connection), entails introducing some kind of exotic matter, measure, or element into routine life and seeing what occurs. It may be just what you want. Or not. In any case, it is a form of magick that can be practiced—and sometimes is—on a strictly psychological basis with no requisite belief in extra-physicality. Some acolytes of Donald Trump consider him a uniquely powerful chaos magickian for his capacity to disrupt norms of behavior, propriety, and speech.

Concurrent with the nascence of chaos magick, English folklorist and retired civil servant Gerald Gardner revived the practice of nature-based religions in the form of modern witchcraft. Following on the 1951 repeal of Britain's last anti-witchery law, Gardner, a nudist described to me as a "lovely old man" by singer-songwriter Mariane Faithfull, wrote the slender but seismic 1954 volume *Witchcraft Today*. He took historical inspiration from British anthropologist Margaret Murray (1863–1963), who maintained the continuous survival of a West European witchcraft cult. Gardner's work and covens ignited worldwide reconstitution of Wiccan and witchcraft-based faiths and practices.

In North America, art student Carlos Castaneda (1925–1998) produced brilliant, vexing, impressionistic memoirs of tutelage to a Native American shaman in the late 1960s and early 1970s. Castaneda tapped the imagination of Woodstock-era seekers who romanticized indigenous wisdom and psychedelia. Although the author's biographical and regional inventions sparked outrage, his spiritual and parabolic insights proved haunting, mysteriously insightful, and not infrequently congruent to perennial tradition. He, too, greets us again.

Peter J. Carroll, a brilliant writer still living, published two books in the late 70s and early 80s, jointly issued in 1987 as *Liber Null & Psychonaut*, which refined Austin Osman Spare's methods of chaos magick, bringing them to a new and lasting audience. Carroll's work demonstrated that twentieth and twenty-first century seekers stand ready to embrace new grimoires provided they are practical and relevant to contemporary needs, as I hope this book proves. A younger generation of magickal experimenters and authors, including Gordon White and Aidan Wachtler, to name two of the most literate, also filled this opening. (Aidan has proposed, brilliantly, that grimoires can be read as literature, whether one intends to practice.)

As I think is clear, magick has never gone away. Recent to this writing, I bought an ancient Roman coin from the reign of Constantine. It has on the back a pressing of Minerva, goddess of wisdom, whom I venerate. Do we in the rational West differ so greatly from the ancients? In the U.S., our currency sports the familiar phrase, *In God We Trust*. The old ways linger. Since religion and magick are, as I think I have demonstrated, inextricably, if fitfully, bound, how does magick figure into the aspirations of today? How do we use magick to become more of who we wish to be—or are? Is there a magickal way that proves direct, effective, and, while no less serious or impassioned than pre-modern paths, also simpler and more ascetic than practices of our ancestry? We will find out—but first a word about risks, warranted and not. But mostly warranted.

CHAPTER THREE

Magick, Ethics, and Risks

I consider it important in a book on practical magick that we consider the question of ethics. I hope this question proves meaningful to you. We are on the brink of plenty of "how to" material. But my wish is to offer a well-rounded treatment. If you are impatient, you are in the wrong place.

I see ethics less as strictures imposed upon you than as principles located by you, granting fuller sense of your relationships, debts (broadly defined), ideals, and self. Ethics should hone your capacities as a thinking, seeking, and powerful being. Power, in order that it not become force, requires ethics. Hence, some of you will detect the inner nature of this chapter: it is not an interlude—but a tool in itself.

What are ethics? I use the term frequently. It seems to me that ethics emerge from the emotions. *Empathy is ethics*. Empathy is at the heart of all ethical principles. Empathy is why ethics differ from morality, which is judgment.

In perhaps the most alluring and underappreciated work to emerge from "Romantic Satanism," a movement revisited in chapter seven, Lord Byron (1788–1824) used his 1821 closet drama *Cain*—a work that earned him excoriation—to introduce the most jarring reconception of Lucifer next to Milton's. Lord Byron's Satan, who befriends the rebellious and ill-fated Cain, is persuasive and penetrating in denying that he was the serpent in the garden but also notes that the serpent greeted Eve as a sexual and political emancipator—an outlook embraced by many proto-feminists and political radicals of the nineteenth century. Like Milton's Satan, Byron's dark rebel is a fiery optimist and something of a populist, who tells Cain, "I know the thoughts/ Of dust, and feel for it, and with you." The play, of course, ends with Cain's tragic and unintended fratricide, leaving the reader to ask: Are competing ideologies and human frictions the inevitable price of awareness?

I mentioned a story in chapter two to which I want to return. In 2009, I was driving down the northern California coast in Big Sur with a friend, parapsychologist Dean Radin. I consider Dean our generation's seminal figure in psychical research and the inheritor of J.B. Rhine, who transformed psi studies into an academic science. During the drive, Dean asked what I was reading. I was then deep into the graphic novel *The Death of Superman* and its spinoffs. For me, the most meaningful part of the saga, I told Dean, is when Superman temporarily loses his powers. The Man of Steel is reduced to a regular human with cape and costume but no special abilities. Rather than retreat, Kal-El continues fighting for fairness and justice—when I was a little kid it was still called "truth, justice, and the American way," which is fine with me.

"Does he have super-emotions?" Dean asked

"He has super-ethics," I replied.

"Ethics come from the emotions," he said.

Those who experience *fine emotions* are better able to experience empathy. In fact, they are the only ones who experience empathy. Empathy and fineness of feeling are, it seems to me, something that people are born with. Gurdjieff, in a different context, called it a "magnetic center." It can be heightened but not produced in its absence. A lover of humanity once accused me of "eugenics" for that point of view. I consider it an observed truth of human nature. We cannot love without tough truths.

Sometimes the experience of empathy is such that I must stop and remind myself what another person may be going through. I may then doubt my capacity to judge. Even online haters are grasping for human contact, albeit of a degraded sort. Such people are almost by definition unhappy. Happy people leave others alone. Empathy might move me to ask questions about what is driving such a person. Nothing will change him or her—but the right perspective, even or especially if silent, can produce unexpected outcomes.

The last place to look for ethics is in what people say. Any person or organization, particularly of a spiritual or religious bent, can point to strictures and declare, we stand for service or peace or social justice or universal love or some generally meaningless macro-virtue. The Talmudic book *Pirkei Avot* or *Ethics of the Fathers* cautions, "Beware the man who bespeaks his own virtue." The greatest act of empathy I have experienced in a religious context goes back to when I knelt before a life-sized statue of St. Jude at a Midtown Manhattan Catholic church; I was in agony. As I was walking out, a young man on his knees, probably from Central America, gave me a fist bump. I cannot tell you have much love was in that act. Contemporaneously, an artist of devotional religious paintings orchestrated a whispering campaign against me that resulted in my being severed from the Association for Research and Enlightenment, or A.R.E., the group dedicated to the teachings of Christian mystic and psychic Edgar Cayce. My talks and writings were erased from organizational media; I was dropped from its prison ministry; a book I wrote gratis as a fundraiser, *Mind As Builder: The Positive-Mind Metaphysics of Edgar Cayce*, was pulled from publication. This is because I am a Romantic Satanist. I have never witnessed an act more bereft of love. It summons a lyric from Jethro Tull's sardonic *Hymn 43*: "If Jesus saves/ Well he better save himself/ From the gory, glory seekers/ Who use his name in death." I have also received private expressions of support from many A.R.E. members for whom I feel deepest warmth.

If the twentieth century taught us anything, it ought to be the chasm dividing principle from action. T.S. Eliot wrote in 1925 in *The Hollow Men*:

> Between the idea
> And the reality
> Between the motion
> And the act
> Falls the Shadow

That is true for every life. In that vein, there's nothing unique about occult, esoteric, or magickal tradition that makes it *more* fraught ethically than any other path, belief, or expression, either ancient or modern. There exists no intrinsic marriage between occultism and grotesque self-seeking, Christopher Marlowe's Dr. *Faustus* aside (a topic considered in chapter seven). In using the Latin terms *occultus* or *occulta* for hidden or secret, Renaissance philosophers, translators, and writers were attempting to reference ancient belief systems of a lost world. They were rediscovering polytheism, including initiatory and nature-based traditions, local gods and customs, spell work and divination, initiatory rites and symbols, some of the most dynamic of which resulted from the Hellenic encounter with Ancient Egypt.

The religious orders that the thinkers of the Renaissance were referencing had vanished. There isn't exactly an *occult* in the Far-Eastern world insofar as Eastern traditions, such as Hinduism, Buddhism, animism, Taoism, Confucianism, Shintoism, did not undergo interruption, vanquish, and disappearance. Such traditions, of course, passed through different permutations, expressions, leadership, politics, rise and fall of empires—Buddhism itself is a reformist movement emergent from Hinduism—but the Eastern faiths existed more or less *continuously*.

When Rome's emperor Constantine converted to Christianity in the early fourth century, eventually, and across generations, Christianity become the dominant and officially recognized faith throughout the empire, which extended from Western Europe to Constantinople, North Africa, and parts of Eurasia. After a time, another Abrahamic religion, Islam, arose in some of the territories just referenced. Judaism remained a numerically marginal but continuous influence due to its progenitive role. The West experienced discontinuity and gradual disappearance of the vast quilt of mystery traditions in the regions trod by Alexander the Great's, and later Rome's, Hellenic armies. Temples, priesthoods, initiatory orders, manuscripts, monuments, oral tradition—all were erased, almost like villages and cities leveled by a tsunami or volcanic eruption. That is among the reasons I cherish Hermetic literature: it contains fragments of Egyptian esoteric philosophy as rendered into an expository language, Greek, that is accessible to Westerners. Hermeticism is among the few written lifelines to our deep ancient past.

It was not until the late 1700s that Napoleon's invading armies discovered what we call the Rosetta Stone in Egypt and provided modern Westerners a key to unlocking hieroglyphics, at least in plainest literalism. The Rosetta Stone is an ancient, handwritten carving in black granite-like stone, standing about three-and-a-half feet high. Produced in 196 B.C., the stele featured a decree heralding the reign of Ptolemy V (210–180 B.C.), among the last of the Ptolemaic line, drawn from the generals of Alexander the Great. The tribute is carved triply in traditional hieroglyphs; Demotic, a phoneticized simplification of hieroglyphs used for official business; and, finally, Greek, language of the ruling class.

Suddenly, the mysteries of the hieroglyphs, previously indecipherable to moderns, cracked open, at least partly. This development occurred deep into the Age of Enlightenment—and in the form of stray threads, as is true for many writings from the once-dominant ancient empires. As noted, we possess incomplete records of late-ancient philosopher Proclus, who wrote about the occult law of *like attracting like*, i.e., image possessing whole. We have only a handful of complete works by classical tragedian Euripides (c. 480 B.C.–406 B.C.), whom Emerson famously quotes ("Zeus hates busybodies") from an extant shard of a play. We possess no writings, if any existed, from Pythagoras (c. 570 B.C.–c. 495 B.C.) and rely strictly on tracts written by students sometimes centuries after his death. We use hallowed names from antiquity, including Homer and Plato in the West and Lao Tzu and Sun Tzu in the East, but possess little knowledge of their historical verity. It was common for ancient scribes—we would not consider them distinct authors in the modern sense—to affix the name of a venerated or legendary sage to their writings in order to lend them gravity, just as the mythical names of Hermes or Hermes Trismegistus (thrice-greatest Hermes) were affixed to late-ancient works by Greek-Egyptian thinkers and curators.

This is the milieu from which emerged what we call occult—i.e., partial or fragmentary teachings from a dimly known antique world.* This reflects the discontinuity I describe in Western religious history. *The notion of occultism or magick presenting a unique ethical dilemma is artifice inherited from the late-ancient twilight of religious philosophies we now possess in odds and pieces.* Practitioners of these ancient faiths never conceived of themselves in juxtaposition to more modern reli-

---

* It should be noted that we also possess remarkable preservations, such as Ugaritic and Sumerian cuneiform on clay tablets, the earliest of which extend to about 3,200 B.C. Later works of epic poetry, such as the "Baal Cycle" (c. 1,500 B.C.–1,300 B.C.) were rediscovered beginning in the 1920s.

gions that damn them. An old truism—maybe overused—says victors write history. I do not know if that is categorically true but certainly victors write *religious history*, at least until our era. This problem limits our ability to understand our pre-Abrahamic past, due not only to cultural framing but also paucity of material.

Amid absence of material—and even among abundance of it—we objectify one another. It is the malady of human nature. That's among the reasons Madame H. P. Blavatsky cofounded the Theosophical Society in New York City in 1875. Whatever else may be said about her, she and Colonel Olcott devised one of the first organizations in modern life that had as its core principle the universality of religions, sanctity of the search, and essential unity of all people. That sounds like ordinary good civics today (although ordinary pillars should never be taken for granted); but to Victorians it represented a radical proposition. Without Theosophy, we would have fewer windows on our past, including in the form of translations.

I think it is important that we endeavor to reclaim useful if calico traditions without apology. That is among the reasons I retain some of the old language. There exist plenty of vocabulary terms suited to our twenty-first century world—and I rarely use them. Certain of the old terms, like occult and magick, and not-so-old ones, such as extrasensory perception and mediumship, possess historical integrity. I refuse to cede them to critics. Even at risk of misunderstanding—and there is plenty—I will not perfume hot-button terms like Satanism; I am not trying to provoke but rather I regard transparency and directness as key principles on the path. (I am by no means counseling loquaciousness; chapter twelve deals with the ethic of silence.)

Every seeker has his or her own commitments—and personal ways of expressing them. But for me, the independent search requires ethical clarity, even more so than what might be required in the mainstream. The traditional faiths and their most vocal exponents often receive a pass, albeit temporarily, because they can point to foundational literature that voices time-honored principles and ethics; current institutions may fail, sometimes egregiously, at their practice, but our culture nonetheless defers to the weight of historically familiar values. We in the modern occult receive no such deference both because of the history described and because we lack the same forms of palatable, canonized literature.

Are precursory ethics necessary on the path? In recent years, I have changed my mind about certain guardrails I once deemed necessary. Years ago, I believed that anyone embarking on an occult or independent spiritual search, possibly solitary and without a congregation or group, possibly experimenting with different forces and possibilities, required some kind of sacred or ethical text as a personal rope line. As I saw it, this could be any work of posterity that could provide ethical guidance—whether the *Bhagavad Gita, Dhammapada, Tao Te Ching, Beatitudes, Meditations* of Marcus Aurelius, or the Talmudic digest I cited earlier, *Ethics of the Fathers*. I felt this necessary to avert gross lapses or dangers.

I do not necessarily disparage or disavow that point of view. But personally speaking, I have come to believe that the search must be wildly free. Your queries and experiments must be remarkably open. In that vein, I am reminded of a statement by philosopher and critic of science Paul Feyerabend: "I am for anarchism in *thinking*, in one's *private life*, BUT NOT in *public life*."* The costs, and they will come, are yours to bear. The benefits are commensurate. This is the price of discovery—not recitative wisdom.

---

* *Against Method*, fourth edition, by Paul Feyerabend (Verso,1975,1988,1993, 2010)

Our generation possesses a wonderful range of translations of ancient literature. But a note to those who, like me, speak English as a first and often only language: not one piece of the wisdom literature I just referenced was written in English. Not one. A wealth of translations exist. Many are effectively free. Go online and there they are. Concurrently, however, we have also fallen into a great deal of *adaptive repetition*, not that our generation is distinct in that regard. With recitation comes thought habit. But: *familiarity is not truth*. Because something is repeated does not mean that it is hallowed or elevated; nor that it reaches us in a manner reflecting the original framing or concerns.

Every religious system, while it may contain universal truths, was devised in a time, place, and culture rife, like any, with local prejudices, needs, and urgencies. As a near constant of human nature, all of our spiritual and ethical framings absorb, sponge-like, the customs, thought habits, politics, and social strictures of those arenas from which they emerged. Often ancient religious and ethical systems are necessarily oriented towards survival. In terms of Judaism, for example, you might be perplexed reading the books of Leviticus and Deuteronomy and wondering at various laws governing diet or what fabrics may be mixed together, laws around sexual practices and timing, and around bodily adornments, and so on. There may be great universal truths in Leviticus and Deuteronomy—I wear passages from the latter encased around my neck—but you will also encounter rules intended to maintain the social fabric of a desert-dwelling people, amid dozens of other desert-dwelling tribes, for whom life and survival were precarious. Social cohesion was critical to survival. Cohesion might announce itself in prohibition against inking or dying one's body (something I obviously haven't abided). Sometimes the need announces itself in prohibitions against homosexuality. It must be understood that, for all the value of codified traditions, including precious rudiments of civic law, we cannot project backwards twenty-first century attitudes, whatever they are, onto religious texts or vice versa. The needs and mindset of ancient people so drastically differed from ours that terms of engagement must occur on a different scale. I have witnessed too many bar or bat mitzvah speeches—a recent wrinkle that did not exist when I was a kid—hinge on up-to-the-minute political concerns, which would have appeared as foreign to the ancients as their needs are to us.

Ancient traditions were born—almost without exception—in cultures of extreme social stratification. Within the cultures that gave birth to Vedism, for example, which in turn gave rise Buddhism, a person was virtually certain to die within the same caste into which he or she was born. Social mobility, another recent concept, was in most cases no more likely than walking the surface of Mars. Hence, certain principles, particularly nonattachment, nonidentification, disassociation from the trinkets and triumphs of outer life, were central to religious tradition, both within Vedic and Abrahamic cultures. I do not consider these principles categorical absolutes.

I do not draw distinctions in my search right now between so-called eternal and temporal, personality and essence, higher and lower, identification and nonidentification, attachment and nonattachment. I personally believe that the individual standing at his or her height—that is, functioning in a manner that is natural, that is suited to productivity and generativity, and, hence, happy—is *the individual in expression*. Our ancient ancestors did not always have that opportunity. I am hardly saying that you cannot find universal truth within some of the traditional strictures I have been identifying—but it is a *question* for me. I believe we really must have questions, and I mean burning questions, on the path. If I catch myself reciting something, I know I am lost. This occurs when I find myself using expressions that come too readily to the lips ("what matters is what we can't see," "you forgive for yourself") because they have been inured into us for generations, so much that such truisms feel as natural as up and down (itself just conceptual). Expressions are limits. We need *questions* that challenge received conceptions, however sacred. At the same time, that doesn't mean that we are free from debts, traditionally or broadly defined; that doesn't mean that we are free to commit violative acts.

I believe deeply in reciprocity. Some call it karma and my term certainly relates to karma. I say *reciprocity* because karma in Vedic teaching is so vast and impersonal that it is difficult—or worse still, *easy*—to speak of it in isolation. For one thing, the opposing ends of karma are so immense that we are rarely granted to perceive its workings. Karma can be near-impossible to negotiate or envisage. In that vein, I offer a response by Lord John Pentland (1907–1984), one of G.I. Gurdjieff's key students, during a group meeting he conducted. Lord Pentland does not use the term *karma* here and I hope I do not err in projecting that onto his statement. But I consider my framing accurate:

> Real feeling is impersonal. It comes from very high in the scale and it connects everything together. The story which I've several times used the last couple of weeks to illustrate that is the story of Brahma. He's supposed to be absolute god in India, and he was taking a nap one day when a very high Brahman—it comes from Brahma, Brahman, it's the highest caste—came with a little child, his son that had died, and said, "Look, Lord Brahma, the first-born son has died. There's something gone wrong down on the earth. You shouldn't have allowed that. Would you look into it?" So Brahma had to get up and dress and so forth and went down to earth and discovered that there was this temple. And a Sudra—that means the lowest caste, untouchable caste—had been affected by some very deep wish and had found his way into

the temple. Appalling thing to happen. So Brahma took one look at the Sudra and he immediately died. One look at Brahma was enough to kill the Sudra. However, this had the effect of fulfilling the Sudra's wish because he died in the temple. So he was saved. At the same time, the little infant immediately was again breathing. You understand?

Well, that is an impersonal story, if you like. Yes? But that's rather strong meat for some of us. That's why I say, although there's relativity, you would have to a little bit expand your horizon to try and get the twin ends of the scale. Yes?*

I believe Nietzsche reflected some understanding of this when he wrote in *Beyond Good and Evil* in 1886: "One *has* to repay good and ill—but why precisely to the person who has done us good or ill?" (From Walter Kaufmann's 1966 translation.)

I consider everything part of a scale. Sometimes we can detect one portion of the scale or arc of existence. The scale of karma that we are *granted to understand* could perhaps be described as reciprocity. Reciprocity, in terms of consequence, means doing nothing to disrupt another's capacity to search. If I have a core ethic on the path, that is it. Doing nothing to circumvent another's capacity to search also means neither condescending to nor denigrating another person. To this I would add not objectifying another person by race or some other benign category. The people who need this statement are always, as a rule, those who think they do not.

Seekers occasionally raise the question of cursing another in a magickal act and wonder about the price or ethics of that—or what conditions might make such an act ethically defensible, if, indeed, any exist.

---

* *Exchanges Within: Questions from Everyday Life Selected from Gurdjieff Group Meetings with John Pentland in California* 1955–1984 (Continuum, 1997; TarcherPenguin, 2004)

I used to reject any such practice. I once abided the notion that the operation of a curse, if it proved effective, would reverberate or "backfire" onto the practitioner. I no longer feel that familiar model is sufficient. It seems to me that everything in life involves payment, broadly defined. What you take, you pay for—or it gets taken out of your skin or psyche. In any case, none of us can elude the inexorable ledger of lived experience. Ralph Waldo Emerson describes this in 1841 essay (and, I think, his greatest work), "Compensation." The Yankee Mystic writes, "The absolute balance of Give and Take, the doctrine that every thing has its price,—and if that price is not paid, not that thing but something else is obtained, and that it is impossible to get any thing without its price . . ." Gurdjieff, too, considered the balance or reciprocity of life, including a lawful aspect to acts of "super effort" and "unflinching perseverance." In Vedic philosophy, varying concepts of karma may speak to lived experience or to experience that extends beyond individual life and appears in cycles of recurrence, not necessarily of a personality-based quality and sometimes on massive scales measurable only across millennia and involving the cosmos as a whole. The Abrahamic religions, particularly Christianity and Islam, often formulate this schema as a cycle of sin and salvation, culminating in eternal life or damnation. The question of culmination or of escaping samsara or karmic cycles appears, too, in Vedism and Buddhism.

Experience persuades me that aspects of the cycle of *preparation and payment* are detectable in quotidian life. To consider consequences as strictly applying to some after-physical dimension reduces the present to a short-time circuit of denial and deferment. Such a life is unworthy of continuance, or as the object of intelligent creation. In any case, I contend that payment is *continually exacted* and that life is also *compensatory if not necessarily redemp-*

tive. Myriad forms of payment, or what might be called suffering, may—and, in my observation, often do—*precede* arrival of a striven-toward or wished-for thing, or form of deliverance. I consider this lawful.

A practitioner may, for example, venture that he or she has duly and objectively suffered at the hands of an antagonist—and perhaps sees every reckoning of continuing to suffer. Is a curse defensible or worthy of a mature, sensitive, striving person? I believe it is. But mind you: the cost is solely on your shoulders. In venturing such a judgment, I would reflect carefully (and privately) on your motives and what is at back of them; the prospect of unknown circumstances that may exculpate or reduce the responsibility of your antagonist; proportionality; the nature of your own actions and incitements; and, finally: whether you are prepared to accept *the costs of wrongness*—or whether you believe that your suffering, or that of others, warrants the magickal response and its proportion.

If you can maturely abide these questions, I believe that the action you decide falls within purview of individual agency. I do not provide formulas for curses in this book; but if you want a hint, think deeply on the principles *like attracts like* and the image contains, or runs continuous with, the whole. You will find that principle woven throughout this book.

When I posted the question on social media of whether a magickian should perform curses, a correspondent replied: "A real magickian won't need to." This called to mind an article I had written several months earlier about Sufi teacher Pir Vilayat Inayat Khan (1916–2004), who I had the honor of knowing several years before his death. It went:

> Pir, or guide, as friends and I knew him, sometimes attracted the ire of orthodox authorities within Islam due to his perceived liberality.

Pir told this story. He once attended a Sufi conference in post-revolutionary Iran. The conference was sponsored by a government-aligned organization.

An "official" imam approached him and said sardonically, "Why, Pir Vilayat, how nice to see you. Tell me, are you still a Muslim?"

Knowing that the man could issue a fatwa against him, Pir said, he replied, *"I'm a bad Muslim."*

Mohammed, Pir explained, taught that Allah holds a special place in His heart for "bad Muslims."

He was off the hook.

We all face a great problem with perspective: how to know whether our actions are beneficent and productive. Yet it must also be said we do not permit that conundrum to disrupt daily life. We seek to work, be generative and productive, to attain or advance toward what we wish. If you are an artist, in addition to excellence of work, you want an audience. If you are in politics, you want a constituency. If you are shop owner, professional, or tradesperson, you want customers or clients. I see no material difference when we resort to magickal or metaphysical methods. We do our best with the perspective granted. That perspective, to amount to anything, requires clarity and focus. As in nature, concentration produces force. You wave air currents out of the way like they are nothing. But air focused into a single, bullet-like point exerts great power. Likewise with light. We move photons out of the way all the time. But light photons concentrated into a laser are searing energy. Same with water. *Concentration is power.*

So, what are you concentrated on? This suggests a different perspective on the expression *know thyself*. It is another of those expressions that seem so familiar. But if you accept the dictum *as above, so below*, if you accept the principle that you, the individual, is attached to all that is, including the cosmic and natural world, it stands to reason that laws you observe in nature repeat within your life, including balance or reciprocity, and the law of focus producing energy and power. What you focus upon and how is very meaningful. Yet it is also tricky because we often disassociate from our wishes. This is where *know thyself* becomes a hotter, more meaningful demand versus just a coffee-mug expression.

It is odd how insights reach us through unexpected byways. One of the formative metaphysical insights of my life arrived this way—and it changed my search. It emerged from a 1972 Soviet-era science-fiction classic, *Roadside Picnic*, coauthored by two brothers, Arkady, and Boris Strugatsky. Russian director Andrei Tarkovsky made the novel into the haunting 1979 movie *Stalker*, with a screenplay by the Strugatskys. The film also forms the basis for a likenamed video game.

Roadside Picnic was written deep in the days of the Cold War when the Soviet Union was officially materialistic or atheistic. The Strugatsky brothers had to submit their work to almost surreal censorship, as Boris recounts in his afterword to a translation published by Chicago Review Press. Reading Boris's record, it is a near-wonder that the brothers retained sanity. Perhaps the bureaucratic madness provided refinement. From within this censorious, philosophically materialistic, authoritarian society, emerged the novel and movie, complementary works that I think evince remarkable metaphysical insight.

The near-future novel depicts an earth where aliens have visited and just as mysteriously departed. The extraterrestrials occupied and abandoned a "Zone" where they discarded advanced technology and inscrutable space junk. Humanity struggles (and mostly fails) to understand these advanced castoffs; the alien devices cause strange, unexpected, and sometimes nightmarish effects. Within the Zone exists a rumored "wish machine," also called the Golden Sphere. It is called The Room in the movie. This otherworldly device grants whatever you want—and only what you want. The wish machine reads your psyche.

The book's anti-hero, Redrick Schuhart, or Red, is a *stalker*, one of the pirates who illegally enter the Zone to scavenge alien technology to sell on the black market. A young protégé accompanies Red into the morphing and dangerous landscape of the Zone. Using an outdated map, the treasure hunters traverse burning ground and other dangers to reach the wish machine. Red asks his trainee what he will request if they make it. When the youth starts rattling off idealized responses about universal happiness, Red cuts him off: "Liar, liar . . . Keep in mind, buddy: the Golden Sphere will only grant your innermost wishes, the kind that, if they don't come true, you'd be ready to jump off a bridge!"

Their harrowing journey succeeds. They reach the Golden Sphere. Upon seeing the object, the youth flies into rapture, rushes forward and asks for world happiness. The alien object—which Red observes is "closer to copper, reddish, completely smooth"—immediately annihilates the boy.

Was it because, as Red suggested, he lied? Or was it because his wish required his own destruction? Red ponders:

> Let us all be healthy, and let them all go to hell. Who's us? Who's them? If I'm happy, Burbridge is unhappy; if Burbridge is happy, Four-Eyes is unhappy; if Raspy is happy, everyone else is unhappy, and Raspy himself is unhappy, except he, the idiot, imagines that he'll be able to wriggle out of it somehow. My Lord, it's a mess, a mess!

Red approaches the Golden Sphere himself to make his wish. Not knowing what to ask, his racing thoughts and conflicts give way to his making the same wish as the dead youth. Did it work? Did it destroy him? Did something else occur? We do not learn. "In reality nothing was ever the way people imagined," one of Red's antagonists muses.

I consider the wish machine real. This book is a little like approaching it; we must do so carefully, with full attentiveness and willingness to bear consequences, which exist at every turn of life, remarkable or mundane. Put differently, *life lived in a certain way* is the wish machine: we advance toward and receive a great deal of what we want, albeit unconsciously in most cases. There exists only the most tenuous bond of memory between wish and event. Deliverance often reaches us, or we it, in a form that is unforeseen or even unrecognized, a topic revisited in chapter five.

All the alien technology left behind in *Roadside Picnic* is compared to rubbish tossed off by road trippers who paused for a picnic. The otherworldly debris produces what seem like miracles—often "cruel miracles" with bizarre consequences and no comprehensible cause-and-effect. This is not unlike the human position regarding religion. We are left with insights, rules, principles, relics, and rituals—but do we possess the means to use them, or do these things remain objects of wonder, confoundment, and, not uncommonly, destruction?

This situation is worsened when we reduce vast complexities to homilies like, "there are no accidents" or "everything happens for a reason." To trifle with such ideas, rather than fall to your knees and sustain them as lifelong questions, is to toy with destruction.

A scientist in the book says: "A lab monkey presses a red button and gets a banana, presses a white button and gets an orange, but has no idea how to obtain bananas and oranges without buttons. Nor does it understand the relationship between buttons and oranges and bananas." Isn't this our relationship with spiritual traditions—and magick? We experience fitful results but possess little, if any, sense of the mechanics at work.

Our only point of agency is through clarity of self and wishes. Self-insight and acknowledgment of desires—while imperfect and maybe at times out of reach—must be striven for. Because *clarity of intent is the single most important (and verifiable) lever of the wish machine.* If we are blind to or denying of our real wishes, the wish machine nonetheless acts upon them. We often become recipients of our alienated desires. We claim no recognition of the fate we have fostered. That is the frightful bargain life offers. The price of self-estrangement is that we insist that our wishes lay in one direction but, ineffably and unfailingly, the psyche and emotions move towards what is *truly desired*, which may lay in another. Self-acknowledgment provides not ease but possibility.

I often tell a story from the life of abolitionist hero, Frederick Douglass (c.1818–1895), when at age fifteen going on sixteen, he stood up to a sadistic slave master, Edward Covey. Frederick did so armed with what he warily called in his memoirs "the magic root." A local man, another slave whom he deeply respected, Sandy Jenkins, pressed the object on him. Sandy "professed to believe in a system for which I have no name," Douglass wrote in 1855. "He was a genuine African, and had inherited some of the so-called magical powers, said to be possessed by African and eastern nations."

Although he never used the term hoodoo, it is evident from Douglass's descriptions across his three memoirs that it was the rock-hard, bulbous root known botanically as jalap root—and within hoodoo as John the Conqueror or sometimes High John. *John de conker* is the pronunciation in oral records and song. In hoodoo, High John is the ultimate protective object, used for everything from personal safety to virility, traditionally carried by a man rather than a woman. In the magickal lore of like attracts or bestows like, conceptually echoing the Hermetic dictum a*s above, so below,* the dried root is shaped like a testicle. You can purchase High John online (I use LuckyMojo.com), or at a botanica in any sizable city.

Carrying the root as instructed on his right-hand side, Frederick stood up to Covey and fought him to a standstill. The "magic root" episode formed the inner revolution of his life. Frederick knew that even though he was, for the time being, a slave in fact, he would never again be a slave in spirit. It took Frederick four more years and one failed attempt to escape. When Frederick as an adolescent experienced his inner revolution, which is the fulcrum of his memoirs*, he remained in bondage. He still suffered a life of cruelty. But he knew above all that he needed to be free within his psyche—and he would be free as a physical fact at the first possible opportunity.

I do not mean to generalize from Douglass's account so much as honor him for universalistic wisdom. There may be things you desperately want that, for any number of reasons, you are unable, economically, socially, or physically, to act on. But that could change. Life is extremely fluid. Life feels static because we are, I believe, alienated from our wishes. Hence, we receive things that we fail to recognize as ourselves. I do not believe the individual can have true ideals, true ethics, or true progress without taking the dictum to *know thyself* to the point of risk and unease. When I ask what you want, I mean not what you are told you *should want* in a tradition—i.e., a decision made by another—but in your unconditioned psyche.

Some of what I have written may invite protest that I am paying insufficient attention to macro social needs or inner preparation. I

---

* *Narrative of the Life of Frederick Douglass* (1845); *My Bondage and My Freedom* (1855); and *Life and Times of Frederick Douglass* (1893).

am not without sensitivity to these points. But I think these bars are often fixed to rungs of rote virtue in our era. Natural disasters and macro crises function amid the myriad laws and forces. Macro forces can, and often do, prove overwhelming. There is, as I see it, no single super law of life. Every force under which we function, including magick, is interrupted and conditioned by other forces, just as gravity responds to mass. Regarding inner preparation, I personally believe that too much fear surrounds spell work and petitionary practices. I encourage specificity to guardrail your outcome. But—and this is key—if you get it wrong, your effort can still be corrected or adjusted, like most things in life. I believe action and need are their own imperative. Reciprocity certainly exists and circumstance takes from our skin what it needs when we fail.

Although I have used a harrowing example from the memoirs of a historical great, I must stress the importance of here-and-now thinking with regard to the life circumstances you actually face, not ideally or in extremis. Use what you know. Confront polarities when and if they arise. It is too easy to reach for categorical extremes when considering the ethic of *acting*. This thought habit devolves into inertia.

Sufi teacher Hazrat Inayat Khan (1882–1927), father of Pir Vilayat and another great twentieth-century figure who helped bring Sufism to the West, was asked by an English-speaking student whether it is necessary to give up riches in order to attain realization. Hazrat told the student, "You do not have riches—how can you give up what is not yours?"*

---

* I must make inadequate tribute to the Khan family. In addition to Pir Vilayat, Hazrat was father to Noor Inayat Khan (1914–1944). While the Khans were dedicated to nonviolence—although Muslim they followed Gandhi's initiative—Noor volunteered for service in the French Resistance during World War II. She was captured and executed at Dachau. Enough cannot be said about the bravery and decency of this woman. She is the subject of a justly detailed article at Wikipedia. Her brother Pir Vilayat, who had also taken a vow of nonviolence, enlisted as a sailor on a minesweeper in the Royal Navy. Pir recalled that his practice of meditation made him an especially good watchman.

Again: deal with actualities. Forget about "what seems" or "what ifs" or what some historic personage, tradition, or custom said. This is your life. The answer of who you are and what you want could vastly differ from what internalized culture or peer pressure induces you to repeat.

I have stressed the ethic of self-honesty. I personally believe that the mature, seeking individual is capable of unembarrassedly answering the question: *what do you want?* I believe that many traditions and gatekeepers deprive the individual of that question—and make it seem as though the individual is incapable of identifying a core self because he or she is in pieces. And we *are* in pieces. Emotions, intellect, physicality, sexuality are all running riot on their own. But the notion that the individual is incapable of knowing what he or she wants is, I think, fallacy. I believe that any emotionally sensitive twelve-year-old could tell you what he or she wants—and it would be meaningful. I do not believe such realization should be taken away from that person.

You might be surprised by what you want. In the confounding and multilayered (and, I think, brilliant) Nicole Kidman movie *Baby Girl*, the protagonist, a high-powered CEO, discovers, after a life pursuing leadership, that she wants to be *told what to do*. That certainly is not all that she wants but it reflects, especially sexually, an unacknowledged facet of self.

Kidman's character, Romy, lets slip early in the movie that she was named by a guru and grew up in cults in a presumptive atmosphere of control. That early childhood experience, I reckon, colored her sense of intimacy and sexual desire, as do all early experiences, especially at periods of sexual awakening. For Romy, subjugation fused with sexuality. Trying to alter arousal is, I think, as futile as trying to change eye color. Magickian Anton LaVey called our early arousal points *Erotic Crystallization Inertia* or ECI, a topic we explore in chapter eleven—understanding it is of great help in magick. Points of arousal are highly individualized, sometimes curious and sometimes confounding, and should not be fought but accommodated within contours of respect and consent.

On a different tack, maybe you have dedicated your life to pursuing learning—yet what you really want is money. Money does a lot of good things. I think gross consumption usually points to an unhappiness or gap in the individual. So maybe the person involved in gross consumption does not really want money. These are maybes. But we so rarely give ourselves the opportunity to really ask.

Artist and British occultist Aleister Crowley wrote many books, but among his most famous utterances is: "Do what thou wilt shall be the whole of the law. Love is the Law. Love under will." As noted, it appears in his 1904 channeled text *The Book of the Law*, which he issued with an introduction in 1938. Crowley's phrase *do what thou wilt* has been misunderstood; part of what Crowley was driving at was not dissimilar to points made by his near-contemporaries Ralph Waldo Emerson and Friedrich Nietzsche, which is that within each of us dwells an essential being, a self buried by conformity, repetition, recitation, peer pressure; and that if you can allow expression of this essential self, that's the emergence of "True Will" which is under the Law of Love.

"Every man and every woman is a star," Crowley further recorded in *The Book of the Law*. I consider it his greatest statement. Yet Crowley, from a perspective of personal conduct, evinced enough ethical flaws—or failures of reciprocity—so that I would not have wanted to be around him. I would not have selected him as my teacher. A lot of people got hurt around Crowley, who engaged in activities that might have been physically dangerous from mountain climbing to drug taking. Disciples got hurt psychologically and sometimes physically. Hence, I do not look to Crowley as a role model. But I cherish his ideas of True Self.

With this in mind, I wrote a new introduction in 2017 to historian Richard Cavendish's (1930–2016) splendid study *The Black Arts* on its fiftieth anniversary. The book has long vexed readers and publishers on account of its title, which sits poorly with occultists who wish to signal the beneficence of their work and not be misunderstood as avaricious or lascivious self-seekers. One British publisher, in what I consider a craven act, altered Cavendish's original to *The Magical Arts*. Did it sell more copies? I doubt it sold a single digit more.*

For any put off by *The Black Arts*, the convivial author quickly explained: "No one is a black magician in his own eyes, and modern occultists, whatever their beliefs and practices, think of themselves as high-minded white magicians"—yet they are driven, as we all are, by the "titanic attempt to exalt the stature of man . . . this gives it [magic] a certain magnificence."

In his shrewd and admiring critical essay on *The Black Arts* in *Book Week* on April 9, 1967, Yiddish Nobel laureate Isaac Bashevis Singer (1902–1991) sided with Cavendish, noting in a too-rare literary review of an occult book: "We are all black magicians in our dreams, in our fantasies, perversions, and phobias."

And, to this I would add, in pursuit of our highest ideals. As Cavendish and Singer detected, we are not very different from the

---

* Never change a title other than for reasons of clarity and quality. Readers are not fooled—nor should anyone wish to fool them!—and copies are not sold by mawkish alterations. In the single greatest regret of my career, I permitted a reprint publisher to change the title of my New Thought history, *One Simple Idea*, from the admittedly less-than-thunderous *How Positive Thinking Reshaped Modern Life* to the inaccurate and cloying *How the Lessons of Positive Thinking Can Change Your Life*—a choice I regret every time I see the book. I hope to correct it some day. The right subtitle is: *The Secret History of Positive Thinking*.

classical magickian when we strive, morally and materially, to carry out our plans in the world—to ensure the betterment of ourselves and our loved ones; to heal sickness; to create, sustain, and, above all, to *generate things* which bear our markings, ideals, and likenesses. All of this is expenditure of power, the striving to actualize inner drives and images.

As you have augured by now, I do not view the search for individual power, including through supernatural means, as negative. Quite the opposite. Historically and psychologically, it is a fundamental human trait to evaluate, adopt, or avoid an idea based upon whether it builds or depletes a sense of personal agency. "A living thing," Nietzsche further wrote in *Beyond Good and Evil*, "seeks above all to *discharge* its strength—life itself is *will to power*..." The difficulty—which everyone must shoulder—is making choices wisely. And paying for them.

We sometimes deny or overlook our power-seeking impulse, associating it with the tragic fate of Faust or Lady Macbeth. (To this I must add that in Goethe's iteration of *Faust*, the sorcerer's fate is ambiguous, which we revisit in chapter seven.) It can be argued that most of our neuroses and feelings of chronic despair, aside from those with identifiably biological causes, stem from frustrated expression of personal power. We may spend a lifetime ascribing our problems to other, more secondary phenomena—without realizing that, as naturally as a bird is drawn to the dips and flows of air currents, we are perpetually attempting to forge, create, and sustain, much like the ancient alchemist or wizard.

"Works such as Cavendish's," Singer wrote, "are a reminder that we are living in an era of amnesia. We have forgotten those vital truths that man once knew and by whose strength he lived." This is what I try, with technical simplicity, to reacquaint us with in this book.

The frustration of magick, as with life in general, is that, while we seem bestowed with almost godlike powers—giving birth, creating beauty, spanning space and time, devising machines of incredible speed and might—we are bound to physical forms that decay. "Ye are gods," reads Psalm 82, adding "but yet shall die as princes." Immortality and reversal of bodily decline is the one magick no one has *yet* mastered. The wish to surpass boundaries of our physicality lies behind some of our most haunting myths and parables, from the Trojan prince Tithonus, to whom the gods granted immortality but trapped in a shell of misery and decay for failing to request eternal youth, to the doomed Victor Frankenstein, who sought the ultimate alchemy of creating life only to bring destruction on all around him. Yet if one reads Mary Shelley's Romantic-era original, Victor is anointed with greater sympathy—and iconic heroism—than is commonly suspected.

A similar intellectual quality appeared in Cavendish. Rather than writing history for history's sake (a valid choice), the Oxford medieval-studies scholar ventured to place his hands and yours on tools of application. Beginning in 1970, Cavendish produced the magisterial twenty-four-volume occult encyclopedia *Man, Myth & Magic*, an illustrated omnibus of impeccable visual quality and scholarly depth. The effort remains unmatched. Vintage copies are among prized possessions in book-collector shops and libraries. In dirtying his hands, Cavendish achieved literary immorality.

My point is: in a life limited and proscribed by parameters, safety ropes, and the wish for respect, I consider it far better to function with dirty than clean hands. Time is short. Halfway measures are no option for the seeker, whatever his or her wishes. Know those wishes. Act on them. *Try.*

CHAPTER FOUR

Sex Transmutation

At this stage in my search, I consider *sexuality* the primary transmitter behind successful magick. By this I mean the urge of sexual desire transmuted toward other ends. Sexuality is *the* critical force—often referenced in obfuscatory if elegant language—that unites the ancient alchemist to the occult revivalist, and hence the contemporary seeker.

In historical occultism, terms abound that whisper this truth. Pioneering occult revivalist Eliphas Lévi posited existence of "astral light" as the vital energy behind magickal operations and key to the Great Work. This comports with near-contemporaneous references to invisible or vital forces such as Edward Bulwer-Lytton's (1803–1873) "Vril" in his liked-titled 1871 novel, *Vril: The Power of the Coming Race*; occult healer Franz Anton Mesmer's concept of "animal magnetism;" Aleister Crowley's "True Will;" Austin Osman Spare's "Kia;" and, most significantly, Arthur Schopenhauer's view of imagination in 1836 in *On Will in Nature*: "Man had not learnt to direct the *light of speculative thought* towards the mysterious depths of his own inner self" (emphasis added).

In his reference to "astral light," Lévi was echoing but not exactly copying Schopenhauer's "light of speculative thought." The occultist *metaphorically named* directed or transmuted thought (and yet it was not wholly metaphorical if considers neurological pathways through which electrical impulses travel in the brain). Lévi, like Mesmer before him, *dramatized a force* that humanity had not yet come to understand: inner workings of mind and existence of a glacial subconscious or subliminal thought-emotive center, or psyche.

In ways both profoundly affecting and dynamic, Lévi interpreted magickal operations as a means of arousing and enlisting this mysterious force, which Lévi also compared to the "serpent of Genesis." Such a force, he reasoned, could be raised through the *sexual urge and directed via focused imagination*. Listen to Lévi from Greer and Mikituk's *Doctrine and Ritual*:

> The astral light is the universal seducer symbolized by the serpent of Genesis. This subtle agent, always active, always luxuriant with life blood, always embellished with seductive dreams and sweet images; this blind force is subordinate to every will, either for good or for evil; this continually reemerging *circulus* of an uncontrolled life, which causes giddiness in the imprudent; this corporeal spirit, this fiery body, this impalpable and always present ether; this immense seduction of nature, how can it be completely defined and how can its action be qualified? Indifferent, in a way, on its own, it lends itself just as easily to good as to evil; it carries the light and propagates the darkness; we can also call it Lucifer or Lucifuge[*]; it is a serpent, but it is also an aureole; it is a fire,

---

[*] A name of uncertain origin, Lucifuge sometimes refers to the prime minister of Satan. In Latin, it is translated as one who flees light.

but one that can as easily belong to the torments of hell as to the offerings of incense promised in heaven. To take possession of it, one must, like the predestined woman, place one's feet on its head.

The image of the woman treading on the head of a serpent appears on the Miraculous Medal, revealed in Paris in 1830 to Catherine Labouré. I have often worn this around my neck. I felt indelible attraction to Catherine's vision for decades upon witnessing it in a bookstore run by the Paulines or Daughters of St. Paul, a Catholic media ministry. I have in my possession, thanks to a close friend and distinguished writer-publisher Gary Jansen, a Miraculous Medal blessed by Pope Benedict XVI. One hangs from a leather jacket of mine—spotted at a reception by a Catholic priest who said, "Well, I'll be damned." I am not against Catholicism—I love Catholicism. As I plan to write in a future book, Catholicism saved my life. Those who hate or proffer conspiracy theories about Catholicism do so because it contains aspects of the Universal Religion, if there is such thing, and I believe there is. Again, Lévi:

> Let us declare here without bandying about that the great magical agent, the double current of light, the living and astral fire of the earth was symbolized by the serpent with the head of a bull, of a goat, or a dog in the ancient theogonies. It is the double serpent of the caduceus; it is the ancient serpent of Genesis; but it is also the brazen serpent of Moses, interlaced with the tau, that is to say the generative lingam; it is also the goat of the Sabbath and the Baphomet of the Templars; it is the Hyle of Gnostics; it is the double tail of the serpent which form the legs of the solar cockerel of Abraxas; finally it is the devil of M. Eudes de Mirville, and it is actually the blind force that souls must conquer to break free of the chains of the Earth . . . All magical work thus consists of freeing oneself from the coils of the ancient serpent,

then placing one's foot on his head and driving him where one wishes.

This force could be termed *emotionalized thought, sexually charged thought, willpower, psyche*, or, as I see it, all these. Lévi believed that the ancient symbols—Tarot (in his reading), alchemical sigils, the pentagram, the serpent, Baphomet, the parabolic myths and ancient fables—were at once reflections of and methods toward arousing awareness and use of this elemental force: *sexuality-thought-will*, symbolized by the serpent and united toward a clarified end. In an empowering innovation, Levi explained how this *élan vital*, this vital force, for which the era had been searching, dwells within the individual where it is summoned by desire, symbol, ceremony, image, and allegory. Power is retained by reserve and focus; it is diluted by excess and dispersal, which is why the great magickian counseled abiding insight, wish, and occult operation in *silence*, a principle explored in chapter twelve.

Since my interest is reducing magick to its practical essentials, I open the methodological section of the book with the clearest, simplest, and most effective ritual I know to harness this universal force. It is called *sex transmutation*. My personal iteration stems from success writer Napoleon Hill's 1937 *Think and Grow Rich* and other references in his talks.*

Hill's concept of sex transmutation shares tantalizing commonalities with the works I have just cited along with classical Tantra, Kabbalah, and Taoism. Hill's key inspiration may appear in a passage from Plato's *Symposium*, as translated by Victoriana's great man of letters, Benjamin Jowett (1817–1893). Socrates recounts the mysterious prophetess Diotima describing the powers of Eros, deity of passion and eroticism:

---

* I recognize Hill's checkered reputation. I do not excuse it but rather consider it in context with the value of his work. For fuller perspective on Hill, see my chapter "The Enigma of Napoleon Hill" in *Happy Warriors: The Lives and Ideas of the Positive-Mind Mystics* (G&D Media, 2024).

> He [Eros] is a great spirit (daimon), and like all spirits he is intermediate between . . . gods and men, conveying and taking across to the gods the prayers and sacrifices of men, and to men the commands and replies of the gods; he is the mediator who spans the chasm . . . For God mingles not with man; but through Love [Eros] all the intercourse and converse of God with man, whether awake or asleep, is carried on.

Hill's method of sex transmutation is simplicity itself. *And it works.* As Hill saw it, the force of life seeking expression is experienced as the *sexual urge*. The sensate experience driving our species toward procreation is *sexual desire*. As such, it is extremely, arguably overwhelmingly, powerful. Sexuality brings great joy and suffering, great harmony and conflict. It is above all the essential *creative urge*. It is the life force pursuing self-expansion. This holds true *not only on a biological level but on all levels*.

We are by nature generative. We build things, foster households, maintain commerce, solve problems, and create new ones. We devise technologies and seek, with greater and lesser success, to manage crises that accompany them. We raze old and erect new. All of these urges, Hill taught, are *the force of life seeking expression*. That force, experienced on the most primal level, is sexuality. Whenever you develop something, whether financial, artistic, architectural, craft-based, or product-based, this same life force is replicating itself through you.

Hill taught that you can *harness* and *direct* this energy wherever you wish—and in a manner that adds more power, enthusiasm, perseverance, insight, intuition, logic, and acumen to any productive effort.

It works like this: Whenever you feel the sexual urge, at times of your private choosing, you *mentally redirect* your desire towards an expression *other than the physical*. You do this through the intellectual act of consciously rerouting your sexual impulse from physical to creative expression. This takes the shape of whatever your wish or effort is at the given moment. This act of transmutation is sexual alchemy.

Hill is not counseling sublimation or repression of the sexual urge. Quite the opposite. Hill noted there exists no greater tonic than sexuality for mood, stress relief, and physical relaxation. This reflected a liberated attitude in 1937. Rather, he is noting that there exist channels through which sexual energy is expressed beyond physicality.

Hill posits that greatly effective people in any area of life—the entrepreneur, the person who excels at a certain art, craft or science, the writer, the actor, the teacher, people who perform at a uniquely high level in their field, and those who evince magnetism and charisma—all of them, *often unconsciously*, are using sexual energy. They are channeling the sexual urge, at critical moments, into their outer efforts. This imbues work and persona with greater vigor, substance, and appeal. This is true of all great salespeople: you know you are being sold something; but you like (or feel subtly or overtly attracted) to him or her—and take the bait. That is sex transmutation, though often without conscious knowledge of the person wielding it.

Hill takes matters further and maintains that people widely considered geniuses, icons, and impresarios are able to rise to that level because sexual energy is at the back of their efforts; although, again, they may be unaware of the power under their command.

For the plural geniuses, Hill uses the arcane *genii*. Genii dates to Roman-Latin usage. It means not only intellectual prowess but also suggests the ancient Roman meaning that genius is a gift bestowed by spirits, genii, or daemons. The same term appears as *jinn* or genie in Arab folklore and culture, again as a spirit capable of bestowing supernatural power on the individual. This suggests the connection

Hill rightly detected in ancient literature between higher forces of life or *Eros* and the individual's capacity for accomplishment.

Toward the end of his life, pioneering psychical researcher Frederic Myers (1843–1901) also pondered the nature and origin of genius. The British scientist came to believe that genius, or remarkable inspiration and application, possessed origin beyond localized intellect. Myers called it the supraliminal mind. In his posthumous 1903 treatise *Human Personality and Its Survival of Bodily Death*, the scientist wrote:

> Genius—if that vaguely used word is to receive anything like a psychological definition—should rather be regarded as a power of utilising a wider range than other men can utilise of faculties in some degree innate in all;—a power of appropriating the results of subliminal mentation to subserve the supraliminal stream of thought;—so that an "inspiration of Genius" will be in truth a *subliminal uprush*, an emergence into the current of ideas which the man is consciously manipulating of other ideas which he has not consciously originated, but which have shaped themselves beyond his will, in profounder regions of his being. I shall urge that there is here no real departure from normality; no abnormality, at least in the sense of degeneration; but rather a fulfilment of the true norm of man, with suggestions, it may be, of something supernormal;—of something which transcends existing normality as an advanced stage of evolutionary progress transcends an earlier stage.

In short, Myers saw genius as interplay of subliminal/subconscious mind—a concept he helped establish—and a supraliminal mind, or what Hill termed Infinite Intelligence, comparable to *Nous* in Hermeticism. In Myers' view, this interplay produces genius, a perspective that jibes with Hill's.

Beat author William S. Burroughs (1914–1997), who knew Hill's work, advocated research into practical applications of the sex-energy concept of *orgone*, pioneered in the 1930s by Austrian-American psychoanalyst Wilhelm Reich (1897–1957). Although it can be reasonably asked whether Hill was aware of Reich's ideas, especially given the corresponding timeline, I have found no such evidence. Indeed, I have pored over Hill's life and work and discerned no definitive giveaway of his sources.

To leave no question regarding the steps of sex transmutation, I am recapping it. You can use this technique almost immediately.

When you experience sexual desire, at times and places of your own choosing, you mentally redirect the urge toward accomplishment of a valued task. Make the mental effort to channel sexual desire along different lines. Simply shift your thoughts away from physical sexual gratification toward another goal, e.g., completion of a piece of writing; pursuit of a client; design of a digital product; creation of your art; acing a job interview; achievement of a physical or athletic goal—whatever it is, you act with the redirected sexual urge focused on your task or aim.

The point is not creating another orthodoxy or "rule" around sex. Sometimes physical expression must be honored. Sexual activity, for pleasure or procreation, is critical for mental, emotional, and physical wellness, as well as for propagation. But in private moments that you alone choose, you can mentally redirect your sexual desire toward a specific task or activity.

Once you have successfully attempted this you may discover new and varying ways of employing sex transmutation. For example, you can use the act of sex transmutation to cultivate a specific mood or personality trait, such as confidence, courage, or enthusiasm. You may attempt this in the near-term for help with a job interview or to face down a bully; or you may want to use this practice in the long-term to remake an aspect of your personality or help someone in crisis. Set no fixed limits on what you may find.

CHAPTER FIVE

Sigil Work and "Established Lines"

British graphic artist and writer Austin Osman Spare (1886–1956) is among the most influential occult figures of the pre- and postwar eras. Through Spare's experiments with breaking structures, rejecting formalism, and seeking to alter reality as we experience it in fleshly form (our only means of experiencing it, he noted), the artist devised an *anti-system* of externalizing will, creating a visual language for the nonrational, and harnessing magick in a manner requiring no belief in the extraphysical—or in anything but empirical results.

French autosuggestion pioneer Émile Coué (1857–1926) ventured a juxtaposition that applies to Spare's way of thought: "The French mind prefers first to discuss and argue on the fundamentals of a principle before inquiring into its practical adaptability to every-day life," he wrote in his 1923 *My Method, Including American Impressions*. "The American mind, on the contrary, immediately sees the possibilities of it, and seeks . . . to carry the idea further even than the author of it may have conceived."*

This approach of *radical application* animated Spare. The artist was, in a sense, an exemplar of William James's philosophy of pragmatism: theory is secondary to outcome. Spare, like James, desired measurable, if not always replicable, results. In so doing, he pioneered the practical occult outlook of the postwar era—and ventured queries that superseded occultism's classical boundaries.

Although Spare believed in the existence of a disincarnate world, one of the most remarkable aspects of his philosophy, emerging in nascence around 1904 when he was a teen, was his *conditioned idealism*. The physical form, he reasoned, is our only means of experiencing the ethereal world or its forces; as such, physicality is sacrosanct. Fifty years later, Spare wrote in *The Formulae of Zos Vel Thanatos:*

> All emanations are through the flesh and nothing has reality for us without it. The soul is ever unknowable because we can only realize by finite form in Time-Space. So, whatever you attribute to the inconceivable is your Ego, as conceived. The mind and its great thought-stream determines everything and permits all things conceivable as possible.

As the artist saw it, reality is as present as flesh and knowable only through its material agencies. This was a concern that also frustrated Kant and Hegel: the psyche, whatever its perceptions, is finally capable only of experiencing itself. For Spare, the task of the occult operation is to bridge the gap between what he deemed *Kia*,

---

* Among other innovations, Coué coined the autosuggestive mantra, "Day by day, in every way, I am getting better and better." Coué's ideas prove subtle—and are supported by contemporary neuro- and placebo science—in ways not widely understood. I profile the mind theorist in my 2024 *Happy Warriors*.

an all-pervading lifeforce similar to Tao, and *Zos,* the manifestation of energy *in self.*

"Magic, for Spare, is about bypassing the ordinary mind and harnessing the innate abilities of one's subconscious," wrote Jake Dirnberger in his excellent 2020 companion *The Pocket Austin Osman Spare.* Hence, the rational mind cannot perform the magickal operation. Another language—symbolic, emotional, and primal—is required.

As with other occultists and consciousness theorists, Spare discovered the bridging force as sexuality, symbol, and disruption of rationality. Around 1913, this insight delivered the artist to his most radical and enduring method: creation of a *sigil* (Latinate for "little sign"), a symbol of desire charged with sexual energy or transcendent emotion, such as ecstasy or fear, and, one could also venture, anger or rage.

Spare's technique is beautiful in simplicity and immediacy. You write a concise statement of your desire, generally no more than a short sentence; cross out duplicate letters; and assemble the remaining characters into an abstract symbol. Another method shared by author and magickian Grant Morrison is to write your desire, cross out vowels, and then cross out repeating consonants. Devise your symbol from there. "Turn that thing into a little image," Morrison said at DisInfo Con in 2015, ". . . and keep reducing it down until it looks magickal. And there are no rules for this thing. Do it until it looks magickal. At that point you now have a sigil. A sigil will work—you can project desire into reality and change reality. It works."

The most popular method for projecting desire onto your sigil was extrapolated by influential occultist Peter J. Carroll (b. 1953): The "charging" of your sigil involves reaching sexual climax over the symbol, usually through masturbation. Other methods of ecstasy include meditation, drugs, and any kind of extra-rational state, such as that brought on through frenetic dance or movement. But masturbation, due to obvious ease and pleasure, has carried the day. Rage, anger, or fear are often considered waste emotions—but they have purposes and they have ignitions; I encourage experimenting in this way, too, when charging your sigil. "Anger is an energy," Johnny Rotten sang in *Rise*.

In Spare's view, magick reaches us only through states of unbridled passion, a perspective in line, more or less, with parapsychologist J.B. Rhine, psychologist Carl Jung, philosopher William James, and other figures of the modern search.

But why should any of this *be*? And, assuming the accuracy of the telling, what is actually occurring? There exist only theories, many borne of personal experience of the practitioner. If one believes that *Zos*— physical man—can function as a capillary of *Kia*—which is likewise comparable to Schopenhauer's "light of speculative thought," Franz Anton Mesmer's "animal magnetism," Edward Bulwer-Lytton's "Vril," and Aleister Crowley's "True Will"—it follows that the sigil serves as a targeting device. "Sigils are monograms of thought," Spare wrote in 1913 in *The Book of Pleasure (Self Love)*, "for the summoning of energy."

In the 1970s, Spare's work grew posthumously associated with the term *chaos magick* as used by Peter J. Carroll in his 1978 *Liber Null*. Chaos magick represents a cut-up and reassembling of self-selected techniques (or what I, in slightly different fashion, call anarchic magick). Cut-up is explored in the following chapter.

Seen from the perspective of chaos theory, to which it is not directly related, chaos magick means that if you alter one particle of existence you necessarily alter everything; there exists complexity and determinism within apparent chaos, an insight with its earliest roots in pre-Socratic philosopher Heraclitus (c. sixth century B.C.). It is impossible for interconnected reality to reflect otherwise. Chaos magick is akin to programming—the introduction of a novel bit of code. One could view the sigil simply as an exotic element dropped into the program of ordinary life. This code could arouse the subconscious, which in turn seeks out-picturing of perspective, suggestion, or, as Spare called it, "true belief." Hence, the chaos practitioner *need not believe in any form of extra-physicality*. Chaos magick could be treated as a strictly materialistic operation. This reflects the terrific *freedom from concept* in Spare's thought.

Spare acknowledged extraphysical phenomena, if not their repetition. "Many experiences I cannot reproduce and in some cases even re-vision," he acknowledged in *The Formulae of Zos Vel Thanatos*. This may offer a yellow light to those who visit by-the-hour psychics. I believe in psychical insight. But it cannot, in my estimation, be turned on and off like a water tap. This is why J.B. Rhine, the preeminent dean of psychical research, stopped working with professional psychics in the mid-1960s. I know a channel or psychic who in my publishing days gave me vital and, I believe, veritable advice that rescued me from a crisis causing health-threatening anxiety. In short, he told me—rightly—to immediately sever all ties with a thuggish author: the kind who wears a suit, wants to save the world, and produces no end of misery for all around him. Trusting my psychic source, I returned to him about year later with a question of deep intimacy. He encouraged me to confess my feelings to another, which I foolishly and selfishly did: the fallout almost ended my life, liberty, and happiness. This is, I believe, why a highly accomplished spiritual publisher cautioned: "You should doubt 50% of what a psychic tells you."

In Spare's system, routine is questioned—while spontaneity of action is critical. Doubt your (or another's) rote acts. Doubt your repeat hits. But: *when feeling strikes—act on your rituals*. To this, I somberly add: do not augment your rituals with rash outer acts. Let magick wend its path, to which we now turn.

It is often said that once you have charged your sigil, you must forget the targeted aim. "Burn every bit of desire out of your system," Anton LaVey (1930–1997) wrote in his essay "Ravings from Tartarus" from his 1992 collection *The Devil's Notebook*, "and then, when you no longer care, it will come to you." As Anton suggests, the point of chaos magick, sigil work, and related techniques is to bypass the rational apparatus of your mind and allow the depths of your subconscious to perform. This occurs, for example, when you think deeply on something, such as the solution to a problem or how to organize a talk, and then, finding yourself in the middle of some other act (like watching a movie or dozing off), the answer appears.

I respect that dimension of the work. But I must add an additional aspect to sigil magick. We not infrequently overlook the arrival of a wished-for thing because it does not reach us in the predetermined form we have idealized in our mind's eye. Prejudice blinds—and sometimes deflects our good. Ancient myths and parables abound with tales of rejected strangers who turn out to be gods, angels, genii, or royalty in disguise. Those who honor the strangers with hospitality are richly rewarded. (Never overlook hospitality as a neglected ancient virtue.) Arrival of your desires can function exactly this way.

Watch carefully for unexpected forms of fulfillment. Something may arrive in seemingly mundane fashion—so much so that you ignore it. Likewise, a wish fulfilled may arrive in a highly unusual or unorthodox way, which contradicts your expectations and perceived forms. This should be kept in mind in matters of intimacy and partnership. I know the hunger of framing a certain person as "the one" and attaching my wishes so deeply to that perceived or unrequited love that I could not fathom a different outcome. Distrust that feeling. In decades on the path, not once—not once—has my "certain" choice in matters of intimacy worked out. Like you, the other person "is a star," as Crowley says, with his or her own system of needs and demands. There is no point in shunning your amorous wishes; what you chase out the front door will return through the back. *But you must remain open to deliverance from other sources of intimacy and love*, which is almost certainly how it will reach you.

There is also likelihood that your intention will arrive through "established channels"—hence the possibility of seemingly common or mundane (and easily overlooked) points of arrival. New Thought pioneer Wallace D. Wattles (1860–1911) in his 1910 *The Science of Getting Rich* observed:

> In creating, the Formless seems to move according to the lines of motion it has established; the thought of an oak tree does not cause the instant formation of a full-grown tree, but does start in motion the forces which will produce the tree, along established lines of growth. Every thought of form, held in thinking Substance, causes the creation of the form, but always, or at least generally, along lines of growth and action already established. The thought of a house of a certain construction, if it were impressed upon Formless Substance, might not cause the instant formation of the house; but it would cause the turning of creative energies already working in trade and commerce into such channels as to result in the speedy building of the house. And if there were no existing channels through which the creative energy could work, then the house would be formed directly from primal substance without waiting for the slow processes of the organic and inorganic world.

The principle of working along "established lines" is one of the subtlest and most important points in practical spirituality. Some people who use spell work or ceremonial magick take this principle a step further. When prescribing a spell or ceremony—which is really ritualized intention, no different from Wattles' formula for "thinking in a Certain Way"—they note that, in order for such operations to work, there must be a *clear avenue of arrival*. For example, if you wish for love but resist company there is no obvious channel of delivery. But if you wish for love and actively circulate among people, you are providing established means of fulfillment.

Each individual must study and consider this step for him or herself. Are you asking for something that fits the context of your life, practices, values, and habits? Are there foreseeable means of delivery? On a different but related note, are you neglecting or overlooking patterns of delivery—or perhaps the arrival of just what you want because it reaches you in unfamiliar ways? Allow yourself freedom in this regard. Focus on the thing or *condition* you wish to attain—not on the limited, mind's-eye form of attaining it.

I want to share a joke that makes this point. During a flood a clergyman fled to the roof of his church to avoid being swept away in the waters. A man in a raft came by and told him to come aboard. The clergyman refused. "God will save me," he said. Someone rowed by in a boat and urged him to come in it. Again, the pastor refused. "God will save me," he said. Finally, a helicopter appeared overhead and dropped a ladder. But the man waved it away. "God will save me!" he yelled. The floodwaters eventually overtook the man and he drowned. Upon reaching heaven he protested to God, "I've served you all my life! Why didn't you save me?" To which God replied: "I didn't save you? I sent the raft, I sent the boat, I sent the helicopter . . ."

Remain open. Take the road when it appears. Reject nothing out of hand.

CHAPTER SIX

Cut-Up Magick

Austin Osman Spare's release from *form* presented distinct appeal to many postwar artists. "Art," writes biographer Phil Baker, "has long been bound up with magic—from cave paintings, which seem to have had magical purpose, to William Burroughs's dictum that 'writing is about making it happen'—and this was more than usually the case with Spare."*

In occult practice, Spare's work arrived as an abrupt and vivifying smash up of liturgy and memorization. The orthodoxy of methods that emerged from the tradition of the Golden Dawn, and even the heterodox Aleister Crowley, could engage the mind but not trigger the passions.

"For this reason," Burroughs wrote in his 1979 *Ah Pook Is Here*, "I consider the Egyptian and Tibetan books of the dead, with their

---

* *Austin Osman Spare: The Occult Life of London's Legendary Artist* by Phil Baker (2011, 2014 North Atlantic Books)

emphasis on ritual and knowing the right words, totally inadequate. There are no right words . . ." For Burroughs and his circle, form ultimately represented systems of control, apparent throughout media and social structure.

Indeed, Burroughs was frustrated by how, with few exceptions, dictatory exposition remained the chief style in writing. In 1959, painter Brion Gysin, encountering Burroughs in Paris (the two previously met in Tangier), crystalized the matter for him, famously observing: "Writing is fifty years behind painting."

Together, they devised and popularized a method, or antimethod, for a process implicit in some earlier modern literature, notably T.S. Eliot's *The Waste Land*. They called it *cut-up*. The technique involves dicing up and rearranging a text, thus summoning an unknown, subliminal, or even oracular meaning. Burroughs summarized the matter in the 1978 book he coauthored with Gysin, *The Third Mind*:

> A friend, Brion Gysin, an American poet and painter, who has lived in Europe for thirty years, was, as far as I know, the first to create cut-ups. His cut-up poem, "Minutes to Go," was broadcast by the BBC and later published in a pamphlet. I was in Paris in the summer of 1960; this was after the publication there of *Naked Lunch*. I became interested in the possibilities of this technique, and I began experimenting myself. Of course, when you think of it, "The Waste Land" was the first great cut-up collage, and Tristan Tzara had done a bit along the same lines. Dos Passos used the same idea in "The Camera Eye" sequences in *U.S.A.* I felt I had been working toward the same goal; thus it was a major revelation to me when I actually saw it being done.

For Burroughs, cut-up offered not only freedom from dominant literary form but a means of expression and perception that violated systemic boundaries of Western conditioning. Again, in *The Third Mind* he noted: "Either-or thinking just is not accurate thinking. That's not the way things occur, and I feel the Aristotelian construct is one of the great shackles of Western civilization. Cut-ups are a movement toward breaking this down."

This reflects an earlier point: insufficiency or ill-suitedness of Aristotelian absolutes in dealing with the occult, to which ineffability, perception, and uncertainty are innate. Any thinker who rejects, prima facie, the extraphysical—itself a position of sentiment—cannot abide suspension of absolutes. Burroughs and Gysin, preceded by Eliot, provided an offramp from this way of thought in both artistic and intellectual efforts. This should not imply release from excellence, an unfortunate extrapolation that has misled countless dilettantes to believe "anyone can do it." Again, Burroughs: "A page of Rimbaud cut up and rearranged will give you quite new images. Rimbaud images—real Rimbaud images—but new ones." And since our psyches are constantly receiving diffuse stimuli, cut-ups, the writer observed, "make explicit a psychosensory process that is going on all the time anyway."

How exactly does cut-up work as a magickal or oracular technique—by which I mean capacity to approach and participate in the "Third Mind"?

During this writing, I decided to revisit a bowl of cut-up phrases that I keep on a mantlepiece. When I was considering titles and themes for my 2022 *Daydream Believer*, I wrote down and cut-up phrases or words that appeal to me and scattered them on the floor to see what emerged. In an observation that intersects with the ideas of Carl Jung's circle (explored in chapter nine), Burroughs wrote, "Perhaps events are pre-written and pre-recorded and when you cut word lines the future leaks out."*

---

* *The Magical Universe of William S. Burroughs* by Matthew Levi Stevens (Mandrake, 2014)

For my exercise on December 2, 2024, I randomly pulled these words from the bowl: *Reconstructionism* ... *Pentagram* ... *Satan* ... *Utopia* ... *Egypt*. Based on my choice, I arranged the five words, which were also random in number, into the shape of a reverse pentagram, considered in the next chapter, like this:

It said to me: *Reconstructionism* is how I view occultism, a revivalist movement of ancient beliefs. The *pentagram* is the occult's most-recognized symbol as well as instigation for my assemblage. *Satan*, which I do not view maleficently, and *utopia* are polarities we must abide in any endeavor or relationship, i.e., friction is the cost of creation. And *Egypt*, finally, is where we shot *The Kybalion* documentary in 2020, and where I am planning to return for a solar eclipse in August 2027. Might that prove a time of galvanizing focus?

When I last did this exercise on January 29, 2023, I pulled five words from the bowl and rearranged them: "Deity of Chaos." The remaining words were "Mind" and "Force." It struck me as propitious that these terms appeared at the exact moment I was immersed in the section on chaos magick in *Modern Occultism*. I reckon that "Mind Force"—*light of speculative thought* or multivarious correspondences—is the "Deity of Chaos": the psyche takes in, assembles, and prioritizes endless impressions. Their stoppage is stoppage of life. These impressions are the alchemist's raw matter—they are unstructured *chaos*. The individual as creator—*as above, so below*—has capacity to refine this material, bringing protean tendencies to bear on it. This is the circle of magick.

Cut-up also reveals meanings not immediately evident. "This," writes Matthew Levi Stevens, "was an attitude he [Burroughs] would extend increasingly to all communications, and eventually all relationships: an early tape-recording from the Beat Hotel has Burroughs and his conspirators discussing a 'creepy letter' which Gysin says he 'can't bear to hear again'—but it is explained that Burroughs 'is going to cut it up—then we'll hear what he's *really* saying!'"

This passage of dialogue appears in the 1977 Burroughs-Gysin book, *The Third Mind*, which, to my embarrassment, I called *The Third Eye* in parts of *Modern Occultism*—but, in the spirit of cut up, I think Burroughs would've been happy:

> *14.* You and Brion have described your collaborations over the years as the products of a "third mind." What's the source of this concept?
> BURROUGHS: *A book called* Think and Grow Rich.
> *GYSIN: It says that when you put two minds together . . .*

> BURROUGHS: . . . there is always a third mind . . .
> GYSIN: . . . a third and superior mind . . .
> BURROUGHS: . . . as an unseen collaborator.
> GYSIN: *That is where we picked up the title. Our book* The Third Mind *is about all the cut-up materials.*

Highly experimental artists like Burroughs, Gysin, and later artist-musician Genesis P-Orridge, integrated into their work the essential ethic of cut-up—which is that *valuable material doesn't necessarily reach you through ordinary or proscribed channels*, including what are deemed serious categories of literature.

In a 2023 Q&A interview with the *New York Times*, novelist Aleksandar Hemon (who either is or is made to sound like one of the assholes of the planet) noted among his reading tastes: "I mainly read books about history, music, and also a lot of poetry, sometimes novels. No advice books, least of all self-help manuals, nor any of those middlebrow smartass books that explain humanity and its evolution and history in under 500 pages and a couple TED Talks."*

While I sympathize with Hemon's impatience toward "news you can use," which dominates TED culture (not to mention its gung-ho materialism), consider what is lost. Standards and measurement matter: exemplary and piss-poor efforts appear in every field or genre; but to categorically reject any "type" of expression is to self-hobble. If one believes that comic books (my father called them "joke books") are childish trash—until recently a widely held view—does that include Will Eisner, Steve Ditko, Robert Crumb, Alan Moore, etc.? I consider it insufficient to rank and thereby exclude modes of expression. Shunning the label "self-help," as Hill's mega-selling book is aptly called, means cutting-off versus cutting-up. "Rejected

---

* "'Vile,' 'Deplorable,' 'Full of Lies': Aleksandar Hemon Is No Fan of Philip Roth," January 22, 2023

stones" not infrequently conceal remarkable insights. This, too, is the ethic of cut up.

Permit yourself freedom to explore different methods of cut up and see what "leaks out." The future? Sublimated insights? Strange associations? Rejectionists insist that Tarot, Ouija, astrology, etc., are "all in our heads." Cut up proves it. But not as expected.

CHAPTER SEVEN

Walking the Lefthand Path

As explored, most Western spirituality stems from Abrahamic traditions—Judaism-Christianity-Islam—along with variations of Vedic, Taoist, shamanic, or Buddhist teachings. At a turning point in my search around 2018, I found these expressions, in both traditional and esoteric iterations, unsatisfying.

I sought a more self-driven path. One of attainment, proteanism, and self-expression. Although I did not embark on my search with this intention—nor with foreordained resistance—I found that my approach coalesced with an outlook referenced in chapter two: the *lefthand path*.

The lefthand path is an ethical and spiritual outlook that could be described as "My Will Be Done." This concept is, I believe, a more honest philosophical antonym to the Scriptural invocation "Thy Will Be Done," which is often invoked with the same meaning covertly or, just as often, unconsciously. We wish to attain—broadly defined—and hope that our strivings comport with those of a Higher Power, or what I call a Greater Force.

The term lefthand, as used here, is rooted in the Vedic Sanskrit *vamachara* ("lefthanded attainment"). Its adoption in the West originated with occult explorer Madame Blavatsky in volume I of her 1888 *The Secret Doctrine*, which popularized the reverse or "horns-up" pentagram in connection with lefthand philosophy; the upside-down pentagram also appears in earlier Western works, such as Eliphas Lévi's 1855 *Ritual of High Magic* and Franz Hartmann's 1886 *Magic: Black and White*.

Some contemporary seekers who identify with the lefthand path believe neither in deity nor extra-physicality but use ritual and symbol for the focus of will. This practice of radical selfhood can be highly integral, such as when working to overcome a limitation or achieve a hallowed form of self-expression. Lefthand practices are not necessarily about "getting stuff," although I defend that approach since an individual's private needs, whatever their nature, may be essential and substantive. Those who walk the lefthand path are often critical of mainstream religionists and "white magic" New Agers who, they say (with validity, I believe), often use obfuscatory or "sacred" language to pursue perfumed self-interest.

A Zen prison minister (now dead) offered a story I value. He was visiting some inmates and one approached him: "I've read all your books and I can't believe I'm meeting you!" The minister replied, "It's not the man but the message." Later, he felt remorse. This inmate had a moment of joy—yet he erased it for some pious "lesson."

In spiritual culture, I distrust overuse of terms like "ego," "nonattachment," and "nonidentification." They are concepts that limit our outlook to decisions made, and for centuries repeated, within Western and Eastern religious frameworks. Such decisions may not be your own. Relatedly, I am uneasy around religionists who avow dedication to "service." Personally, and after many years on the path, I have never encountered someone claiming the mantle of service who was not concealing a shiv behind his or her back. I write that as plainly as I have experienced it. In short, every spiritual principle (and the company espousing it) requires scrutiny by seekers in every generation.

As noted, all religions, whatever universal truths they offer, arise from and respond to particular cultural circumstances. Cultural circumstances facing most ancient believers involved almost certainly dying within the same caste they were born into. The invisible world was a leveler and means of justice. I reject that perspective: of temporal life as illusory and the ineffable as absolute truth. I consider life, seen or unseen, one whole, united by the principle that invests existence with purpose: *self-expression.*

The lefthand path is often conflated with the "dark side" or Satanism, although these comparisons are usually proffered with too little subtlety and understanding to be meaningful. While the lefthand path is not necessarily Satanic, it by no means precludes exploration of Satanism on a seeker's own terms. I likewise recognize that the concept of Satan—rooted in the Hebrew השטן (*ha-sa-taan*), literally "The Satan" or *the adversary* (sometimes *the prosecutor*), or the Latin-derived term Lucifer, or *light bringer* (originally a condemnation of the ancient king of Babylon as a falling star)—is fraught with cultural landmines. While the term Satanism, depending on your perspective, summons images of maleficent darkness, absurdly fictitious abuse scandals*, anti-conformist libertinism, or any number of other associations, there is, I believe, an authentic, if diffuse, esoteric tradition of Satanism in the West, from antiquity to

---

* E.g., see "It's Time to Revisit the Satanic Panic" by Alan Yuhas, *New York Times*, March 31, 2021; "I'm Sorry" [the recantation of a former child witness] by Kyle Zirpolpo as told to Debbie Nathan, *Los Angeles Times*, October 30, 2005; "Why Satanic Panic never really ended" by Aja Romano, *Vox*, March 31, 2021, and "The McMartin Preschool Abuse Trial: An Account" by Douglas O. Linder at Famous-Trails.com. I consider the matter further in my 2023 *Modern Occultism*.

modernity, encompassing intellectual, ethical, literary, and spiritual dimensions.

In addition to re-soundings of ancient themes, I find the esoteric tradition of Satanism enduring in the work of Romantic poets and writers, such as William Blake (1757–1827), Percy Bysshe Shelley (1792–1822), and Lord Byron (1788–1824), who posited the Satanic as a force of rebellion, usurpation, overturning of staid or calcified structures, persistent questioning, rejection of conformity, and refusal of hive mentality. This is my perspective.

An antecedent for this outlook of radical selfhood appears in John Milton's (1608–1674) 1667 *Paradise Lost*, where Satan famously declares: "Here we may reign secure, and in my choice/ To reign is worth ambition though in Hell:/ Better to reign in Hell, then serve in Heav'n." In actuality, the precursor to Milton's lines may come from the mouth of Julius Caesar (100–44 B.C.), at least as posthumously recorded by ancient historian Plutarch (c. 46–119 A.D.):

> We are told that, as he was crossing the Alps and passing by a barbarian village which had very few inhabitants and was a sorry sight, his companions asked with mirth and laughter, "Can it be that here too there are ambitious strifes for office, struggles for primacy, and mutual jealousies of powerful men?" Whereupon Caesar said to them in all seriousness, "I would rather be first here than second at Rome."*

Yet I also distrust a go-it-alone approach to life. I believe in cosmic reciprocity, or what is sometimes called karma, as explored in chapter three. My spiritual, by which I mean extra-physical, outlook abides a core of human commonality, something reinforced by

---

* *Plutarch Lives*, Vol. VII, Loeb Classical Library, translated by Bernadotte Perrin, Harvard University Press, 1919

my interest in psychical research, which is explored in Appendix A. Hence, my search is nonviolent. That does not mean abstaining from self-defense but rather doing nothing to knowingly deny another the same reach for human potential that I reserve for myself. In that regard, I do not seek to love my neighbor. But I do seek to *leave him alone*; except if solidaristically called to his defense.

For similar reasons, I question the imperative of forgiveness. I believe that the moral suasion to forgive often places the individual in an unnatural position and produces inner division that gets diverted into other, often hostile or self-negating behaviors. That does not mean forgiveness is unwarranted in given situations. Nor that it has not healed wounds. It means only that I reject forgiveness as a blanket rule, spiritual requirement, or ethical necessity. I find a more natural and realistic ethic in *abiding*: using injustice as a goad to something greater.

New Thought mystic Neville Goddard observed in a lecture of March 17, 1972, the year of his death, that a drama teacher once cruelly debased him. The British-Barbadian youth, who had traveled alone to New York City at age seventeen to study theater, spoke in an Anglo-Caribbean accent, which his instructor deemed a career-killer:

> My own disappointments in my world led up to whatever I am doing today. When the teacher in my school, I could ill afford the $500 that my father gave me to go to this small school in New York City, and she made me the goat. She called me out before an audience of about forty students. And she said, "Now listen to him speak. He will never earn a living using his voice."
>
> She should not have done that, but she did it—but she didn't know the kind of person that she was talking about. Instead of going down into the grave and burying my head in shame, I was determined that I would actually disprove her.

It did something to me when she said to me, "you will never earn"—to the class, using me as the guinea pig to show them what not to do—and so, she said, I spoke with a guttural voice and I spoke with this very heavy accent, and I will never use my voice to earn a living . . .

We all went to this school and this teacher simply singled me out to make some little, well, exhibition of what I should not be doing in class. But I went home and I was so annoyed that I had lost my father's $500 or $600 that he gave me for the six-months course, but I was determined that she was false, that she was wrong. So, I went to the end. I went to the end and actually felt that I was facing an audience and unembarrassed that I could talk and talk and talk forever without notes, no notes.

When I first wrote about Neville in 2005 for *Science of Mind* magazine he was a near unknown even within many New Thought circles. My boss, himself a New Thought minister, needled me that I was only interested in the teacher due to his obscurity and that my article might find commensurate readership. I used his comments in the same way that Neville used his drama teacher's. As it happened, the article ignited a *Nevillelution*. Neville is today one of the most highly regarded spiritual orators of the twentieth century—and among the most widely read metaphysical voices of our own. His vast range of recorded lectures amass hits in the millions online.

The mystic taught a radical system of thought causation in which your *imagination is God*. He used expressly Christian terms and points of reference, even if dramatically redefined. This has led some seekers to ask how I can consider myself a student of Neville's thought.

I sometimes maintain correspondence with incarcerates. One who was freed recent to this writing wrote me in April 2022 with the below passage. Although it isn't necessarily how I would put things myself, I found her observation keen. An outsider may see my work better than I do. It is quoted with the writer's permission:

> . . . you really aren't deviating from the teachings of Neville Goddard, and I find it amusing that people miss that. He, as you know, taught about Christ consciousness and that if you want it enough you can manifest it. You have taken this teaching and put it as "My will be done," over "Thy will be done," and yet it is the same teaching on manifesting. The phrase "Do what thou wilt, an it harm none" is much the same words.

My correspondent's closing reference is from the Wiccan Rede, an ethical code enunciated in 1964 by English Wiccan Doreen Valiente who employed elements from Gerald Gardner and Aleister Crowley.

"People speak of socialism," wrote political theorist Michael Harrington (1928–1989) in his 1989 coda *Socialism: Past and Future.* "We should speak of *socialisms*." The same could be said of Satanism. One-dimensional use of the term, often hitched to self-elevating fantasies of anti-Satanists (who vastly outnumber their imagined targets), is as ridiculous as equating Bernie Sanders and Pol Pot because both are called socialists. Based on personal experience, most anti-Satanists dwell upon lurid accounts of abuse, filled with historical and legal gaps and inventions, in ways I've never witnessed among those they target. I venture that some who collect and brandish these records nurture a prurient interest of their own, perfumed and reprocessed through activist "research."

The most sensational and longest-running case to emerge from the Satanic Panic—and also the longest running in U.S. history—involved California's McMartin Preschool, of which journalist Heather Greene wrote in her 2021 *Lights, Camera, Witchcraft*:

> In 1983, accusations were made against owners and childcare workers at the McMartin Preschool in Manhattan Beach, California. They were accused of ritual child abuse, including sodomy, rape, and other forms of molestation. Stories circulated of animal sacrifice, secret tunnels, blood drinking, the placing of pentagrams on children's bottoms, and more. In 1984, 384 McMartin preschool children of the 400 interviewed were diagnosed as having been sexually abused. Arrests were made. Despite all early doubts as to the credibility of the children's testimonies and the legitimacy of various reports, the McMartin trial continued for seven years, becoming the most expensive and longest running criminal trial in American history.

All charges were dropped in 1990. No one can restore the lives stolen from the falsely accused. Despite myriad debunking, related canards endure in willful suppositions and circumstantial leaps of conspiracy narratives. Implications sometimes emerge on the geopolitical stage. In justifying his attempted annexation of four regions of Ukraine, Vladimir Putin announced in a speech of September 30, 2022, "The repression of freedom is taking on the outlines of a 'reverse religion,' of real Satanism," claiming that Western liberal outlooks amounted to "denial of man."*

---

* "Putin's speech on annexation paints a stark picture of a face-off with the West" by Anton Troianovski, *New York Times*, September 30, 2022

As alluded, I am attempting to redefine the Satanic in more esoteric terms, according to concepts, principles, and points of view understood by Romantic poets and writers who framed the Satanic current as one of legitimate rebellion, rejection of received concepts, and pursuit of what Crowley termed True Will. Historical and esoteric reading of Satanist metaphysics or philosophy is defensible on those grounds.

Many of us grew up learning the story of humanity's fall from grace in the biblical parable of the Garden of Paradise. The serpent—long culturally associated with Satan—seduces Eve, and then she Adam, into eating forbidden fruit from the Tree of Knowledge of Good and Evil. This ur-myth appears in the sparsely detailed Genesis 3. When revisiting the formative story, you will find, in virtually any translation, that the serpent's argument is based in truth: the first couple do not perish for eating the apple and their eyes are, in fact, opened to good and evil. Or, as William Blake wrote in another context in *The Marriage of Heaven and Hell*, "the doors of perception were cleansed." Moreover, Eve, contrary to a cultural shibboleth, does not seduce Adam who requires little coaxing. The serpent suggests, as augmented in other texts, that Yahweh displays cruel hypocrisy by forbidding illumination of mind, even as its availability sits in the garden's midst.

It is not clear whether the Tree of Knowledge of Good and Evil and the Tree of Life, both of which appear in Genesis, are two distinct trees or one and the same. One of the earliest exponents of the "one tree" theory was German theologian Karl Budde (1850–1935), followed by bible scholar Claus Westermann (1909–2000), both traditional figures, widely recognized in the field. What if the Tree of Knowledge of Good and Evil and the Tree of Life are one thing?

What kind of life are Adam and Eve conscripted to in paradise without knowledge of good and evil? In such a state, they could not create, compare, produce, and measure. Also true is that they do not know friction. They eat from the tree, they are expelled from Eden, and they beget two sons, Cain and Abel. Differences are introduced into the world. Cain explodes in rage at his brother with whom he had deep fissures. His brother is pious, theological, and favored by God. Cain is independent, a loner and a rebel, and unsuited to worship. Cain loves his brother yet harbors radical differences with him because their parents ate from the Tree of Knowledge of Good and Evil. Cain does something he regrets for the rest of his life. This pathos is reexamined from Cain's perspective in Lord Byron's 1821 closet drama, *Cain*.

Yet if knowledge of good and evil had not been introduced into paradise by the adversarial force, not only would there have been no differences between Cain and Abel but in a very real sense there would have *been no Cain and Abel* because everything and everyone would be extensions of a certain *sameness*. There seems no purpose to creation absent distinctions of evaluation and measurement, of production and counter-production, and of friction, which inevitably arises from choice, will, and agency.

Hence, it is possible to view Genesis 3 through a different lens. *It is not a Jewish book or a Christian book*—those are early modern terms—it is, like all primeval mythical works, a parable of human development and selfhood. All great spiritual works emerged from humanity seeking origin and purpose. If we approach Scripture that way, we can detect across history a slender thread of insight that invites new understanding of our foundational Western myth.

I encounter some seekers who embrace my defense of occult or metaphysical practices by which they feel understood but reject any consideration of Satanism because that word for them, as with the word *occult* in general culture, is so sullied by convention it cannot be revisited. When I began my explorations in 2018, the marketing director of a Manhattan New Age center told me that a "beloved astrologer" threatened to sever ties with the venue unless I canceled or altered the name of a talk on Satanism. I refused and my talk went as planned. The world kept turning. I am working to reform this prejudice. It may be a windmill too great to tilt at; but my effort is underway and you do not turn back once you have embarked on an errand. In a humorous domestic kerfuffle, I was told, "You're not gonna convert Western civilization to Satanism!" Point taken.

Amid such considerations, it may be fairly asked: What about sacrifice for others? What about "giving back?" These things arrive of their own volition, often (more often, I aver) without proclamation or intention. If you realized how many beings underwent sacrifice, suffering, and death for the circumstances that allow you to read these words in material comfort, you would place a different value on your life and what debt you owe for it. I find that most sacrifices, where they actually occur, are intimate and silent.

There exist a handful of diffuse Satanic organizations, from the foundational and, today, professedly atheistic Church of Satan formed by magician and artist Anton LaVey (1920–1997) in 1966 (Anton was less cut-and-dried on questions of theism); to the more occultic and spiritual-oriented Temple of Set founded by the recently deceased Michael Aquino (1946–2019); to the activist-driven Satanic Temple, which focuses on First Amendment rights and countering Satanic Panic fictions. I value these and other groups but belong to none and write as a solitary seeker.

Why piece together an individual lefthand philosophy? Why not simply embrace Aleister Crowley's *Thelema* ("do what thou wilt . . .") or Ayn Rand's radically capitalistic Objectivism? I deeply respect Thelema and share much with it; but I harbor general aversion to some of the more stringently ceremonial and liturgical expressions of Crowley's thought. This may result, in part, from an orthodox bar mitzvah as a youth, an experience I cherish but do not accept as a template. In any case, I like a statement cited earlier by philosopher and critic of science Paul Feyerabend: "I am for anarchism in *thinking* . . ."

Regarding Ayn Rand, I am smitten with her persona, which I consider an act of protean self-creation that represents her greatest work (and compares well to another iconic Russian, Madame H.P. Blavatsky). But I am not in line with philosophical materialism or atheism, which are at the heart of Rand's outlook. I believe we participate in both tactile and extra-physical realms. As I see it, our ancient ancestors were right in identifying and personifying energies or intelligences in nature. I seek relations with a Greater Force.

Recent to this writing, an artist I love, Duncan Trussell (who calls Lucifer "diet Satan"), asked whether there isn't risk in what I am attempting? Especially given mainstream interpretation of the Satanic. I venerate an unprejudiced question, our rarest resource. I abhor rhetorical questions, a device that falsifies this precious means of exchange. I responded to Duncan's question in two ways. First, religious models—like scientific ones (e.g., string theory, cosmic wormholes)—are just that: models of reality, not reality itself. What we call time is just measurement of time—the thing itself is vastly more elusive. Neither I, nor any seeker, is obligated to abide conceptualizations, nor matter how oft repeated. *Familiarity is not truth.* Never confuse tradition with habit. In that vein, readers may notice paucity of a common word in this discussion: Devil. The Devil is an Old-English term. It is steeped in exoteric prejudices. Beyond proper names or vernacular expressions, I rarely use it. I am sometimes sweetly called a "Devil worshipper." That misses the mark.

But I am not indifferent to larger cultural attitudes. Hence, I must respect the question of risk, which I have asked myself. In short, I determined several years ago that I may be courting risk. I accept that. I privately elected to follow this road as a seeker—I vowed to follow it—and to testify to what is found. That is my self-chosen effort. If the lefthand path possesses an operating principle it is uttered by the Great Rebel of *Paradise Lost*: "Can it be sin to know?" I will never defer to thought systems or customs that forbid the fruit of measurement or punish its consumption.

An October 5, 2019, *New York Times* column, "How to Sell Your Soul to Donald Trump" by Frank Bruni, referenced the popular legend of medieval wizard Faust making a pact to serve Satan in exchange for power and renown. The idea of selling your soul to Satan is among the most familiar parables in Western culture—but where does it actually come from?

There exist many versions of the Faust drama, most notably by playwright Christopher Marlowe (1564–1593) and philosopher Johann Wolfgang von Goethe (1749–1832). The latter is widely regarded as dramatically superior and subtler.

For his part, Marlowe was writing partly in support of a backlash against Renaissance occultism. His *Doctor Faustus* is a lyrically beautiful if one-dimensional morality tale about the dangers of dabbling in dark forces, for which the protagonist pays with damnation. Goethe's *Faust* is more psychologically and ethically layered. In it, Mephistopheles and Faust circle each other, sharklike, neither quite trusting the other. They finally strike a bargain in which the Dark Lord agrees to grant Faust unbounded happiness and knowledge—with a peculiar catch that binds Mephistopheles to his word: if Faust ever occupies a moment so splendid that he wants to live in it forever only then will he go to his death and vest his soul to Satan. That moment never quite occurs and the sorcerer is saved.

Was there a real Faust? Very likely, but historians have never fully agreed upon who. Rough consensus settled around Johann Georg Faust, a German alchemist, astrologer, theologian, and magickian who died around 1541. Central European legend held that the mysterious figure made a pact with Satan for knowledge and power. This Faust probably formed the model for Marlowe's stage character.

Lots of modern figures are rumored to "sell their souls"— many such stories populate folklore and literature. Baroque violinist Giuseppe Tartini (1692–1770) related one of the most alluring. The composer's famously complex Violin Sonata in G minor, better known as the Devil's Trill Sonata, was, he said, played for him in a dream by Satan. To his agony, Tartini on awakening could reconstruct only a shadow of the original. A similar mythos of Satanic inspiration surrounds the career of violinist Niccolò Paganini (1782–1840), who astounded audiences with his technical prowess and ability to play without sheet music.

In yet another exhibit of Madame Blavatsky's omnipresence, the occultist adapted Tartini's narrative into a short story, "The Ensouled Violin," originally appearing in *The Theosophist* in January 1880 and in her posthumous 1892 collection *Nightmare Tales*. As it must, Blavatsky's horror tale hosts a legend of its own, which is that it was cowritten, along with several other collaborations, by the hidden Cyprian adept called Master Hillarion.

One of the most popular modern iterations of soul selling involves American bluesman Robert Johnson (1911–1938). As popular legend goes, the guitarist met or conjured the devil at a crossroads and vowed to serve him in exchange for preternatural musical skills. Although Johnson recorded a song called "Crossroads," it was not about soul selling but hitchhiking. But another blues master, Tommy Johnson (1896–1956), performed a similar—though more elusive—act of magick, recounted by his brother LeDell to biographer David Evans in his 1971 *Tommy Johnson*:

> If you want to learn how to make songs yourself, you take your guitar and you go to where the road crosses that way, where a crossroads is. Get there, be sure to get there just a little 'fore 12 that night so you know you'll be there. You have your guitar and be playing a piece there by yourself... A big black man will walk up there and take your guitar and he'll tune it. And then he'll play a piece and hand it back to you. That's the way I learned to play anything I want.

Ledell does not specifically reference Tommy engaging in soul selling *or* encountering Satan. Rather, Tommy drew upon a practice found in the Black magickal tradition of hoodoo. Due to phonetic and cultural intersections, hoodoo is sometimes confused with Vodou. As noted, Vodou is an Afro-Caribbean religion with its own deities, priesthood, and liturgy, properly spelled Vodou in Haiti and Voodoo in the American South. The term hoodoo is lowercase. Its etymology is unclear. But hoodoo may come from *huduba*, a term used among the Hausa people of West and Central Africa meaning to arouse resentment against someone. In blues songs, singers sometimes lament being "hoodooed"—i.e., crossed and tricked by spell casting. Hoodoo was and remains a syncretic, spell-working system originated by enslaved people in the U.S. Within the framework of hoodoo, Tommy, at least in his brother's account, was practicing a retention of Western and Central African magic in which a seeker summons a deific protector, sometimes in the form of Ellegua or Eshu, who guards the crossroads and dispenses wisdom and artistry, similar to Hellenic gods Hermes or Mercury.

A sketchy but nonetheless intriguing online legend has Bob Dylan following Tommy Johnson's footsteps and selling his soul to Satan for fame and artistry, at least according to his elliptical (and fascinating) 2004 interview on *60 Minutes*:

Ed Bradley: Why do you still do it? Why are you still out here?

Dylan: Well it goes back to the destiny thing. I made a bargain with it, you know, a long time ago and I'm holding up my end.

Bradley: What was your bargain?

Dylan: To get where I am now.

Bradley: [laughing] Should I ask who you made the bargain with?

Dylan: With, you know, with the chief commander.

Bradley: On this earth?

Dylan: On this earth and in the world we can't see.

This is, of course, a shaky interpretation. But Dylan, the perennial trickster (in the mold of Hermes and Eshu), won't let on for sure.

Where, finally, does the idea of selling your soul to Satan originate from, at least in the Western mind? The likeliest and earliest source is the Old Testament book Isaiah 28:15, in which nonbelievers are said to elude bad tidings by striking a deal with nether-forces. It appears this way in a 1985 translation by the Jewish Publication Society (JPS):

> For you have said, "We have made a covenant with Death, Concluded a pact with *Sheol*. When the sweeping flood passes

through, It shall not reach us; For we have made falsehood our refuge, Taken shelter in treachery."

Sheol references the Hebrew concept of the afterworld—sometimes translated *nether-world* as in JPS's 1917 translation—and is not synonymous with more modern concepts of Hell, the term used in the King James Bible. Although notions of a personified Satan had not fully taken shape in the biblical era, the idea of a maleficent pact spread among early Christians and probably formed the basis of "selling your soul."

As a historian and participant in occult and esoteric movements, I never dodge the all-important question: *does it work?* Well, I have provided background and tools. Never permit past convention to curb current experiment. If your spiritual journey involves a relationship to some personified energy, from whatever time, place, or culture, I offer this observation: It could be that deity does not afford you favors but grants you the strength to attain favors. Or favors themselves may also come. Are you prepared for them? I prescribe no medicine I have not taken myself.

In closing, I know that some reading these words may find, as I once did, that their search seems at a dead end. They feel that they have cycled-out or failed to reach a wished-for destination. Allow me a tangent: It seems to me that art is expression that plants new ideas in the viewer. I was inspired this way by witnessing a production of Japanese underground theater maestro Shuji Terayama's play *Duke Bluebeard's Castle* at the Japan Society in New York the night before recording this book. (I have also experienced this with the work of musical expressionist Geneva Jacuzzi.) As I viewed Terayama's play, I realized how to end this chapter—with a prayer of salutation for any who wish to use it. This address can precede your petition:

> *God of Wishes Fulfilled*
> *God of the Outsiders*
> *God of Reciprocity*
> *God of Retribution*
> *Grant what I ask*
> *Which I am prepared*
> *to pay for*

Keep in mind: in some cases, payment has already been made and the ask has been earned.

CHAPTER EIGHT

Spontaneous Deity Petition

At this point in my search, I have come to believe not only in the importance of passion and sexual energy in magick but also *spontaneity of action*. A practitioner must act when the feeling strikes regardless of surroundings or timing. Extemporaneous action not only allows you to harness the psyche's forces but also deters staidness and recitative orthodoxy.

In my view, the greatest danger to magickal practice is orthodoxy. Orthodoxy asserts itself insidiously, including, or even especially, within settings chartered to escape it. This chapter on deity worship and petition is a battle cry against orthodoxy. In that vein, I call my personal system *anarchic magick*. If you like my approach, I invite you to honor it by throwing away my term and using your own.

I do poorly with timed rituals and spells. I never fully know when I will be prepared to bring passion and a sense of internal morale (call it faith) to the wish at hand. Mind and emotion united prove a powerful combination. Hence, you must remain open and ready to practice, the same way a sculptor, painter, writer, or musician must have his or her tools at hand for when inspiration requires action. Spontaneous practice is very powerful. I find it much more efficacious than stratified and planned-for spells or rituals.

Let me recount a spontaneous episode that galvanized so much in my current life. On a winter afternoon about eighteen years ago, I climbed to the top of a stone tower on the banks of the Charles River in Weston, Massachusetts. The Victorian-era oddity (or *folly* as the style is sometimes called) was built in 1899 to commemorate a Viking settlement that some believe Norse explorer Leif Erikson founded on the banks of the Charles around 1,000 A.D.

Named Norumbega Tower, after the legendary settlement, the 38-foot column had iron bars on its windows and doors to keep out snoopers, ghost hunters, and beer-drinking high schoolers. All I knew was that I wanted to go inside. I slithered my six-foot-two-inch frame through a loose grill, discovered some graffiti left by Satan-worshipping metalheads (love them), and climbed a dank stone stairway to the top.

At that time in my life, I had one great desire burning in my heart: to become a writer. I had already been active in this direction, but I was not young — I was past forty. I swore from the top of that tower that I would establish myself as a known author. I asked all forces available to me on that frigid winter day, seen and unseen, physical and extraphysical, to come to my aid.

Something swelled up within me at that moment: I felt in sync physically, intellectually, and emotionally and at one with my surroundings; my wish resounded clear, strong, and assured, as though lifted by some unseen current. It was a totalizing experience, which went beyond the common. In the years immediately ahead, I did become known as a writer—I was published by Random House and other presses, won a PEN literary award, and received bylines in publications such as *The New York Times*, *The Wall Street Journal*, *The Washington Post*, and Politico—outlets rarely drawn, if not culturally averse, to my occult topics.

My act that winter day was entirely spontaneous and of the moment. I neither planned nor prepared for it nor was I reciting ceremonies, spells, or rituals from a book.

Not long after, I had a related experience. I was suffering a sense of failure in my efforts to break into nonfiction television and movies, where I hoped to host, write, and treat the occult and esoteric themes I love. In July 2017, I wrote these words in the margin of a copy of Napoleon Hill's *Think and Grow Rich*: "My TV plans have not been sound—I am at cross purposes. I need a new vision of what will work, and what is right/compatible with my ideals." Just around that time, I visited the Museum of the Moving Image in Astoria, Queens, in New York. As part of the exhibit that summer day, movie-set trailers were parked out front and visitors were allowed to enter makeup and green rooms typically used by on-set actors. Inside the museum (in addition to the life-sized, head-rotating doll from *The Exorcist*) appears a delightful walk-in exhibit that expressionistically captures the interior of vintage movie palaces. I found myself alone in that space. It was a propitious moment in which I felt emotion welling up in me. I again prayed to all forces within and without to bring me the screen success for which I yearned. I repeated something similar when I entered—and stole moments of privacy in—the location trailers.

The road that followed was hard, twisting, and, at times, sufficiently difficult so that days occurred where I vowed to give it all up. In a park on New York's Lower East Side, after suffering betrayal on a screen project from someone I had considered a close friend, I wrote on April 21, 2021, in my notebook: "My DCA [definite chief aim] has failed. It is eating me alive. I need a turn of corner . . .

I need a *new* DCA. TV is not viable. Kybalion movie = headed south." But an authentic wish is a strange thing: you cannot give it up. It has a hold on you. It owns you, in a sense. You are indebted to it. Hours or at most a day later, the wish came roaring back, as it had other times. On April 23, 2021, I wrote, "I cannot move away from my DCA."

As I write these words in late 2024, I just got off a Zoom call with an executive at the A&E Channel, where I have a development deal. I host a Discovery/HBO Max show, *Alien Encounters*, which, among other things, has appeared in Max's top-ten streaming shows. I play myself in the 2024 installment of the found-footage horror franchise *V/H/S/BEYOND*, which got nominated for a Critics Choice Award. I play a newscaster in the Sundance-premiering 2023 Paramount thrilled *My Animal* directed by Jacqueline Castel. I am featured in the 2024 docuseries *Beyond: UFOs and the Unknown* on MGM+, executive produced by J.J. Abrams. My 2022 feature documentary *The Kybalion*, brilliantly directed by Ronni Thomas and shot on location in Egypt, premiered as the #3 documentary on iTunes. I have legitimate and ethical management at SpectreVision, a media company cofounded by actor Elijah Wood. Jim Perry, Daniel Noah and other principals there collaborated with me on a dream-come-true podcast, *Extraordinary Evidence: ESP Is Real*. I appear regularly on *The UnBelievable* with Dan Aykroyd on the History Channel. Dan, in an interview of November 15, 2024, with *Decider*, said: "I love Mitch Horowitz. He's great . . . I kind of relate to him in a way. I just like his look, you know?" (While moving by itself, Dan's comment arrived several months after producers at a production company told my manager they were unhappy with my leather-jacketed look. They asked him to lie and say it was *his* idea that my leather go. He refused. Thank you, Antonio D'Intino.) As of this writing, I was just named an on-camera analyst for the History Channel show *The*

Proof Is Out There and my manager is negotiating my appearance on an occult-themed true-crime docuseries. And so on.

The effort never stops and arrival is always tantalizingly a step away—but progress? In early 2024, when I stepped into the talent trailer on the Roswell, New Mexico, set of *Alien Encounters*, the sense of symmetry was uncanny and emotional. My eyes teared.

On other occasions, I have dedicated myself to highly involved spells. I have scouted and bought myriad ingredients, sometimes staying up all night performing the prescribed operation. Success proved spotty. For me, the more textbook or involved a ritual, the less I am able to summon or sustain passion. Nothing works as directly or completely, in my experience, as self-devised, *radical spontaneity*.

In anarchic magick the world is your temple, quite literally. Within the environs of that temple, I believe deeply in petitionary prayer, of a radical sort. In my view, we overlook great wisdom and possibilities if we neglect the petitionary outlook of our primeval ancestors. As noted earlier, the ancients personified energies as deities, giving them names like Set, Minerva, Jupiter, or Kali, and sought relations with these deific beings. Nearly every parable and story about deities from the world over depicts them possessing the same human foibles we all have: rage, jealousy, pride, certain strengths, certain weaknesses. Hence, it stands to reason that there is an emotional component to these intelligences. If so, then, once again, it could be that the old gods are lonely and hunger for your attention. This presents the *possibility* to foster relations with these timeless energies, ascribed different names across different cultures, but generally representing archetypal traits.

I offer this exchange I once had with an online 'zine *Secret Transmissions*:

Q: Mythology is intimately intertwined with magic, whether it's Norse, Greek, Egyptian, Celtic or other. But let's say that you don't feel compelled to join a group ruled by a specific pantheon but are nevertheless deeply moved and inspired by these deities and want to make them a part of your spiritual life; how might that be achieved?

A: Well, to share a personal story, many years ago on Canal Street near Manhattan's Chinatown, I discovered an old office building that had a beautiful profile relief of Mercury above its entrance. Apropos of what I was saying earlier, I harbor questions about the lingering energies of the old gods.

I made a practice, for many weeks, of taking the subway to that slightly out-of-the-way place every morning and praying to that image of Mercury. I used to stand on the sidewalk in plain sight and pray in front of a very nice and indulgent Latin American woman who sold newspapers from on top of a milk crate in front of that building.

I don't know whether she thought I was crazy—there is a greater tolerance and embrace of occult religious methods in Latin America, so I might not have seemed very odd to her. In any case, I venerate the personage and principle of Mercury, and this was a means of expressing that, as well as petitioning favor. I felt some satisfaction, though no sense of conclusion, from this act.

I encourage privately determined acts based on your sense of need, aesthetic, dedication, and passion. Your practice of worship, like any kind of intimacy, is exquisitely personal. You do not require my or anyone's help selecting a deity. You already know who to select. Ask yourself. It's there.

For those who wish to make petitions based on seasonal cycles, I will cite Jewish folkloric and Talmudic sources to direct you to four she-demons (I use demon neutrally) corresponding to the four *Tequfot* (singular *Tequfa*) or equinoxes and solstices.* They are:

> Lilith = vernal equinox
> Naamah = summer solstice
> Igrath = autumnal equinox**
> Mahalath = winter solstice

Fall equinox traditionally honors Igrath. This "mistress of sorceresses"*** rules the autumnal equinox from sundown to midnight, during which time she can be petitioned. Igrath is the queen of demons and guardian of prostitution or sex work. Lilith, who rules the vernal equinox, is the queen of night, controlling nocturnal animals and mating with men. Lilith and Igrath were once imprisoned like genies in a lantern. Should you wish to make a petition on the equinox, this supplies a hint of tribute. Naamah—whose name means pleasant—is the archetypal seductress. Ruler of the summer solstice, she charms through music. Naamah can be petitioned not only on the summer solstice but also as part of any sex magick ritual. And, finally, Mahalath, guardian of the winter solstice, is the outsider and consort to those in second or third marriages. She responds to stringed instruments. My wish is that you determine and act on your own affinities, or share mine if you like.

As alluded, you can experience worship, which I define as self-expansion (*as above, so below*), in any setting, including a movie.

---

* See *The Hebrew Goddess* by Raphael Patai (Wayne State University Press, 1990). Also see: https://luciferianapotheca.com/blogs/news/how-to-celebrate-the-spring-equinox-w-lilith-ahriman

** Igrath may also be phoneticized "Igrat" or "Agrat."

*** *Jewish Encyclopedia* (1901–1906).

Michael Muhammed Knight, an innovative scholar of Islam, began his conversion at age fifteen after seeing Spike Lee's *Malcolm X*. "Can a film be sacred scripture?" Mike wondered. I say emphatically yes. I find a similar experience in the character Abel played by Oscar Isaacs in *A Most Violent Year*. Abel embodies the kind of self-sufficiency and hard-won ethics that I venerate. The movie takes me to an elevated state and opens me to a wish. A podcaster told me that she saw qualities in artist Courtney Love that she felt drawn to emulate, even to *worship* in the sense of expanding oneself. Traditionalists be damned, I say that all this represents a legitimate spiritual act.

Most traditionalists (I use the term colloquially, not to describe the thought movement called Traditionalism) do not know what spirituality is. They know a system, usually one that makes them feel protected from perceived dangers, such as irrationality or irreligiosity, and call it truth.

If I have an ethical ancestor, I hope it is Ralph Waldo Emerson who wrote in 1841 in his essay "Self-Reliance" (today out of favor):

> I remember an answer which when quite young I was prompted to make to a valued adviser, who was wont to importune me with the dear old doctrines of the church. On my saying, What have I to do with the sacredness of traditions, if I live wholly from within? my friend suggested,—"But these impulses may be from below, not from above." I replied, "They do not seem to me to be such; but if I am the Devil's child, I will live then from the Devil."

If I have a natural adversary, it is an English professor who wrote me several years ago to complain about the paucity of analytic notes that appeared in a small collection of Emerson's essays I once published. He wrote it is "impossible" (his word) to read Emerson without analytic notes. I cannot imagine anything less Emersonian. But even my Moriarty's pedantry facilitates my search. We need polarities. To exist is to be in polarity.

In 1790, William Blake wrote in *The Marriage of Heaven and Hell*: "Opposition is true Friendship." Only through being tested, opposed, and thrown onto our hidden reserves do we get anywhere. But opposition must be worthy. Argue with a fool, make a fool a colleague. That is what drove me to anarchic magick. Years of study within more formalized orders and systems, both alternative and traditional, forged my conviction that every principle must be challenged, tested, and measured. Including the old saw that a senior colleague in an esoteric group once used on me: "There are no shortcuts." I do not know that.

That said, before entirely throwing out the rulebook you must master the rulebook. This principle appears in the process of many artists, writers, and thinkers. It is part of my own approach. I have argued that the astrologer should know something about astronomy. The Kabbalist should possess a working grasp of Hebrew. The Tarot reader should know the authentic history of the cards (even if it challenges one's sense of romance). The witch should be versed in ancient nature faiths. Knowhow fosters true choice. And yet, I am loathe to erect any new tollgate to experience. *Result is all.* You require no other defense, if you require any.

Anarchic magick means that you can, and sometimes must, abruptly depart one line of practice and just as abruptly begin another. Under the right conditions, such a schismatic act bestows special power. Beginners and latecomers to any field often become its innovators. For a secular example, consider Gaston Glock, inventor and manufacturer of the Glock handgun. As explored in journalist Paul M. Barrett's *Glock: The Rise of America's Gun*, the Austrian engineer had, until well into middle age in the 1980s, dedicated his career to producing metalware, including curtain rods and knives. He knew almost nothing about firearms. But when the Austrian military issued a call for a sleek, new-generation sidearm, the manufacturer was intrigued. Unheeding of what "could not" be done, Glock took three months to develop a prototype of his lightweight plastic pistol, which went on to revolutionize handguns.

Embracing a pursuit belatedly—and proceeding to learn everything about it—spurs innovation and spurns prejudice, allowing you to leap past pitfalls and conventions. I approach UFOs not as an "expert" but as a historian who has the benefit of belonging to none of the field's factions. This mode, called "beginner's mind" in Zen, serves the dedicated seeker as much in spirituality as in worldly affairs, of which I see no ultimate difference.

Traditions arise from experiment but do not replace it. I encourage experimentation backed by some kind of education or immersion in what you are attempting. Above all: permit no one (including me) to dictate that some formal precondition is necessary to commence a spiritual practice—who is saying that, and what is the nature of his life that gives him authority to do so? Brush past experts and begin your search or practice *now*, wherever you like—do it with maturity, dedication, intellect, grit, and seriousness. Be undeterred by fee of entry, metaphorical or otherwise.

Cultivate awareness of physical surroundings to detect your natural temple, or places where prayer, affirmations, setting of intentions, or appeals to a Greater Force may occur. I have already cited two of my own. In closing, I offer one more. It appeared in the main branch of New York Public Library. On the third floor of the beaux-arts edifice appears a ceiling mural of Prometheus, who stole fire from the gods to illumine humanity. Prometheus is a cosmic figure with special relevance to strivers, seekers, and Satanists. Positioned around him on the floor below are marble lampposts with cloven hooves carved into their base. In this setting, you can touch one of the cloven hooves, perhaps arousing your natural tendencies, and send Prometheus an intention or appeal for something you intensely desire. I have said prayers in this space. One time, an old college girlfriend noticed me and approached after: "I didn't want to disturb you," she said. "It looked like you were praying." She was right.

Are you willing to try this, or something like it? Or are you too serious to venture such a childlike exercise? The wish for respectability, observed spiritual teacher Jiddu Krishnamurti (1895–1986), is the greatest deterrent to selfhood and progress.

Maybe it's a little inflated, but I'm touched by the declaration of anarchist revolutionary Mikhail Bakunin (1814–1876): "I cleave to no system, I am a true seeker." I take that as the informal motto of anarchic magick.

I invite you to run past everything you know, forget all your respectable spiritualities and see what you find. When you do find something—I am confident you will—do not coddle and nurse it for too long. Do not remain still. Here again is Emerson from the epigraph to "Self-Reliance":

> *Cast the bantling on the rocks*
> *Suckle him with the she-wolf's teat;*
> *Wintered with the hawk and fox,*
> *Power and speed be hands and feet.*

CHAPTER NINE

The Logic of Tarot

The use of Tarot as an occult or divinatory device is a modern innovation, as is its mythos as an ancient book of wisdom. The first Tarot decks, not yet bearing that name, emerged in Northern Italy in the early 1400s. That is the earliest physical evidence of Tarot we possess.

The first Tarot cards were called *carte de trionfi*, cards of triumph or trump cards. By the early 1500s, the deck was often called *Tarocchi*. Around 1530, its center of production shifted from Northern Italy to Marseilles, France. Late in the century, the French term Tarot gained prominence. We possess several variants of the Marseilles Tarot today.

The images of Tarot—the pope, priestess, death, lovers, the juggler, the tower—have some continuity with the archetypes of Hermeticism but visibly emerged from passion plays, carnivals, and stained glass of the early medieval period. That said, the visuals themselves convey allegorical meaning—they are recognizable in almost any culture. But equally important to understand historically, is that Tarot at its inception was not used for divination; that usage did not develop until more than three centuries later.

Some seekers take umbrage when historical writers note that Tarot began as a household game in the early Renaissance. To call Tarot a "game," however, does not capture the depth of what that concept could mean in the Renaissance. In 1616, late-Renaissance alchemist Michael Maier (1568–1622) published an allegorical work called *Lusus Serius,* Latin for a "serious game." This connotes the creativity and profundity that may arise from playfulness. We speak of "playing" an instrument but that does not mean musicianship is frivolous. We reference a drama as a "play." That does not refer to a minor charade. Something deeper is at work.

People possessed few domestic objects in the medieval and Renaissance period; hence, everything was imbued with significance. To term something a game does not debase it; any more than to say a passion play, i.e., a medieval or Renaissance-era religious drama, means an ordinary entertainment. Even a household object with obvious utility was, at least for the wealthy, decorative, purposefully designed, and valued—not frivolous or disposable. I note this as someone who deeply respects the mystical allegory and divinatory dimensions of the cards. But it is important to reach terms with the history of our devices and realize, too, that vintage does not equate with truth any more than novelty does with frivolity

I should also note that various playing decks were, at times, also used for divinatory purposes; so, it cannot be ruled out that Tarot was used privately in this manner. But, as seen in chapter two, the explicitly occult conception of Tarot emerged in 1781 through publication of *Le Monde Primitif* and was built upon in 1789 with publication of the *Grand Etteilla Tarot,* the first deck expressly intended for divination.

With the advent of the Grand Etteilla Tarot, querents experienced a deck more fully illustrated, vivid, and dramatic, laced with early Romantic and anglicized Egyptian imagery. Older decks from Marseilles and Northern Italy tended toward sparser illustrations. Indeed, beyond the 22 trumps, the suit cards or minor keys, which included variations of staffs (wands), coins (pentacles), cups, and swords, were mostly spare and utilitarian in style. The late-fifteenth century Sola Busca deck was more fully and alluringly (even hauntingly) illustrated; but the popular Marseilles decks were more ascetic. Seekers wouldn't start to encounter richly illustrated decks until the late-nineteenth and early twentieth centuries, culminating in the modern ur-deck designed by English artist Pamela Colman Smith (1878–1951) and Brooklyn-born British occultist Arthur Edward Waite (1857–1942), issued in late 1909. Smith's accessible yet byzantine paintings are key to Tarot's growth as a popular tool. It is the deck I personally use.

To avoid confusion about Tarot's development, I deemed it necessary to open with this pocket history. But let me be clear: as a contemporary seeker, I, like most reading these words, employ Tarot as a divinatory device. I believe that, like the ancient oracle I Ching, Tarot's pictogrammatic images and their random spread possess value as a tool of understanding and foresight. Experience has led me to reject arguments that Tarot is merely a Rorschach or instrument of cognitive bias—or at least not that alone.

My method—and the one I recommend—is a simple three-card spread taught to me by artist Robert M. Place. His book *The Tarot*, which I published in 2005, is vital reading for both its historicism and symbolical insight.

Here is the three-card method. Shuffle the deck with a passionately felt question in mind. Avoid asking routinized or repeat questions. The psyche is a compact of intellect and emotion and both should be in play. Spread out the cards face down in an arc, row, or semi-circle. While thinking of your question, randomly select three cards, laying them face down from left to right. Allow pure randomness to prevail; select from impulse and nothing more. In the same order, then flip your three cards over. If you encounter a reversed card, turn it right-side up. This method does not use reversed cards, which I (and Place) consider a modern artifice and needless source of anxiety. Tarot's seventy-eight cards are sufficiently broad in symbolism and vast in combinations to convey whatever meaning may be deciphered. Then look for a storyline or narrative, as though you are reading a three-paneled comic strip. Look for a flow of movement, i.e., the direction that the characters, if any appear, are gazing or proceeding. This does not require linearity: your story may flow in any direction. You may sometimes receive a spread that I call "wings," whereby the center card is a point of convergence impacted or elucidated by the cards on either side, which may be facing it, turning away from it, or qualifying its meaning.

In frankness—you can judge the accuracy of my reading—recent to this writing I queried whether my aforementioned television show *Alien Encounters* would be renewed. As I write these words in November 2024, the answer remains unknown. I received this spread:

In this case, I follow the flow of movement, starting with the left card: Eight of Cups. The card conveys a melancholic figure who sampled many cups but must now move onward to seek satisfaction. He has crossed water and is headed for higher ground. This suggests delayed deliverance or gratification. The center card, Six of Wands, shows a red-cloaked figure riding a white steed and bearing garlands in a victory parade, a symbol of triumph. This is a propitious card, which, as it happened, I drew after the aforementioned friend nuked a screen deal. The rightward card, Ten of Wands, shows a burdened figure carrying a load of branches toward his destination in the background—the load is arduous but the destination is reasonably near and arrival is presumed. In an innovation that Smith brought to several of her depictions, you will see in the Ten of Wands that the background image shows the bottom border of a curtain or backdrop of scenery. I interpret this to mean that what is witnessed is not fixed or fundamental but rather passing.

My interpretation is that news of renewal will be slow in coming, a circumstance that has already proven true. The center card suggests decisive victory: either of renewal or of something commensurate. The last time I drew this card, renewal and victory *eventually* arrived. The third card, however, suggests that triumph will be hard-won and arduous, though not excessively so. This may indicate a hectic or long-term commitment, or some process of extra effort required in completion.

Now that I have provided history and practice, I turn to the question: Why should Tarot work at all, if indeed it does? In terms of long experience, I believe that something more than projection is occurring. One July 4th weekend I offered free readings to social media followers. The response was beyond what I expected. I ended up doing hundreds of readings across seventy-two hours. Anecdotal though it is, the responses that came back were remarkable. A woman who asked about her career path got cards symbolizing justice; she had already enrolled in a police academy. Another who wanted to know where to relocate got cards with two rivers; she had been considering Two Rivers, Wisconsin. Lots of replies were less specific but no less penetrating—including a reading I did for myself that forecast multiple benefits from a project I was unsure of taking on but which has since brought me many opportunities. If there were lots of unremarkable null readings—a charge often leveled by woo critics—they did not reach my attention.

For a time thereafter, I charged modest fees for my readings ($20) and then let prices inch up. But sometimes when someone wrote me in need I just could not charge that person. Moreover, I do not wish to be in the role of presenting a stranger with vital life information. A story appears in the Talmudic book *Pirkei Avot* or *Ethics of the Fathers* about a student who encounters a skull floating in the dank waters of a cave. "How did you get here?" the student asks the skull. "I drowned others with my words," the skull replies, "until my words returned to drown me." I do not want to be that skull.

In addition to personal conviction and experience, I have a theory of why Tarot readings glean insight and even foresight. It is based on an observation made by some of Carl Jung's students. Jung and his immediate circle worked with the I Ching. Like Tarot, the ancient Chinese oracle tells a parabolic story through pictograms. Some of the psychologist's students theorized that it is possible that a pictorial representation, such as a pictograph or sketch, captures a moment in time—but more than just a linear moment. A pictogrammatic image captures, for a fleeting interval, an impression of past, present, and future; an I Ching pattern or a Tarot spread can function as a kind of multi-dimensional snapshot conveying what is happening at a given moment unbound by straight-arrow time. Such an image is not flawless or immune to change, but it is a reasonable iteration of what is occurring beyond boundaries in which we typically think.

Among the themes considered in the following chapter as well as the closing one is that linearity is an illusion, albeit a *necessary illusion* for five-sensory beings to navigate life. Most of the time, we gather information through limited instruments of sensory measurement—sight, smell, touch, taste, sound—and naturally conclude that we know what's going on. Yet quantum theorists, using much finer instruments of measurement, reveal to us a particle world in which infinitesimally small objects occupy states of "superposition," or limitless possibilities and potentialities, which become localized only when a sentient observer takes a measurement. Likewise, serious researchers of psychical abilities have produced vast statistical records of individuals acquiring information in anomalous ways—gleaning images, coordinates, or symbols from a near-infinitude of possibilities without limitation by time, order, or distance. (Key data is reviewed and sourced in Appendix A—I ask, in fact, demand that none of my statements be taken on faith.) Furthermore, theories of speed, light, distance, and gravity have demonstrated—and in some cases proven—that time itself is relative, and time necessarily bends based on speed or extreme gravity. Hence, it is no casual statement to observe that linearity *isn't a real thing*. That's where Tarot reenters.

If a Tarot spread can be seen as a random *measurement*—and what else is it?—then it follows that its pattern of images may time-stamp an event from among a near-infinite range of possibilities. The localization may be affected by the attitudes and emotions of the reader, as much as any other factor, which is why some are said to possess a "gift" for reading the cards. These localized possibilities are unbounded by conventional concepts of time; they can shift or change based on intervening intentions or forces. But they are a reasonable "weather report" of what is occurring beyond our liner thought system and, hence, what is likely to be experienced.

Tarot is psychologically penetrating because its imagery consists of archetypes that are recognizable and emotionally meaningful to people from nearly every culture. Death, the Magician, the Emperor, the Wheel of Fortune, the Lovers, and so on, are a visual code that proves evocative to nearly every psyche. When we use Tarot, we use a universal language. I should, of course, note that I am specifically referencing images found in the major trumps of the Florentine and Marseilles decks of the early Renaissance, built upon earlier Hermetic influences and, as noted, re-envisioned with occult splendor by artist Pamela Coleman Smith in the early twentieth century.

I believe that Tarot and the I Ching share common capacity to tell a story of human relations using a primeval code of archetypal images. The readings and images that these devices produce are not playthings or random hits. They are, I believe, psychological and quantum measurements of the human situation at a given moment.

Jung put in this way in his 1949 introduction to Richard Wilhelm's groundbreaking study and interpretation of the I Ching:

> The ancient Chinese mind contemplates the cosmos in a way comparable to that of the modern physicist, who cannot deny that his model of the world is a decidedly psychophysical structure. The microphysical event includes the observer just as much as the reality underlying the I Ching comprises subjective, i.e., psychic conditions in the totality of the momentary situation. Just as causality describes the sequence of events, so synchronicity to the Chinese mind deals with the coincidence of events. The causal point of view tells us a dramatic story about how D came in existence: it took is origin from C, which existed before D, and C in its turn had a father, B, etc. The synchronistic view on the other hand tries to produce an equally meaningful picture of coincidence. How does it happen that A', B', C', D', etc., appear all in the same moment and at the same place? It happens in the first place because the physical

events of A' and B' are of the same quality as the psychic events C' and D', and further because all are exponents of one and the same momentary situation. The situation is assumed to represent a legible or understandable picture . . . It is assumed that the fall of the coins or the result of the division of the bundle of yarrow stalks is what it necessarily must be in a given "situation," inasmuch as anything happening in that moment belongs to it as an indispensable part of the picture. If a handful of matches is thrown to the floor, they form the pattern characteristic of that moment. But such an obvious truth as this reveals its meaningful nature only if it is possible to read the pattern and to verify its interpretation, partly by the observer's knowledge of the subjective and objective situation, partly by the character of the subsequent events.

Hence, there exists a necessary interplay of observer, event, image, and interpretation. Jung's observation, while divergent from ancient Chinese philosophy, which posits disincarnate or spiritual agencies, has something in common, if indirectly, with the perceptual basis of quantum theory.

On a related note, I like this observation from a 1992 exchange between Terrence McKenna and Ram Dass:

> *Terrence*: So you download the unspeakable into language and let the chips fall where they may?
>
> *Ram Dass*: They don't fall where they may; they fall in a perfectly harmonious pattern.
>
> *Terrence*: That's them falling where they may.*

---

* "A Conversation Between Ram Dass & Terence McKenna" in Prague during the International Transpersonal Conference in June 1992, YouTube.

Before moving on, I want to say a word about one of the most beguiling cards in Tarot: the Wheel of Fortune. The image depicts animals, sometimes of a mythical nature, rising and falling along a rotating wheel. The revolving wheel of life is, of course, an archetypal theme in the Western and Eastern mind.

The Wheel of Fortune also captures an important principle about the fundamentally cyclical nature of experience. In that sense, it harbors psychological and social truth.

In essence, all of life—nature, the cosmos, and human existence—follows a law of cycles, which dictates that events within and without you change, flow, and repeat like seasons, tides, or planetary bodies. Hermeticists and the Transcendentalists understood that if you wish to glean the laws under which you live—including those that govern your psyche and daily life—study the revolutions of nature. As go tides, weather, seasons, and circular routes of the cosmos, so goes your existence.

This whispers truth about work, ambition, and effort. The revolutions of the Wheel of Fortune in Tarot tell you to *purposefully remain in your place*. If you are earnestly and diligently working, training, drilling, rehearsing, preparing, and doing your labor, the Wheel of Fortune dictates that, eventually and inevitably, the cyclical law of rise and fall will reach you where you stand. In time, this law will lift your fortunes in their desired direction. Also lawful are reversals. Any gambler or statistician can tell you about "runs of luck." Runs lawfully reverse. So be careful. The flipping of a two-sided object must eventually even out, for good or ill, depending upon your perspective.

But there is a way of riding the law of cycles. Hardworking people sometimes complain that their schools or workplaces are not meritocracies; that life just isn't fair. And they are right—to a point. I have personally, and sometimes frustratingly, witnessed feckless or mediocre people survive or even thrive in competitive situations. But this occurs only if they manage to stick around long enough (e.g., they may benefit from an indulgent boss, compensatory coworkers, or plain accident). The law of cycles, or the Wheel of Fortune, passively works in their favor. It is a peculiar feature of life, and particularly of career, that failures are often forgotten while successes are remembered. In terms of perception, one success mitigates a lot of failure. This is because people sense, without fully knowing why, that success will strike again (as will failure). They want to be there when it does. This gives you a hint of how to ride the Law of Cycles.

Consider: if a mediocre person, by just hanging around, experiences success at unexpected (though lawfully apportioned) hours, imagine how much greater a success you can experience if you persevere as a figure of excellence. The prepared and driven person is better primed to reap the fruits of lawful upturn in the law of cycles versus a mediocre one.

And, again, while downturns are equally inevitable, they are more often forgotten. Successes linger in the mind, including the group mind, in hopes of reaping their return. This is why an artist, entrepreneur, campaign manager, or solider can build his or her reputation on a sole success, no matter the reversals that precede or follow. This happened to Winston Churchill (1874–1965), albeit on an epic or, as some may see it, catastrophic scale. Churchill committed horrendous military blunders in World War I in Turkey, which took the lives of literally tens of thousands of Allied soldiers. Considered inept in domestic politics, the wartime leader was voted out of office immediately following World War II. But Churchill's success as the desperately needed and foresightful hero of World War II lingers.

This is why Churchill told a group of boarding school students at his alma mater Harrow on October 29, 1941: "Never give in, never give in, never, never, never, never—in nothing, great or small, large or petty—never give in except to convictions of honor and good sense. Never yield to force; never yield to the apparently overwhelming might of the enemy."

This might sound like English bluster (which I personally believe we need more of today), but the leader recognized a greater truth to which he alluded in the same speech: "You cannot tell from appearances how things will go." As it happens, Churchill was voted from office immediately following the war. And later returned. This is because appearances, like everything in nature and life, are constantly and lawfully changing. Understand that and you understand the Wheel of Fortune.

When you encounter the Wheel of Fortune in Tarot, based on whatever deck you use, you are being reminded of life's lawful inevitabilities and the imperative to abide them. The message is: *remain steadfast and prepared*. When things go well, prepare for winter. But one thing the card does not reveal, at least explicitly, is that the purposeful individual can ride these cycles, knowing that the apex will always return.

Since I am focusing here on worldly issues, let me conclude on related if somewhat tangential note. We often ask ourselves where to best dedicate our labors. I suggest a different question: not where but *with whom*. Relationships are the key to fortune. Seek neither topic nor investment but *excellence in collaborators and workmates*. Colleagues are your best determinant of success. But that is not all. When entering a workplace ask yourself: Where is the healthiest profit center here? Participate in that center. When the scythe falls, it is rarely in the boom area of a organization.

This chapter has dealt with "randomness" and the rise and fall of cycles. I now want to take matters a step deeper. Everything we have considered here is, in a sense, a device for marking off or measuring time and events. But—what if time and events are not what we think?

CHAPTER TEN

Backwards Causation

The expression "never give up"—echoing Churchill—holds esoteric meaning. This is not only because our concept of linear time is illusory—but because what appears lost can be gained. What appears settled is anything but. We often rue the 20/20 nature of hindsight as though it provides no payoff beyond melancholic wisdom of what *could have been*. But time, rather than an arrow moving in a sole direction as classical physics dictates, is, in fact, a matrix of infinitude through which we may, and always do, step in *any* direction via measurement, perception, observation, and *continuance of effort after presumed fact*.

Keep in mind that "feeling" something—such as personal independence or, for that matter, the earth's motion, proves a poor guide to actuality. Writing in his second epilogue to *War and Peace*—in the concluding lines of the work itself—Leo Tolstoy (1828–1910) noted humanity's earlier necessity of acknowledging heliocentrism to save itself from absurdity, which he compared to modern man's psychological predicament:

In the first case it was necessary to renounce the consciousness of an unreal immobility in space and to recognize a motion we did not feel; in the present case it is similarly necessary to renounce a freedom that does not exist, and to recognize a dependence of which we are not conscious.

I believe that Western culture occupies a similar position today, more than a century after Tolstoy's death. In order to save ourselves from absurdity, there must soon come acknowledgment of nonlocal and extraphysical aspects of existence—and with it acknowledgment that time is not the restrictive linearity it appears.

"Cycles," said esoteric Egyptologist R. A. Schwaller de Lubicz (1887–1961), "are the only way to beat time and space. Yes, the only way to beat those two is on their own ground. And cyclical consciousness places it there. Time is not like a river that flows by and in which you cannot step twice. Time is a spiral, and space as well, a spherical spiral. Can you imagine a spherical spiral? Try!"

Schwaller's point is further suggested by *Tao Te Ching*, in a passage at once familiar and elusive: *timing is everything*. Likewise, the symbol of the ouroboros or spherical serpent biting its tail. And the cyclicality of the I Ching (itself an esoteric time-keeping device) as well as the Mayan Long-Count calendar.

I quote Schwaller from the extraordinary 1987 memoir *Al-Kemi: Hermetic, Occult, Political, and Private Dimensions of R. A. Schwaller de Lubicz* by André Vanden Broeck. I encountered this book in 2005 at a transition in my life. It fortified my conviction that occultism, at its subtlest, is intellectually sound. I was not always certain. In his 1947 essay, "Theses Against Occultism," Frankfurt School philosopher Theodor W. Adorno wrote, "Occultism is the metaphysic of dunces." He was wrong—yet he opened me to an idea that has expanded despite not being dwelt on: how intellectuals I admired growing up were, like the most ordinary minds, locked into judging category of query versus scale of quality.

I reencountered *Al-Kemi* nearly twenty years later and the day before my fifty-ninth birthday; the book evokes strange memories filled with vulnerability. Its mysterious author, Vanden Broeck, was then living in retirement at a hotel in Mexico managed by his son. His publisher gave me his fax number. "I do not participate in the internet," Vanden Broeck wrote me. He sent a friendly fax in response to my initial outreach noting that he used to live on New York's Hudson Street where my publishing company was then located. Thereafter he went silent. I had the impression, perhaps retrocausal in nature, that he did not wish me to write an expository appreciation of his book. His publisher, too, previously friendly, went silent. My path is not theirs. It is one of exposition.

Ancient logic is splitting one to get two. Modern logic is adding one to get two. Exposition is not *l'expérience* (which can also mean experiment) but, as Schwaller observed, it is next best. "The reason for this lack of contact," André wrote in *Al-Kemi*, "holds no mystery: he [Schwaller] did not believe in language. Yet it is through language, both his and mine, that I discovered him."

This chapter attempts—with clinical data (how modern!)—to offer the language of Schwaller's ineffable truth of time as "spherical spiral" versus progressing line. It is my effort to drag the ineffable into what literary critic Irving Howe—another intellectual hero growing up—in his 1986 *The American Newness* called "the shallows of the explicit." That is the job I have assumed. It was offered and I accepted it.

The rational world we know quietly changed in 2011. This change came at the hands of Cornell psychologist Daryl J. Bem. The parapsychologist is the reverse-image of the founder of pseudoskepticism, stage magician James Randi (1928-2020). Both men grew up Jewish-misfit-boy magicians. Following a childhood of humiliation by bullies—forcing Daryl's Denver family to move homes—he, like James, took refuge in stage magic. But unlike the faux-skeptic, the grown Bem determined not to bleed the world of mystery but to study its contours.

After a long and distinguished research career, Bem suffered unprecedented professional and media evisceration when his 2011 paper in a scholarly journal detailed a decade of clinical evidence for precognition and retrocausality, in which *future events* cognitively impact *present ones*.* Bem seemed fated to repeat his early years, now at the hands of *media bullies*, from Slate to the *New York Times*, who, absent evidence and ignoring their critics (like me), deemed him the poster child for bad science.

A decade on, however, the unthinkable occurred: Bem's findings were widely replicated and proven confirmatory in a large-scale meta-analysis.** His work is physics-meets-alchemy as evidence demonstrates that *actions you take in the future affect the present*. Just as Einstein, Schrödinger, and innumerable mystics taught, 1) time is not linear, and 2) all events are infinite at once. Professional skeptics, like a clunky Soviet bureaucracy, endure; but in 2011 the dialectics (if I may) of immateriality turned: realities of interdimensionality, psi, and humanity's ineffable existence are the genie that cannot be rebottled.

---

* "Feeling the Future: Experimental Evidence for Anomalous Retroactive Influences on Cognition and Affect" by Daryl J. Bem, *Journal of Personality and Social Psychology*, 2011, Vol. 100, No. 3

** "REVISED: Feeling the future: A meta-analysis of 90 experiments on the anomalous anticipation of random future events" [version 2; peer review: 2 approved] by Daryl Bem, Patrizio E. Tressoldi, Thomas Rabeyron, Michael Duggan, first published: 30 Oct 2015, latest published: 29 Jan 2016, last updated: 23 Jul 2020, *F1000Research*

Here are basics. For about ten years prior to publication, Bem conducted a series of nine experiments involving more than 1,000 participants into precognition or "time reversing" of widely established cognitive or psychological effects, such as memorization of a list or responding to negative or erotic stimuli flashed as images on a screen. Bem's discoveries demonstrated the reach of cognition across boundaries of linear time.

Bem, as with other researchers, including the aforementioned Dean Radin of the Institute of Noetic Sciences (IONS), identified factors that seem to correlate with precognition, such as the body's response to arousing or disturbing imagery. As Bem wrote of previous experiments in presentiment of stimuli: "Most of the pictures were emotionally neutral, but a highly arousing negative or erotic image was displayed on randomly selected trials. As expected, strong emotional arousal occurred when these images appeared on the screen, but the remarkable finding is that the increased arousal was observed to occur a few seconds before the picture appeared, before the computer had even selected the picture to be displayed."

In one of Bem's trials, subjects were asked to "guess" at erotic images alternated with benign images. "Across all 100 sessions," he wrote, "participants correctly identified the future position of the erotic pictures significantly more frequently than the 50% hit rate expected by chance: 53.1% . . . In contrast, their hit rate on the nonerotic pictures did not differ significantly from chance: 49.8% . . . This was true across all types of nonerotic pictures: neutral pictures, 49.6%; negative pictures, 51.3%; positive pictures, 49.4%; and romantic but nonerotic pictures, 50.2%." You will note the slender but statistically significant effect referenced here, which is typical of parapsychology experiments. The measurable impact is not like

Zeus throwing lightning bolts at earth but rather a detectable "signal in the noise," which requires precise measurement and circumstantial cultivation.

The response to either arousing or disturbing imagery is suggestive of the *emotional stakes* required for presence of a psi effect, to which pioneering parapsychologist J.B. Rhine alluded in the appendix to a British edition of his 1934 monograph *Extra-Sensory Perception*:

> Since my greatest interest is in stimulating others to repeat some of these experiments, I should like to mention here what has seemed to me to be the most important condition for ESP. This is a spontaneity of interest in doing it. The fresh interest in the act itself, like that of a child in playing a new game, seems to me the most favorable circumstance. Add now . . . the freedom from distraction, the absence of disturbing skepticism, the feeling of confidence or, at least, of some hope, and I think many good subjects can be found in any community or circle.

This begins to suggest the bridge, however delicate, between parapsychology and the causative nature of the psyche, which I consider the root of magick. In both categories—parapsychology and thought causation—*passion is critical*. Stakes must exist and emotions must be in play. In his 1937 general-readers' book on ESP, *New Frontiers of the Mind*, Rhine emphasized the role of spontaneity, confidence, comity, novelty, curiosity, and lack of fatigue. (And, as it happens, caffeine.)

Bem's horizons, however, extended further. In the most innovative aspect of his nine-part study, the researcher set out to discover, in experiments eight and nine, whether subjects displayed *improved recall* of lists of words that were to be practice-memorized *in the future*:

Inspired by the White Queen's claim, the current experiment tested the hypothesis that memory can "work both ways" by testing whether rehearsing a set of words makes them easier to recall—even if the rehearsal takes place after the recall test is given. Participants were first shown a set of words and given a free recall test of those words. They were then given a set of practice exercises on a randomly selected subset of those words. The psi hypothesis was that the practice exercises would retroactively facilitate the recall of those words, and, hence, participants would recall more of the to-be-practiced words than the unpracticed words.

Bem found a statistically significant improvement of recall on the lists of words studied in the near future: "The results show that practicing a set of words after the recall test does, in fact, reach back in time to facilitate the recall of those words."

In experiment nine, this retroactive effect heightened when researchers added a refined practice exercise. ("A new practice exercise was introduced immediately following the recall test in an attempt to further enhance the recall of the practice words. This exercise duplicated the original presentation of each word that participants saw prior to the recall test, but only the practice words were presented.") The results improved: "This modified replication yielded an even stronger psi effect than that in the original experiment." In general, future memorization heightened current recall.

Within a year of Bem's publication, a trio of professional skeptics published a rejoinder. Playing off of Bem's "Feeling the Future," their paper sported the media-friendly title, "Failing the Future."* The skeptics reran Bem's ninth experiment. They wrote in their

---

* "Failing the Future: Three Unsuccessful Attempts to Replicate Bem's 'Retroactive Facilitation of Recall' Effect" by Stuart J. Ritchie, Richard Wiseman, Christopher C. French, *PLoS ONE*, March 2012, Volume 7, Issue 3 abstract: "Nine recently reported parapsychological experiments appear to support the existence of precognition. We describe three pre-registered independent attempts to exactly replicate one of these experiments, 'retroactive facilitation of recall', which examines whether performance on a memory test can be influenced by a post-test exercise. All three replication attempts failed to produce significant effects . . . and thus do not support the existence of psychic ability."

The authors omitted a critical detail from their own database. By deadline, they possessed two independent studies that replicated Bem's results. They made no mention of the opposing studies despite their own preset ground rules for doing so.

As even his critics noted, Bem opened his database and software and provided instruction manuals free to anyone who wished to rerun his experiments. As of July 2020, Bem's experiments (including the original trials) showed replication in a meta-analysis encompassing 90 experiments in 33 laboratories in 14 countries. "To encourage replications," Bem and his coauthors wrote in the abstract of their follow-up paper, "all materials needed to conduct them were made available on request. We here report a meta-analysis of 90 experiments from 33 laboratories in 14 countries which yielded an overall effect . . . greatly exceeding" the standard for "'decisive evidence' in support of the experimental hypothesis."

This book is about magick not magic. But I must offer two anecdotes that suggest potential uses of backwards causation.

About eighteen months before this writing, I heard from a professional Thai kickboxer, Spencer Hanley. Spencer's fights appear all over digital media. At the time, he was training for a match outside Houston, Texas. He had nine days before the bout and wrote seeking advice on sharpening his mental game. Spencer felt good about his training but needed guidance to stay "on" mentally.

I suggested a simple exercise called the 30-Day Mental Challenge. It appears in Appendix B. The challenge requires writing and signing a contract committing you for thirty days to directing your thoughts along progressive, positive, and productive lines. Spencer said he would do it. But his fight was only nine days away. He needed something more immediate. This *is* immediate, I explained. A trick appears in this exercise that allows you "to beat time and space." And I guaranteed him that no one in the opposing corner was even thinking about it.

In short, I continued, there exists an entirely real prospect that what you do in the future, i.e., following a given event, may improve your cognition and performance during the event itself. Referencing Bem's study, I noted that the clinician supplied recent, juried, and replicated data to support *a retrocausal effect in cognition*. As demonstrated in his lab experiments—and confirmed in largescale meta-analysis—*future* actions benefit *present* cognition. This is "impossible" insofar as superposition is impossible; particles (e.g., positrons) traveling backwards in time is impossible; surpassing lightspeed (e.g., quantum entanglement) is impossible; and, of course, ESP, so widely validated in bulletproof data, is impossible. If we eliminated everything that classical and Newtonian physics (if not Newton himself) deems impossible, we would erase world-class science, including quantum computing.

It must be noted that Bem's trials focused exclusively on cognition. I consider it a reasonable experiment (or *l'expérience*) to seek similar benefit in physical or athletic ability. Plus, Spencer was seeking help with his mental-emotional preparedness, which is not unrelated to cognition. In any case, tendrils of connection are not strictly linear and experiments with retrocausality may evince results that violate standard perceptions of past, present, and future. Spencer vowed to try.

He won the fight. He dominated the match and appeared relaxed, good natured, and respectful toward his foe. Of course, he might have won anyway. But I like this wrinkle: for his entry song, rather than the usual death metal or drill rap many fighters choose, Spencer selected the pop classic "Heaven Is a Place on Earth." One of the ringside announcers said: "The fact that he's coming out to Belinda Carlisle makes me so happy." Several weeks after the match, and before my writing about it, I received DM voicemails from someone I had never met or followed: singer-songwriter Belinda Carlisle. Other than a high-school crush (Jones Beach Theater on Long Island, summer of '82) and enduring love for her music, I had no currency with the artist. In two detailed and thoughtful messages, she said she was reading my books and was a fan. Dying happy in 3, 2, 1 . . .

More recently, a friend wrote to say she was applying for a deeply needed and desired job at a New York City religious organization. She recounted:

> I was on unemployment insurance and stressed TF out on a real first chakra level, the whole thing being on the same wavelength as shit I've been dredging and clearing for WAY too long . . . When I had that thought about the job, it felt like *"that's for me."* Or more like "I WANT THAT," with maybe a twinge of "Why can't *I* have that?"

In short, she was hopeful but nervous. Time passed and for some reason the job went to another person. She felt despondent. I offered the same basic advice given to Spencer with the wrinkle that she continue to hone her skills and presentation, and actively burnish her qualifications for the position. (She also gamely applied for other openings.) If it did not help, certainly it could not hurt. She agreed.

About a week later, she wrote me ecstatic. The boss "emailed me again and said that he had what he hoped was good news. It was the same job but with more hours. Amazing Grace Attack!!"

This episode calls to mind an exercise prescribed by Neville Goddard called "the pruning shears of revision." Neville advised *revising* a regretful event by imaginatively reliving it "from the end" of how you would like it to have gone. Hence, a disappointing encounter could be transformed into a positive one through entering and experiencing the "feeling state" and imaginative scene of a happy outcome. Assuming the efficacy of Neville's method, and in the light of the factors I have a cited, what is actually occurring?

What if the antecedent event and its alternative each proceed in real but different dimensions? Your alteration forms or perceives another dimensional strand or string—try to imagine reality as an endlessly and concentrically expanding ball of twine—with the "anchor strand" from which you first experienced the event circumstantially untouched. Perhaps your perception "leaps" to or weaves another strand, every bit as real and contextual as the anchor strand. This occurs without upending your sense of self, history, or location because it is as real as the other outcome. But it is now localized and experienced by you as solid, solitary, and unchanging. You may no longer recall the negative event.

Another possibility is that what *is* touched, what *is* altered, is the emotional antecedent of the event. So that your anchor reality and the psyches of those you encounter within it—independent beings who crisscross within your perception of reality or intertwined strings, as you do within theirs—are leavened by alteration of experience even though the forensics may be unchanged. Hence, if you consider a piece of evidence from the past, like an email, it may reflect the same incident, i.e., current reality evinces the same empirical markings. But because you wove or identified a new strand—you selected a different dimensional storyline and thus launched another among infinite timelines—there may exist a *reverberation* in which salving qualities either appear or are felt at the anchor point. (There is also, by this logic, another reality—one among an infinite number—where altered circumstance, either jarring or salving, is, in fact, experienced.) Within the reality of your inceptive thought point, the emotive ripple is felt. Healing can occur. The opposite is also true, so we must be careful when we consider the question of changing our past or when we idly revise, rerun, or reinforce scenes.

From the perspective of the figures in the famous Schrödinger's Cat thought experiment—the observer and the cat—they are singular, local, and concrete. But quantum laws dictate that this is only *a point of view*. In actuality, these figures, beyond their personal perspective, are multi-dimensional. So are you and me.

Neville equated revision with forgiveness. In his mystical reading of Scripture, to forgive does not mean to excuse but to *re-vision* an adversary or fractious encounter according to your ideal. I am not always emotionally or ethically certain that I *want* to undo or reverse an event so much as resolve it on my own terms. This is a fact of human nature with which we must honestly reckon. Do you want peace—or victory? Is one exclusive of the other? Our emotions always pull in the direction of authentic desire. Our inner or outer voices often conceal our motives; our emotions expose them.

I believe that there are times we actually *want* to retain negative situations, themes, or memories. For example, a perceived adversary may be someone for whom you harbor deep feelings, even love. What is love but the opposing polarity of hate? In both situations, another person shapes, marks, and even gives direction or purpose to your life. Love and hate are, in a sense, the same rhythmical and emotional continuum.

Relatedly, we may wish, without acknowledging it to ourselves, to retain, review, and even re-live a difficulty. That dynamic may also occur because the disturbing episode afforded us no emotional closure so we continually rerun it in search of resolve. Closure is a subjective feeling that arises from exiting a situation with some personally conceived degree of dignity, approval, or maturity. It is a restoration of self, objectively accurate or not.

Other times, you may savor conflict, which might provide a feeling of *aliveness* or even a thrill of having escaped. Such an attachment could present myriad or conflicting emotions. Fear and allure are also part of the same continuum. Finally, a trauma cycle may evoke feelings of injustice, which you fitfully, and often unconvincingly, use your imagination to fix or restore. This can lead to "what ifs?" in which you reimagine telling someone off or rescuing yourself from trouble through foresight or a quick response.

None of what I just described is *revision* in the manner defined by Neville. But nor am I exactly criticizing these approaches either. A wise man once said that justice is nothing but a mental idea, i.e., a necessarily limited or peripherally blind perspective based on selfishness or perceptual boundaries. I have abided his statement for years. I am unsure it is true, at least as an absolute. I believe that the mature individual possesses a valid scale of reference for how he or she is treated in life, and likewise has some conception of just and unjust scenarios pertaining to autonomy of psyche and body as well as ethical standards.

From the perspective of larger currents of reciprocity, an event may satisfy one's thirst for justice, albeit indirectly. This may be what Nietzsche had in mind when he wrote in *Beyond Good and Evil* a passage noted in chapter three: "One *has* to repay good and ill—but why precisely to the person who has done us good or ill?" This is a disquieting principle. Why should payment be extracted from an uninvolved pedestrian? To this objection the philosopher might reply: Why then should good tidings be granted to any such person?—as in the popular concept of "pay it forward." Perhaps *both* consequences are unwarranted on an intimate scale but arise from matters beyond our perception. Nietzsche's ideal may reflect the *impersonal scales* of life found within concepts of karma in Vedic theology. In traditional Hinduism and Buddhism, karmic balances of equilibrium are unseeable, ineffable, not infrequently harsh, and occur across vast reaches of time. In that vein, I might reframe Nietzsche's statement from "one *has* to repay" to "nature *has* to repay." Both Nietzsche and the wise man I quoted earlier remind me that I must bow to limits of perspective. That said, I will venture this: When someone humiliates you, consider that it may be retrocausal from what that person is *going to suffer.* Time is a "spherical spiral."

What I *can* conclude is that the effectiveness of Neville's pruning-shears approach rests upon the *authenticity and emotional clarity* of the individual's wish to undo knots. This is why, again and again, I emphasize self-honesty. It is the solution upon which every choice and possibility rests, at least insofar as we can be said to function independently.

In season six of *Better Call Saul*, Walter White calls a "time machine" both a "real and theoretical impossibility." His "theoretical impossibility" is based on Einstein's second law of thermodynamics. According to this law, backwards movement in time is a virtual impossibility. This is because molecules placed into an agitated state, or heat, cannot of themselves return to their previously static state. Just as Humpty Dumpty does not reassemble, entropy does not reverse.

But the master's conclusion, as usual, must be viewed through the lenses of both classical and quantum physics, as well as understood for its subtlety. As author L.D. Deutsch notes in her pristine 2025 study *Time, Myth, and Matter*: "Einstein's theory of special relativity does imply that all moments in time exist in some permanent location along the temporal dimension of the block universe." (I cannot say enough to recommend Deutsch's book: if I were a hiring manager, I would require every employee to read it so they would know what reality is.)

When referring to "time" we are referencing measurement of time versus the thing itself (whatever it may be); likewise we reference the unitary "arrow of time"—itself a measurement concept—to explain the near-impossibility of unbreaking an egg (again, Einstein's second law of thermodynamics). But time is more unruly and fantastical, as seen within quantum versus classical physics; Einstein considered the quantum field open ended or at least incomplete.

A series of conferences, "Quantum Retrocausation," convened by the University of San Diego (USD) and American Association for the Advancement of Science (AAAS) have been exploring the question of time reversal and retrocausality. As of this writing, papers from the latest in 2017 are collected in the *American Institute of Physics (AIP) Conference Proceedings* volume 1841, issue 1.* The preface by USD physics professor Daniel Sheehan notes:

> Quantum Retrocausation III is the third in a series of international symposia convened at the University of San Diego under the auspices of the Pacific Division of the American Association for the Advancement of Science (AAAS), to discuss the intersection of time and consciousness ... Its focus was on a specific aspect of time—retrocausation—because it is here that time and

---

* The table of contents appears here: https://pubs.aip.org/aip/acp/issue/1841/1

consciousness intersect to beget several of the most compelling experimental mysteries and theoretical puzzles in physics.

Retrocausation is the proposition that the future can affect the present in a manner analogous to how the past affects the present via causation. It is well known that the fundamental equations of physics are time-symmetric—that is, they possess time-forward (retarded) and time-reversed (advanced) solutions—yet this belies our temporally asymmetric experience of the world, which progresses unidirectionally toward the future. Physics almost universally adopts this prejudice by discarding advanced solutions as "unphysical". This symposium challenges this assumption.

Various 'arrows of time' have been recognized by physics for more than a century... These presume solely causation, thus precluding retrocausation. This is understandable insofar as the former helps provide the narrative structure consonant with our experience and physical theories; however, causation itself—and, by extension, retrocausation—has been philosophically suspect since at least the time of Hume. Causes are invisible, they are inferred from events but are not intrinsic to them; correlations, by contrast, can be directly measured. Causes are reasons given to well-established correlations, signposts for the stories we tell to make sense of the world and physical theory. Thus, retrocausation may be as illusory as causation—and perhaps just as necessary.

In QRC-III retrocausation was discussed within the context of quantum mechanics, a subject, not coincidentally, also largely defined through correlations, puzzles and paradoxes, e.g., Einstein's bubble, Schrödinger's cat, EPR, Wigner's friend, Wheeler's delayed choice, quantum eraser, interaction free measurements, and many others. While this list bespeaks the depth and richness of the field, it also evidences its theoretic incompleteness; after all, paradoxes are the seeds of truth, not its fruit.

This query seems to me the most exciting facet of natural philosophy today—and the springboard for a new era in understanding. Again, as Sheehan notes, "paradoxes are the seeds of truth, not its fruit."

In writing this chapter, I am further struck by the prescience of Neville Goddard's ideas. In one of the final lectures of his life, delivered April 3, 1972 (he died October 1, 1972), the mystic recounted a remarkable story from 1949, which, as is often the case with Neville's accounts, bears the marking of truth. It elucidates the core of this chapter.

> I'll go back now to 1949. I was in Milwaukee, and I gave a series of lectures on the Bible. And this couple, he was a physicist, the head physicist, of Allis-Chalmers. They're a huge, big manufacturing firm making these turbines, sometimes bigger than this interior, and he was the head of the chemical department, where they would send waters from all over the world, who bought the turbine, and he would analyze the water to discover the problem that they faced; because the water, as it came through the stream, gathered the chemicals, and then the chemicals deposited itself within the turbine; and so they would send him samples of the water, and then he would analyze the water, and then send them the solution to their problem.
>
> Well, being a trained chemist, and the head of the department, he didn't take issue with me, but he said: "Neville, I can't quite go along with you because as a chemist, it's in conflict with my training. You tell me that I can go forward in time, that you can move backward in time, that all things are, and everything is

now, at this very moment. And yet you are telling me that you can make things change, and it is in conflict with my training." We have a law known, said he, and we call it entropy. And entropy means that the past is fixed and unalterable. You cannot change it. If that could be changed, it throws everything out of kilter in my lab. I must know the past is unalterable, like braiding a lady's hair, and the braided part, that's fixed. The rest is the future, not yet braided. We are waiting to see how it will develop from the braided part because that is completely fixed and unalterable. And you tell me it is not; that the whole vast world exists now, past, present, and future, and that you can go into these sections of time, in a world that is finished. Well, I can't go along with that.

That's perfectly all right. I'm not a chemist; I'm not a scientist, so I cannot argue the point with you. I only know my visions. And I teach vision as I have actually experienced it. And I can go into these spots. I have gone into these places and the past has not passed away. And it's fixed, as you say, but I'm quite sure one could go back and revise that past and change it.

And I can go forward into the future that I do know and set it up to walk across a bridge of incident; when I come to that point in time where I have entered, it takes on the color, the tone, and the reality that I assumed it to be when I entered that state.

Can't be done. But he was a very honest man, as most of these fellows are; they're trained to be honest. How else could they achieve what they do achieve in science unless they're perfectly honest with themselves?

Well, in the month of November, I received a letter from him and he sent me the science newsletter dated October the 15th. And it was all about the positron. And the one who wrote it was Professor Richard Feynman, he was then a professor of physics at Cornell University. Twenty years later, only last year, they granted him the Nobel Prize in physics for that paper.* It took them twenty years to recognize what he said as theory back in 1949. And if I can quote it, this is it: "The positron is a wrong-way electron. It's 'wrong way' in every sense of the word. It moves backward in time. It moves from where it hasn't been and speeds to where it was an instant ago. Arriving there, it is bumped so hard its time-sense is reversed and it moves back to where it hasn't been."

Now that is not Neville speaking; that is Professor Feynman. For that, he got the Nobel Prize last year. He said: "It's not only backward in that sense, but even its charge is backward. It's a positron; it's positive and not negative. And yet it is an electron."**

When they first observed it or rather had it as theory, they did not want to admit it, but yet it fitted in with Einstein's theory, mathematically, so they had to in some way accept it, but no one had ever photographed it. Then came someone who photographed it in their studies of the cosmic rays, and here it was the actual positron. It seemed as though two were developed at a certain point. And it wasn't, said he. That one coming back, which was the positron, should, if it is bounced, it should be deflected and continue on its course, but deflected course. On the other hand, if it's bounced so hard, it's not deflected; it's reversed and moves forward in a normal manner to where it hasn't been.

Well, I told him that I was sitting at home, and I would go into a section of time, even this year, for instance. This is now only April. I put myself in Christmas. I would feel the stores are

---

* The paper to which Neville accurately refers is, "The Theory of Positrons" by R.P. Feynman, *Physical Review*, Volume 76, Number 6, September 15, 1949. In 1965, Feynman received the Nobel Prize for physics, shared with Julian Schwinger and Shin'ichirō Tomonaga, for their "fundamental work in quantum electrodynamics, with deep-ploughing consequences for the physics of elementary particles." Neville's talk appears in the anthology *Neville Goddard's Final Lectures* (G&D Media, 2022), which I edited and introduced.

** Electrons carry a negative charge.

all dressed for Christmas. I could hear the music of Christmas, all the carols. I'd walk through Saks Fifth Avenue in New York City, go into Best, go into the other, and I would feel all that I would feel if it were true that it's Christmas, that it's the month of Christmas. And then when I feel that it's all Christmas, then I would feel that things are as I desire them to be back in the month, say, of March or July, which was certainly not Christmas season. So, take a hot, hot day in July, and I'm feeling it to be cold, and snow on the ground, and all the dressings for Christmas. And then I would open my eyes, and bounce back, and shock myself because it seems so real to me that, when I came back and opened my eyes upon July, and it's hot, I thought, now, are you kidding yourself? No, when I went forward in time quite normally, waiting out the days, the months to the month of December, things happened as I actually had assumed that they would. I went forward and determined, predetermined, what would happen.

Well, when he sent me this, he wrote a sweet, lovely letter saying, Neville, I must confess: I didn't see it; no one saw it until Professor Feynman in his lab discovered this. But he discovered it by theory, and you tell me you know it by vision. You're not a scientist, and yet all that you said to me—which I could not believe, and even this moment it's difficult for me to believe, here comes the great professor, a theoretical physicist, and he is the one who wrote this paper. For that, he got the Nobel Prize last year. He worked on our atomic bomb; he worked on the hydrogen bomb. Then he asked the government to relieve him of the secrecy imposed upon him because of his position, and he came here to Caltech and taught at Caltech: theoretical physics. He said I want the freedom of imagination. I didn't want to be confined with the secrets of government so that I could not express myself. Leave me alone, all in theory. So, he goes blindly on with his mathematics and his theory, bringing out these concepts, all theory. Well, mine is not theory.

As a further matter of testimony—this time yours—does retrocausality or backwards causation really work? You already possess evidence that it does. The chapter you just finished reading is a product of it. When I began this chapter, I worried about having sufficient time to complete it satisfactorily, to plumb the possibilities, to refine its ideas. It occurred to me: *continue after the fact*; invest the written exploration with its claim in action. You can judge the result.

CHAPTER ELEVEN

Total Environment

Positive *Thinking Weaponized* is how I have described the magickal outlook of artist, provocateur, and Church of Satan founder Anton LaVey (1930–1997). As I see it, the shaved-headed, goateed Satanist took the principle of New Thought philosophy—*thoughts are causative*—and wed it to a sense of meaningful theatricality and self-invention.

Never assume that Anton's pageantry was of a low sort. Public relations and propaganda theorist Edward Bernays (1891–1995) emphasized the need for disruptive events, claims, or behavior by whomever wishes to influence mass opinion. In 1990, five years before his death, the PR maestro told historian Stuart Ewen: "A good public relations man advises his client . . . to carry out an overt act . . . interrupting the continuity . . . of life in some way to bring about a response."*

This Anton did, but not as a blind end. He believed that well-wrought fantasy—heightened through real-life garb, designed

---

* *PR: A Social History of Spin* (Basic Books, 1996).

surroundings, and even life-sized dolls (he was a philosophical progenitor of virtual reality)—proved superior to unsatisfying sexual relations or lame outer experiences. He termed such invented realms "total environments."

Anton's magick requires self-awareness of a kind rarely found in modern occult literature. In *The Satanic Bible* in 1969 he wrote of the *Balance Factor*:

> One of the magician's greatest weapons is knowing himself; his talents, abilities, physical attractions and detractions, and when, where, and *with whom!* . . . The aspiring witch who deludes herself into thinking that a powerful enough working will *always* succeed, despite a magical imbalance, is forgetting one essential tool: MAGIC IS LIKE NATURE ITSELF, AND SUCCESS IN MAGIC REQUIRES WORKING IN HARMONY WITH NATURE, NOT AGAINST IT.

Historian Stephen E. Flowers, adds in his 2012 *Lords of the Left-Hand Path* that LaVey's is *pragmatic magic*—"All elements in his magical system are there to act as triggers for certain psychological events." And further that the practitioner aims at "making only slight alternations in the right place at the right time to 'tip the balance' in one's favor."

Regarding ritual, Anton's approach ran parallel to Austin Osman Spare's chaos theories. Rites can assume nearly any form—Anton used a potpourri of historical Satanic references, self-devised dramas, and sometimes an adapted system of Enochian, a magickal language recorded by Elizabethan mage John Dee—but nonnegotiable ingredients are *passion* and what might be called *creative forgetfulness*. Anton taught that a ritual or ceremony must immerse you in feeling *satisfied* that you have gained the thing wish for. In this regard, sexuality and self-sexuality are core tools in his rituals. Once you experience the longed-for sense of satedness, you drop the matter. "Burn every bit of desire out of your system," to revisit his essay "Ravings from Tartarus" from his 1992 *The Devil's Notebook*, "and then, when you no longer care, it will come to you."

If fantasy or ritual (and, I would add, prayer or petition) does not bring full satisfaction, it must be performed again. Or you must find another way of diverting yourself from distraction with your aim. A ritual fails, he wrote, "Because it matters so much to you." Again, Anton:

> How can one avoid caring? There are many tricks which can be employed. Creativity is one. When you are in the process of creating something your brain must function on a creative level, not on a rote or repetitive one. Your mind cannot be possessed by one thing and yet entertain new thoughts — unless the object of your creation happens to be in the likeness of your obsession. Here we find an ideal combination, for if the hands can create a facsimile of the desired objective with such dexterity as to be convincing then it is as good as done.

As he suggests, the point of chaos magick, sigil work, and related techniques is *bypassing* the rational apparatus of the mind and allowing the depths of the subconscious to perform. Another valuable hint for effective magickal practice appears in Anton's previously noted concept of *Erotic Crystallization Inertia* or ECI. In short, the practitioner peels back memory to determine earliest instances of sexual arousal. In his widow Blanche Barton's 1990 biography *The Secret Life of a Satanist*, ECI is described as the "point in time and experience in which a person's emotional/sexual fetishes are established."

ECI moments also harken to when the individual experiences key feelings of vitality, at-homeness, and conscious ease. This can occur in peak social situations and during tasks or efforts when you feel distinctly seen, mature, understood, capable—and hence powerful. He encouraged recreation of these moments and settings in both personal rituals and general surroundings, further clarifying the notion of "total environment." *This also requires shunning settings, people, and situations that detract from your sense of vitality.* And be ruthless about it. By contrast, relationships among people who possess complementary ECIs often prove propitious and satisfying.

Toward the end of the first of the don Juan books by Carlos Castaneda—a self-invented figure like Anton—an episode unfolds that I think metaphorically captures this point. Carlos's teacher, Yaqui Indian sorcerer, don Juan, tells his student that he most locate a point on the teacher's porch that provides him unmistakable safety and strength. Each person has his own such spot. This is one of many passages that I think give a sense of the grace and gravity of Carlos's work, whatever its documentary reality or source. He writes:

> After a while he calmed down and explained to me that not every place was good to sit or be on, and that within the confines of the porch there was one spot that was unique, a spot where I could be at my very best. It was my task to distinguish it from all the other places. The general pattern was that I had to "feel" all the possible spots that were accessible until I could determine without a doubt which was the right one.
>
> I argued that although the porch was not too large (twelve by eight feet), the number of possible spots was overwhelming, and it would take me a very long time to check all of them, and that since he had not specified the size of the spot, the possibilities might be infinite. My arguments were futile. He got up and very sternly warned me that it might take me days to figure it out, but that if I did not solve the problem, I might as well leave because he would have nothing to say to me. He emphasized that he knew

where my spot was, and that therefore I could not lie to him; he said this was the only way he could accept my desire to learn about Mescalito as a valid reason. He added that nothing in his world was a gift, that whatever there was to learn had to be learned the hard way.*

After many arduous hours, Carlos locates his "spot of happiness"—a development that saves his life. In a harrowing episode toward the end of the book, a shape-shifting sorceress seeks to gain dominion over Carlos's soul. Standing on his power spot, he wards her off with a ferocious war cry and flinging of a stone. Don Juan later appears to tell Carlos he prevailed.

"But how did I win?" he asks. Don Juan replies: "You did not move from your spot. Had you moved one inch away you would have been demolished. She chose the moment I was away as the best time to strike, and she did it well. She failed because she did not count on your own nature, which is violent, and also because you did not budge from the spot on which you are invincible."

Understanding ECI provides key help in working with both sigils and sex transmutation. But, as suggested, the matter extends further. Settings that evoke power, potency, and vitality appear to have measurable benefits, including therapeutically. In studies by Harvard psychologist Ellen Langer—the subject of controversy but their results never upended—elderly subjects experienced physical and mental improvements—including increased strength and flexibility, recovered memory and cognitive function, and improved mood and vitality—when immersed in nostalgic settings populated with stim-

---

* *The Teachings of Don Juan: A Yaqui Way of Knowledge* (University of California Press, 1968)

uli from their youth, including vintage books, music, and movies. In Langer's work, settings that evoke *feelings* of youth actually seem to summon the reappearance of youthful traits, extending even to improved eyesight.*

As some of Anton's students observed, the very act of "costumery" can evoke similar feelings of wellbeing. This implies dressing and comporting yourself in a manner that affirms idealized self-image. Too often our wished-for concepts of self are disrupted by therapeutic or spiritual truisms about what we are *supposed* to value, thereby short-circuiting authentic exploration or restricting it to familiar patterns. A more radical and, I believe, helpful approach is trusting your personal aspiration, building it, and permitting *no one* to summarily or even briefly disrupt it. If they do, you have left your power spot. Cut off such people and return to your ideals.

Within both alternative and traditional spiritual cultures, we often hear that what matters is what we cannot see, and that outer life consists of illusion and temporality, which the seeker learns to regard with less significance as he or she advances. I do not believe that customary principle honors or encompasses the full nature of our existence. In some respects, the ideal of nonattachment is a carrot forever dangled before the seeker; we are perpetually pursuing it without getting closer. I believe the principle of nonattachment places an unnatural demand on the seeker. We must be wary of *uncritically* importing or cherry-picking concepts from ancient religious traditions, both Eastern and Western. We encounter certain concepts, often in translations of translations of ancient literature, which we are taught to consider sacrosanct and inerrant. In actual-

---

* See "What If Age Is Nothing but a Mind-Set?" by Bruce Grierson in *The New York Times Magazine*, October 22, 2014. Researchers often dispute older studies, such as Langer's 1981 aging study, based on newer standards of methodology. But this phenomenon affects our view of all past clinical work, as it will affect how future researchers view today's practices, since methods inevitably progress. More recently, researchers have linked *reversal* of greying hair to destressing: "Quantitative mapping of human hair greying and reversal in relation to life stress" by Ayelet M Rosenberg, et al., *eLife*, 10:e67437, 2021.

ity, many religious concepts must be understood and evaluated from within the context in which they arose.

As noted, all religions are the product of human hands. Religions are attempts to codify and structure our relations with the ineffable. Every faith emerges from its own locality and time, reflecting civic, legal, and social needs of a distinct public. Enduring religions offer universally applicable lessons; but virtually all religions bear traits and markings of the prejudices, attitudes, and crises of their birth. Hence, I insist that religious precepts must be verified in every generation. Otherwise, we perpetuate habit as much as tradition.

For many ancient people, especially in caste-stratified societies, the search for self-worth was relegated largely to a scale of extraphysical values and detachment from worldly goods or rank. These urgencies do not necessarily comport with life today. Nor are they, I believe, intrinsic to human nature. As I see it, the highest role of men and women is to be *generative*: to be co-creators within our sphere of existence, in matters both visible and unseen. In that vein, I consider *self-expression* sacred. Scripture says God created the individual in his own image. If one takes that concept seriously, it stands to reason that we are intended to self-create, at least within parameters of our circumstance.

I believe there exists total interplay between inner and outer. At this point in my search, I do not think of separations between inner and outer, higher and lower, essence and personality, attachment and nonattachment, identification and nonidentification, spiritual and material. It is all one thing. If spirit or psyche can impact flesh, it follows that flesh can impact spirit or psyche. *As above, so below.*

Contrary to much teaching within the alternative spiritual culture, I do not believe we are called to deemphasize the so-called exterior as we pursue the fullest sense of life. I consider that artifice. In actuality, attainment of greater selfhood facilitates your ideals, actions, sense of possibility, and manner of relating to others.

Perhaps I am wrong about all this. Perhaps I have misread the purpose of religion and conflated it with my own psychological or self-centered needs. That, too, is a risk willingly taken. I wish to quote again from a dialogue between Castaneda and don Juan, beginning with Carlos's question:

"Is there a special way to avoid pain?"
"Yes, there is a way."
"Is it a formula, a procedure, or what?"
"It is a way of grabbing onto things. For instance, when I was learning about the devil's weed I was too eager. I grabbed onto things the way kids grab onto candy. The devil's weed is only one of a million paths. Anything is one of a million paths [un camino entre cantidades de caminos]. Therefore you must always keep in mind that a path is only a path; if you feel you should not follow it, you must not stay with it under any conditions. To have such clarity you must lead a disciplined life. Only then will you know that any path is only a path, and there is no affront, to oneself or to others, in dropping it if that is what your heart tells you to do. But your decision to keep on the path or to leave it must be free of fear or ambition. I warn you. Look at every path closely and deliberately. Try it as many times as you think necessary. Then ask yourself, and yourself alone, one question. This question is one that only a very old man asks. My benefactor told me about it once when I was young, and my blood was too vigorous for me to understand it. Now I do understand it. I will tell you what it is: Does this path have a heart? All paths are the same: they lead nowhere. They are paths going through the bush, or into the bush. In my own life I could say I have traversed long, long paths, but I am not anywhere. My benefactor's question has meaning now. Does this path have a heart? If it does, the path is good; if it doesn't, it is of no use. Both paths lead nowhere;

but one has a heart, the other doesn't. One makes for a joyful journey; as long as you follow it, you are one with it. The other will make you curse your life. One makes you strong; the other weakens you."

In a slightly oddball but beguiling 1932 book *TNT: It Rocks the Earth*, journalist and financier Claude M. Bristol noted how artists, businesspeople, and leaders convey a purposeful, intentional image to their audience, listeners, and constituents. Bristol used Mahatma Gandhi as an example. He observed that Gandhi, who at that time was fomenting peaceful revolution in what is today the largest democracy in the world, was known for nonviolent political change and universal polity. Bristol said that it is not at all cynical to point out that, in addition to Gandhi's political, diplomatic, and ethical greatness (and flaws), he also crafted a purposeful image. His walking stick, sandals, spectacles, cropped hair, and robe came from the lower rungs of India's caste system. Gandhi's adoption of that appearance—which markedly contrasted to his Anglican style of dress and hair when young—contributed to his stature on the world stage. Bristol wrote that cultivating a sense of showmanship can prove enormously helpful to the striving individual. I am sure Edward Bernays would have agreed. Bristol did not mean this in a degraded or cynical way. As a newspaperman, he was blunt and direct.

Gandhi's successor—and one of my personal heroes—Jawaharlal Nehru (1889–1964) did more than any other leader of the twentieth century to attempt a state that practiced indifference toward—and hence freedom of—religion. Nehru was close to Jiddu Krishnamurti, tutored by Theosophists in adolescence, and collaborated with Annie Besant. This influence warrants greater exploration. Nehru, too, cultivated a studied look on the world and national stage. His accessories and attire—including the famous collarless Nehru jacket worn by The Beatles—drew from across India's social and religious cultures, an important statement in unifying an already-splintered nation including Hindus, Muslims, Sikhs, and Christians.

For those of us who struggle with issues of self-image, as I once did, it can seem very distant to be told to "believe in yourself," be confident, throw back your shoulders, stick out your chest, and march through life with a sense of self-possession. There are, of course, affirmations, self-suggestions, and visualizations that can improve self-image. In addition, as I have been suggesting, there exist physical steps that heighten self-image and make you more persuasive, formidable, and relaxed.

We all have things that we like about our appearance and gait, and other things about which we are insecure. Each person must deal with these complexities, some of which are culturally conditioned. But even within such parameters, you possess greater freedom and possibilities than you may realize. As considered in chapter three, we live within a framework of cosmic reciprocity, or what is sometimes called karma. I believe the same is true of your personhood. We are made to feel that we are in pieces; there is truth to that—but the interplay of so-called inner and outer is so intimate and total that I believe we misunderstand human nature when we reference those things separately.

In that vein, let me ask you a question. Are you dressing as you wish? When you get up in the morning—whether weekday, workday, weekend, or vacation—are you comporting yourself in a manner that feels natural and relaxed? How exactly do you want to dress in the world? How do you want to wear your hair? How do you want to wear your makeup? What image, what persona, are you comfortable projecting? Do not get lost in thinking that I am "merely" referencing outer shell. I see no difference between kernel and nut. It is one interplay. You are granted the gift, as co-creator, of crafting your image. It reverberates throughout your being.

So, again, I ask: How do you want to dress in the world? How do you want to comport yourself? What gait do you want to assume? Do you want to wear bodily adornments like jewelry and tattoos? Even if present circumstances make it impossible for you to dress and present how you wish, you should still know *what that way is*. Live from that mental picture. The day will come, perhaps sooner than you realize, when you will act on it. But that day will not arrive unless you really ask the question.

What I am describing involves other cues and signals, such as tone of voice. When I was in college, I interned at a newspaper in Central New York. I knew a police reporter who was effective and talented; he cultivated respectful relations with the cops and found his way through the folds of difficult stories. He was a man of slight build, very slender, and short. In conventional terms, he might appear to cut a slight figure. But he spoke in a rich, sonorous voice—a very deep bass voice. It got people to listen. It impacted his character. I never knew whether it was natural or affected, but it colored his dealings with the world.

On many occasions I have observed striking and charismatic people who, if they possessed a less-developed personal style, might have been considered unremarkable, at least on first impression. But their ability to cultivate a style or look, to create something memorable—eyeglass frames, tilt of a hat, manner of dress—made them magnetic. And it did more. It made them self-possessed and better able to approach people for what they wanted. A now-dead relative served in the U.S. Army with future Secretary of State Colin Powell (1937–2021). He told me you could always see Powell was going places. How? I asked. "Oh, the way he crooked his hat," came the answer.

We populate our perceptions with images, parables, and ideals that we wish to cultivate within. Of course, we live in a consumer-driven, often-conformist, and media-flooded environment. But what I am describing has been true in some measure from time immemorial. Every culture, from the Mayans to the Polynesians, from the Hebraic to the Hellenic, had its ideals of beauty and adornment. There is nothing wholly new in the human situation. If a certain image or idea attracts you, allow yourself to experiment with it. What you discover may be the opposite of conformity: you may find that you are engaged in an act of self-selection and self-creation, which allows you to surpass boundaries set around your functioning.

There may be peers who do not like what you have done and run you down. Those are the very people to get away from, as explored in the next chapter. It debases you and holds you back to remain near people unresponsive to your true self. And it reveals their previously unspoken attitudes toward you, who was always that self in nascence.

The expression "be yourself" resounds in our culture. We hear it so often it can seem banal. But, like many familiar expressions, its depth emerges only in application. As some readers know, I dress the same on TV as I do in life, usually (though not always) wearing a leather jacket. Indulge my repeating a story, which I think warrants it. Producers at a production company that makes two shows on which I have often appeared kept pressuring me, for unclear reasons (something about it being too "subculture" for the "conservative" network), to drop the leather. One of them told my manager to lie to me and say it was his idea to ditch the jacket. He refused. So did I. I rejected their offer to reappear on a show. Several months later, in an interview of November 15, 2024, Dan Aykroyd (on whose show *The UnBelievable* I appear on the History Channel—*the same network*) said: "I love Mitch Horowitz. He's great . . . I kind of relate to him in a way. I just like his look, you know?" I did not see Dan's vivifying comments until the show runner sent them to me. That's what "being yourself" means, at least in part.

Mind you, I have also made concessions—when asked respectfully. While hosting season one of *Alien Encounters*, I was asked by Discovery producers to drop my leather for a blue-flannel shirt—the same one I wear under my leather jacket in winter. I agreed. But on the condition, affirmed by my reps, that my hand tats would not be concealed (I got them to ensure my colors always fly), my hair would remain untouched, and I wouldn't have to remove my earrings. It is still me. I am not "playing" anyone other than myself, just as in V/H/S/BEYOND, where I am credited on screen as host of *Alien Encounters*—but this time in leather. See how things come around?

Rather than fearing an off-center look would limit my possibilities, my instinct ran opposite. My partner Jacqueline Castel, a feature-film director who has twice premiered at Sundance and whose latest thriller, *My Animal*, was distributed by Paramount, told me: "Anyone who wants to be a public persona should be able to be reproduced as an action figure—and be immediately recognizable." The characters that we venerate—celebrities, sports figures, authors—are easily identified. They bear recognizable traits, like Nehru or Gandhi. This is true of our archetypes, including in mythology: Mercury holds a caduceus or wand with serpents wrapped around it; Pan holds a lyre or harp; Hercules, a club; Diana, a bow and arrow of the hunt.

As you adopt the clothing or look that makes you comfortable, or brings out traits you wish to cultivate, you will find that your tone of voice grows easier and more commanding; your gait and posture become more relaxed and confident; you catch second looks from people; and your expressiveness trends more natural and persuasive, whether you are an artist, writer, diplomat, or salesperson.

Here is a rarely uttered truth: *people approach you for what they do not have.* We look to others for what we need, for what we consider missing or under-expressed in our lives. The definition of "cool" is *not needing* something from another. Hence, you do yourself no favors by seeking to overly accommodate other people, because they are not coming to you for what they already possess. If you present yourself as an iconic or self-directed persona, you not only become more appealing, but your self-crafted image, as you hone it, eventually reflects who you really are. It is not a mask. It is the shedding of a mask.

Misinterpret none of this as carte blanche to behave in an aloof or withholding way. No one who tolerates that for long is worth having as a friend, colleague, or patron. It is a cardinal rule of mine never to withhold enthusiasm—confident and creative people understand what it means to reward another's labor or effort with recognition. On a related note, I abhor the "mind games" in *The 48 Laws of Power*, the bible of wannabes. An old boss would use them on me, e.g., showing silence in the face of my or another's triumph or taking credit for another's work. I hated it. Do it to me today and I'll bounce you out the door. I believe that the actuality of self allows you to be *naturally* powerful without resorting to mind-fuckery.

All of what I have written hinges upon *frankness about your aim*. You must not be pollyannaish with yourself. Be blunt about what you want. Keep it private. The psyche is perhaps the last place in our hyper-connected, tracked, and algorithm-driven culture that privacy still exists. If you won't exercise it there, where will you? Halfway acknowledgements, like halfway measures, net nothing. I heard from a thoughtful reader and freelance producer of reality shows,

Leslie Spann, who offered a recollection that touches on this topic. It appears with her permission:

> I worked on a weight-loss show—the show was about eighteen-year-old kids who graduated from high school and were going off to college. These kids had been overweight all of their young lives and they were wanting to lose weight, with a personal trainer, before they started their "new" lives as college students. Long story short, I was working with one of the girls who had been told her whole life she had a "pretty face." This is something many overweight girls/women hear and most of them hate hearing it because it really means, "You have a pretty face. Too bad about your fat body though." While talking to this girl, I asked her why she really wanted to lose weight. We were in the presence of her parents and her trainer. Her trainer had been really frustrated with her because she wasn't "giving it her all" during her workouts. When I asked why she wanted to lose weight, she gave the standard answer many people give, "For my health." I said to her, "That's bullshit. You are eighteen years old and are tired of being told you have a pretty face. You want to be hot. That's what you dream about when you think about losing weight. It ain't because of your health, because you're eighteen for chrissakes. Of course you want to be hot! That is part of what someone who is eighteen and going off to college to start her life SHOULD want—and that is absolutely nothing to be ashamed of. Embrace that and really understand that there is ZERO shame in wanting to love the way that you look and feel in your body!"
>
> Well, this was transformative for her. Her whole face lit up and there was a palpable shift in her energy from then on. She was literally set free in that moment. She needed permission to want what she actually wanted—rather than to want the thing for the socially acceptable, lame-ass reason. I tell you this because

> I feel like it's such a beautiful example of what I've heard you talk about . . . when you are discussing the power of being honest about what one wants in their deepest heart of hearts.

I have observed that as you pursue your aim, you may find that friends and coworkers are always trying to distract you with media or events that interest them but not you. We can absorb and retain only so much. What appeals to you in media, as in company, usually involves expanding your sense of self. And, with it, your sense of power. This cannot occur if you are bound to other people's agendas. To return to Anton LaVey's philosophy, he put it this way in a 1986 essay "Don't Recycle Your Brain" from his newsletter *The Cloven Hoof*:

> I refuse to partake of trendy or pop input. Not so much because it usually replaces valued old information, but because it will "mediocritize" me. It will dilute my special kind of knowledge bank (which has allowed me to remain unique) to a sort of common knowledge catchall. It will render me more adaptable to the common denominators of the herd, but much less adaptive as a role model to others. Rather than being possessed of data that gives me social distinction, I will be able to discuss the same movies, plays, singers, TV shows and stars, current events, sports, etc., as everyone else. Thus, I won't look like everyone else, but the moment I open my mouth, I'll sound like them.

Anton's principle stipulates that new intake must be "augmentive" of your ideas, concepts, and techniques. This does not mean you shouldn't experience something wholly new; such a break provides fresh perspective from which to measure your ideas and thought forms. The point is you do not just *give away* your attention or selfhood to whatever comes along or whatever peer activity beckons. You view media, entertainment, social outings, design, adornment, and so on, as units that augment your aim, style, personhood, total environment, and power. The ideal is to craft, to the fullest extent possible, your surroundings and self. This effort, so commonly neglected in our spiritual and therapeutic traditions, may deliver you to exactly what you are seeking.

CHAPTER TWELVE

Silence

Earlier, I quoted from a 2004 *60 Minutes* interview with Bob Dylan. I want to return to something further the artist said:

> *Ed Bradley*: You use the word destiny over and over throughout the book. What does that mean to you?
>
> *Dylan*: It's a feeling you have that you know something about yourself nobody else does. The picture you have in your mind of what you're about *will come true*. It's kinda the thing you kinda have to keep to your own self—because it's a fragile feeling and you put it out there, somebody will kill it. So, it's best to keep that all inside.

This is as good an explanation I know for the importance of maintaining silence around your magickal operations, self-work, and personal ideals. In *The Doctrine and Ritual of High Magic*, Eliphas Lévi explained how the *élan vital* for which his mid-nineteenth-century generation had been searching, dwells within the individual where it can be aroused by desire, symbol, ceremony, image, and allegory. *This power is retained by reserve and focus; it is diluted by excess and dispersal.* Lévi provided a statement of aim for the dawning magickal culture:

> *One must KNOW in order to DARE.*
> *One must DARE in order to WILL.*
> *One must WILL to have the Empire.*
> *And to reign, one must BE SILENT.*

Silence—it is the easiest treasure to hold and to squander. When harboring a key idea of self or plans, we often commit the kneejerk error of seeking emotional validation, as I once did. At one point in my publishing career, I dreamed of starting an independent press dedicated to classic, below-the-radar reprints. I rigorously researched the market, copyright issues, and prevailing and unfolding technology. I never started the press but based on its premises devised a boundingly successful reprint program at Penguin Random House, rescuing my imprint (then called TarcherPenguin) during the 2008 Great Recession, which shuttered the national book retailer Borders. My proudest accomplishment is that no one at my shop lost their jobs during that time. Sharing my vision of an indie reprint press with a close friend, however, I found he ran it down and diminished it with snide remarks. He sometimes dropped such asides into otherwise relaxed conversations, blindsiding me. In retrospect, I realize I was foolish. You cannot disclose your plans to another, whether friend or family, but only to professional colleagues with real expertise (whom you might have to pay for it).*

---

* An exception are close colleagues united in what Napoleon Hill called a "Master Mind" group.

Human nature often seeks to destroy or devalue what it cannot personally attain. Hence, when you disclose your wishes to another there is likelihood—barring special circumstances—that he or she will either subtly or ham-fistedly attempt to shatter it. So goes commerce, so goes magick.

My most painful memory as a child recalls this process. At age four or five, flowers were delivered to the attached house where we lived in Glen Oaks, Queens, in New York City. I have no idea who sent them or why. Tucked into the soil was a clear plastic pitchfork, which my mother gave me as a toy. I went outside to play—those were days when a five-year-old was permitted outside alone—and saw two slightly older boys across the court of houses. I proudly brandished my little pitchfork and said, "Look what I have!" They yelled, "That's a baby toy!" and began throwing rocks at me. I fell to the ground; my pitchfork broke in two. I ran back upstairs to our second-floor apartment crying to my mother. She bandaged my knee and used Scotch tape to mend the pitchfork. But it was ruined. If I had the episode to live again (and there exists a real prospect of it) I would have charged at the boys as aggressively as their attack was unprovoked.

This process repeats. And people near you will do to your dreams what those boys did to my pitchfork, if you permit it. *Remain silent.* As alluded, this is true—especially true—of family and friends. Napoleon Hill wrote these words in *Think and Grow Rich* in 1937. Remember them:

> "Opinions" are the cheapest commodities on earth. Everyone has a flock of opinions ready to be wished upon anyone who will accept them . . . Close friends and relatives, while not meaning to do so, often handicap one through "opinions" and sometimes through

---

See my *Power of the Master Mind* (G&D Media, 2018).

ridicule, which is meant to be humorous. Thousands of men and women carry inferiority complexes with them all through life, because some well-meaning, but ignorant person destroyed their confidence through "opinions" or ridicule.

I believe that the success maestro is overly generous. If you are looking for sources of cruelty in your life, start with those emotionally closest to you, including friends, family members, and work colleagues. In that vein, nothing—nothing—matters more to your sense of self than what you are now about to read: *you must escape cruel people*. It is a point I make again and again. If I am emphatic, it is because people often fail to realize how much they stand to lose—and gain.

Strictly speaking, this is neither ritual nor operation—but it is so important and yet *so neglected* that you may find no greater recommendation in this book. Even as therapeutic language and concepts abound in our culture, personal cruelty is among the most *underdiscussed* aspects of our society. It is neglected in therapy, spirituality, and ethics. The problem of cruelty is often explained away or layered over with discursive and indirect solutions. Except one: *getting away from cruelty without compromise*.

We are taught to consider this solution *last* and even then to over-ponder its consequences. Yet it is as close as the breath you are now drawing. Act on this and your life, happiness, and sense of self will improve dramatically. You will rediscover yourself as a person of conviviality and relaxedness. This works when nothing else does. I vow from experience.

If you are in proximity to people who dimmish you, make you feel inferior, make subtle jokes at your expense, devalue your efforts or aims, deliver backhanded compliments, pretend to forget your job, or what you said five minutes earlier—whatever it is such people do to *reduce you*—I can say assuredly: *you are not imagining things,* although your antagonists will assert that you are. *Plausible denial is the chief tool of bullies.* Hence, when you identify cruel people, never confront them or tell them you see through them. They will only twist your claims against you ("you're too sensitive . . . I was just joking . . . well, you once said . . ."). The point is not to engage and get wounded again—it is to separate.

If you absolutely cannot separate from someone at present, for reasons of economics, domesticity, or livelihood, revisit the story about Frederick Douglass in chapter three. Swear silently to yourself that will you separate from this person as an fact within—tell neither them or anyone else of your oath—and you will become free as a physical fact at the soonest possible opportunity.

Cruelty and hostility run riot in social circles because antagonists enjoy it—and victims accept it. In the face of cruelty, most of us behave like sheep. But have you ever really observed sheep? One kick from a sheep can break a grown-man's ribs.

The term gaslighting is perhaps overused today, but it points to an important dynamic, which people found more difficult to express years ago. I think one of the underlying factors in gaslighting is pernicious vanity, i.e., the party doing it experiences a sense of self-elevation or false magnanimity by *denying* the validity of another's suffering, thus proffering an image of self-remove, which doesn't otherwise appear when stakes are personal. That such vanity comes at the expense of another's wounding is deplorable. Some gaslighters take matters further: they collect "pets" that bite, by which I mean friends or employees whom they know are damaged and hurt others; they perversely enjoy witnessing this wounding while adopting a pose of faux-Solomonic indifference or denial. There exist, of course, other forms of gaslighting. But these are particularly widespread and pernicious. When you detect them, walk away—immediately.

On a related note, I believe that most of us foster too many relationships. I do not know where the idea came from that we must host dozens of relationships. Social media worsens this. We engage with more people in a day than our ancient ancestors might have in a lifetime. Within this swarm of contact festers the malady of human nature, as suggested earlier: deriving false power from debasing others.

You possess power to limit your relationships. Nothing matters more in relations than feeling seen and appreciated; nothing is more corroding than feeling debased, including subtly. There exists no law that you must abide relationships other than those that honor you. It is far better to be nobly alone than to compromise with bad company.

A complementary and, in some ways equally powerful step in ensuring your sense of selfhood and operations, is abstaining from gossip and trash talk, especially online where it runs riot. When done for entertainment, tale bearing and rumor mongering are *poison* whose very act ensnares you in falsehoods and half-truths.

Spreading or listening to hearsay degrades you in ways deeper than realized: watch for how fitful, anxious, and physically depleted you feel after an hour gossiping. You are skittish because you have degraded another while failing to salve your own wounds. The gossiper implicitly assumes that exposing another person's problems and weaknesses dilutes his or her own. Instead, you pierce the reputation of another—rarely knowing the full truth—which instigates guilt. To escape the cycle of guilt, the gossiper, like an addict returning to the bottle, takes another swig and talks trash again, further damaging his sense of self.

In choice cases, open discussion of hurtful episodes *does* provide clarity and empathy. Overdone, however, such disclosures become morbid excesses, to which our culture is so attached that it ascribes prestige to announcements of victimhood. Twentieth-century spiritual teacher Vernon Howard (1918–1992) observed, "Show me the victim and I'll show you the bully." I realize that some want to argue with that statement. But if you sit with it, esoteric truths appear. As a teacher, Vernon offered seemingly simple maxims and asked students to live with them for six months.

We seek a false sense of vitality from being "in the know" about things. But there is a means to real vitality, and hence power, without excessive talking or exchanging in the commerce of cruelty. Ralph Waldo Emerson's essay "Power," which appeared in his collection *The Conduct of Life* in 1860, prescribes how to gainfully assert your will life.

Emerson named four key elements to exercising personal power. The first—and that which sustains all others—is to be "in sympathy with the course of things." Displaying his instinct for Taoism and other Eastern philosophies, Emerson believed that an individual could augur the *flow of life* and seek to merge with it, like a twig carried downstream. "The mind that is parallel with the laws of nature," he wrote, "will be in the current of events, and strong with their strength."

The second element of power is *health*. Emerson means this on different levels. He refers broadly to vitality of body and spirit; the state of physicality and personal morale that sustains risks, seeks adventure, and completes plans. But he also means routine bodily health, without which your energies are sapped and all your attention must go toward recovery.

The third element is *concentration*. We deplete our energies by spreading thin our aims and efforts. In "Power," an imaginary oracle says: "Enlarge not thy destiny, endeavor not to do more than is given thee in charge." Within this appears an esoteric truth about both action and speech: *dispersal reduces force.*

The fourth and final element is *drilling*. By this Emerson means repeating a practice until you can perform it with mastery until all conditions. I cannot find the original source, but martial arts legend Bruce Lee is credited with saying: "I fear not the man who has practiced 10,000 kicks once, but I fear the man who has practiced one kick 10,000 times."

When you discover what you ought to be doing in life, i.e., the nature of your wish, all of this will come naturally and you will spend less time on self-depleting actions in talk, relationships, or pursuits. In a surviving fragment of a Euripides tragedy, the dramatist observes: "Zeus hates busybodies and those who do too much." Guard your energies.

CHAPTER THIRTEEN

Tipping the Scales of Luck

Magick and folklore prescribe myriad charms and talismans to boost luck. I grew up with them. In a photograph from age four or five, a lucky rabbit's foot dangles from my belt. Visitors to the Franklin Roosevelt Presidential Library and Museum in Hyde Park, New York, can view a rabbit's foot that FDR carried during his first presidential campaign in 1932.

Today, I carry a silver Mercury dime in my wallet, a money-attracting device within the tradition of hoodoo. My dime, issued during the leap year of 1940, is considered especially powerful. As you can see, I take superstition seriously, if a bit playfully. Some superstitions or "old wives' tales" retain elements of folk religion or old ways. Superstitions keep us humble in a strange world where we experience delusions of control.

In that vein, harbingers of "good luck" have always fascinated me. Before continuing to the fuller purpose of this chapter—*cultivating good luck*—I briefly consider the best-known tenets of good and ill omens, and their origins. My perspective is: Abide omens of luck—

and practice behaviors that tilt the scales of luck toward you. Magick reaches those who practice, or at least attempt, impeccability.

1. Breaking a Mirror

Ancient Romans believed human life renews itself in seven-year cycles, following cycles of the moon or the schema of the then-known planets: Moon, Mercury, Venus, Sun, Mars, Jupiter, and Saturn. Because a reflection was considered someone's "magickal likeness"—*like attracts like*—it followed that if a person's reflected image got shattered, so did the next seven years of the subject's health or luck. A broken mirror was far less likely than today, as metallic mirrors were more common in ancient Rome, but looking glasses were still known. Mirrors inspire myriad superstitions. Victorian parents feared exposing infants to mirrors, believing a mirror could trap their reflection and stunt their growth. Or, worse still, kill them by imprisoning their young souls. Even today, traditional Jewish families cover mirrors for seven days after the death of a loved one to avoid the departed soul wandering into the reflection and getting lost en route to eternity. This also gives an idea of why soulless vampires cast no reflection.

2. Knocking on Wood

Knocking on wood to protect your luck is one of history's most enduring superstitions. It emerges from millennia of mythology and religious belief that trees are sacred. Ancient people, from Chaldea to Sumatra to the British Isles, believed trees housed gods and nature spirits, who ruled the seasons. People often sought favors by laying hands on the trunk of a sacred tree. Many cultures also believed *evil* spirits lurked in wood—and when "knocked on" a malevolent spirit or mischievous fairy was shaken out. Another source of wood symbolizing spiritual power comes from the cross of Jesus. Many Christians today will rub a wooden cross to seek penance or protection.

3. Walking Under a Ladder

It is commonly said that walking under a ladder brings bad luck. Ancient Egyptians believed that a ladder perched against a wall forms a *sacred triangle*—and to walk beneath it disrupts its spiritual energies. Early Christians avoided the underside of ladders due to depictions of a ladder propped against the Holy Cross; some believed the Adversary lurked at the bottom. In ancient Asian societies, prisoners were hanged from the top steps of a ladder—onlookers were forbidden to pass beneath for fear of encountering the victim's ghost. In France, convicts were forced to walk beneath the ladder leading to the gallows, the prisoner's final *unlucky* act.

4. Spilling Salt

For thousands of years, salt has been an object of magick and superstition. In the antiquity, salt functioned as a preservative for both food and mummification, connecting it to immortality. In Rome, salt was used to augment pay, forming the root of *salary*. In Europe's Middle Ages, villagers sometimes spread a line of salt outside their doors believing that witches, who had obsessive-compulsive traits, were delayed by counting every grain before entering. The ultimate bad luck is to *spill your salt*. Leonardo da Vinci's painting "The Last Supper" shows Judas knocking over the salt, a harbinger of betrayal. To uncross yourself from spilling salt you must toss a pinch over your left shoulder, blinding the troublesome spirit behind you. I do it unfailingly.

5. Sneezing

In the West, *bless you* is the common response to a sneeze. This practice, or something similar, exists worldwide, from African Zulus to Florida Seminoles. The Romans used to say: "Jupiter preserve you!" In early Christianity, the devout would follow their sneeze with the sign of the cross. The tradition involves more than health: Egyptians, Greeks, and Romans believed that the soul dwells in the form of breath—and a sneeze could expel it from the body. Wariness around sneezing foresaw what modern medicine eventually proved: sneezing spreads communicable diseases.

6. Opening an Umbrella Indoors

Dozens of superstitions surround umbrellas, indoors and out. From ancient Persia to China, the umbrella was a luxury possessed by royalty. They used it not to block rain but to protect from the sun's rays, which they thought contained invasive spirits. Many still cringe at opening an umbrella indoors, believing "bad juju" is expelled as it springs open inside. This taboo has a more quotidian origin. The first rain umbrellas were large and tightly sprung—when opened indoors an umbrella could shatter the decorative adornments of "Victorian clutter," like lamps, frames, vases, figurines, and baubles.

7. Horseshoes

Ancient Greeks invented horseshoes not only to protect the animals' feet but to honor horses as sacred. To the Greeks, the horseshoe's design itself was holy: its U-shape was associated with the crescent moon, symbolic of fertility, new beginnings, and good fortune. The crescent shape held such mystical significance that people spanning Egyptians, Babylonians, Hindus, and Celts incorporated it into architecture, statues, and depictions of gods. The ancients commonly began agricultural festivals on a new crescent moon. Hanging a horseshoe outside one's home dates to the plague years in Europe, when it was believed to ward off illness. The practice stuck and lucky horseshoes appear in homes and businesses worldwide. Some say hanging a horseshoe upside-down causes the luck to "leak out." In hoodoo, this is disputed: you can hang a horseshoe however you like.

8. Jumping the Broom

The expression "jumping the broom" means getting married—but it comes from an old custom that the newlyweds literally *jump over a broom* to prove that one of them is not an evil double. In folklore from both Europe's Middle Ages and traditional African cultures, vampires and wicked spirits, as with witches, are considered obsessive-compulsive. A malevolent spirit could be exposed by its having to stop to count the broom's bristles. In the West, a newlywed husband often carries his bride across the threshold, which the Romans considered crawling with sinister spirits. Bridesmaids' dresses also extend to Roman antiquity, where adorned maidens were supposed to deflect or distract wicked spirits from the bride.

9. Rabbit's Foot

Ancient people from the Aztecs to the Chinese ascribed magickal properties to the rabbit, considering it a symbol of cunning, survival, and fertility. German and Scottish folklore placed special emphasis on the rabbit's relative, the hare, which was believed capable of casting an "evil eye" on people, probably because it is among the few animals born with eyes open. In America, carrying a rabbit's foot grew popular in the nineteenth century through hoodoo. Many actors, famously superstitious, kept a rabbit's foot in their makeup boxes as an applicator. When powder puffs grew popular, some retained the old rabbit's foot for luck. As noted, Roosevelt carried a rabbit's foot during his 1932 presidential campaign. He gave it to friend and confidant Margaret Suckley to hold for his second race in 1936.

10. Wrong Side of the Bed

In the annals of superstition, climbing from bed on the *left* side invites negative consequences, giving rise to the expression "getting up on the wrong side of the bed." This stems from Ancient Egyptian belief that the "left side" belongs to the forces of death and destruction. (This also relates, albeit indirectly, to lefthand magick within Vedic tradition.) Some modern hotel and casino designers arrange guest rooms with the *left* side of the bed facing the wall, helping guests rise on the side of luck. Old European custom requires exiting your bed on the *same side* as you entered it or the cosmic circle of sleep will be disturbed, until the following night when the cycle can resume as normal.

11. Wearing Black While Mourning

A wide range of ancient cultures, from China to Persia, considered death contagious. People who prepared or were otherwise near the recently dead were shunned. In Rome, mourners wore black to warn others to avoid them. (Some superstitions had altruistic qualities.) According to Old European superstition, you should give away your colored clothes while mourning for a quick passage of sorrows. Others warn against wearing mourning clothes beyond two years or you risk new tragedy. Another European custom holds that you should never accept a gift during your loss or you invite new death. And if you wear mourning gloves they must be made of *cotton* (versus more expensive leather or silk) or your whole household could perish. While myriad ancient customs surround gifts and fabrics, *in meaning* these practices demonstrate humility and absence of preening or gaiety following a death.

12. Black Cats

Egyptians considered cats sacred to the gods. Several deities, including Bastet and Sekhmet, appear as cats. On the earthly plane, cats proved hygienically important, keeping rats, mice, and other pests out of grain supplies. Between the eleventh and fourteenth centuries, Europe's cat population exploded. At times, the animals overran the continent and were seen as pests themselves. In England, elderly or single women—prime targets of witch trials—were considered caretakers of cats. So arose the legend that felines are witch companions or familiars. Another English tradition holds that Satan was thrown from heaven into a blackberry bush, perpetuating evil associations with the color black, as well as the notion that both black dogs and cats hail from the netherworld.

13. Thirteen

Fear of thirteen may be humanity's most widespread and enduring superstition. Its earliest known origin is ancient India, where it was considered unlucky for thirteen people to dine together. In Norse mythology, the maleficent Loki is the thirteenth guest at a banquet of gods, which ends in argument and violence. The most famous origin involves Judas Iscariot, the so-called traitor apostle, who was thirteenth man at the Last Supper. Returning to Roosevelt, the president's secretary Grace Tully wrote in her 1949 *F.D.R. My Boss*: "The Boss was superstitious, particularly about the number thirteen . . . On several occasions I received last-minute summonses to attend a lunch or dinner party because a belated default or late addition had brought the guest list to thirteen."

Jesus was crucified on Good (or Holy) Friday, which got linked, accurately or not, with number thirteen. In late 1306 or early 1307, Pope Clement summoned the grand master of the Knights Templar, Jacques de Molay, to Avignon under pretense of discussing a new Crusade. In 1307, on a dawn raid of Friday the thirteenth of October, secret agents of King Philip IV arrested Molay and all of his fellow Knights in France, contributing to the ill-omened Friday the thirteenth. So enduring is fear of thirteen that even today some hotels are designed without a thirteenth floor.

Now that I have reviewed some of the more prominent folklore around luck, we turn to thirteen behaviors and principles that cultivate good luck. As I see it, what we call luck or fortuitous circumstance is not blind chance but a network of causative factors, which are identifiable and cultivable. As put in the 1908 occult classic *The Kybalion* (explored in Appendix C): "Chance is merely a term indicating cause existing but not recognized or perceived." This relates to chaos theory—in which a particulate or exotic element traceably alters the whole—although the word *complexity* might be substituted for *chance*. In any case, nothing lasting occurs in a vacuum. Magick, as noted, favors those who attempt impeccability. Hence, I prescribe thirteen behavioral rules for fostering luck:

1. Luck is learnable.
2. Good chemistry is lucky.
3. To be lucky you must be noticed.
4. Prepared minds win.

5. Sobriety is lucky.
6. Persistence beats odds. (This does *not* apply to gambling.)
7. Failure can be lucky.
8. *No* is not always final.
9. Enthusiasm and pessimism are a fortuitous combination.
10. Humiliating people brings bad luck.
11. Recognizing others improves luck.
12. You must help "fate" find you.
13. Lucky people are decisive.

We now explore each:

1. Luck Is Learnable

A neurosurgeon at the University of Arizona College of Medicine told me never to take notions of luck lightly: "I've seen many patients live or die on an operating table based on what we call luck." He once canceled a scheduled surgery when a crow landed on the road before his car. Does that sound foolish? Not in his world where a hair's-width chance divides life from death.

We have difficulty saying what luck really is. Good or bad luck, most would agree, is accidental. Yet barring extreme exceptions, is anything truly accidental when cause-and-effect are detectable behind every event, even if only afterwards?

Obviously, no one can control myriad and vast factors behind every occurrence. Yet I have observed certain practices and habits that regularly improve good luck or put differently, sway circumstance. This is true even when the recipient is unaware of what is occurring. A famous actor told my friend his key to success: "Determine the things that make you lucky and then do more of them." Implicit in his statement is belief that identifiable actions, habits, relationships, and environments are, by nature, lucky. Look back on the passage I quoted from Carlos Castaneda about the "spot of happiness."

Talent, intellect, persistence, and social factors matter; but pivotal events in people's lives, and sometimes the entire arc of their adulthoods, result from practice or neglect of the principles considered here. If followed, these practices place motivated people into the current of destiny or flow of good luck. Remember: magick finds the impeccable.

2. Cultivate Chemistry

The company you select plays a tremendous part not only in the values you live by but also in the opportunities you experience.

Never take for granted the powers of relationship and collaboration. Things we attribute to talent alone are, in reality, due to the intangible but vital chemistry that arises from complementary efforts, well-balanced weaknesses and strengths, personal affinities, and shared visions. It also arises from being in the profit center of a particular business.

Good chemistry is good luck. Scan your life for it. When you find or already have it, value and maintain it. Mick Jagger never recorded a successful solo album. Neither did Joe Strummer. Consider that. If good chemistry sours do not fear letting it go. But do so only after careful observation. An old colleague with whom I enjoyed years of collaboration published several of my books; he refused to do a small editorial favor for me while I was on the road. I realized our run of luck had ended.

3. Get Noticed

You cannot profit from opportunities unless other people, including those of influence, know who you are and what you are doing.

This does not mean becoming a slave to social media or a tiresome self-promoter. (Although I must note that a not-insignificant number of self-promoters *do* meet with success.) Rather, you must honestly and plainly make clear to others your actions and enthusiasms.

A friend employed in audio publishing once told me she was not getting noticed on the job. She realized that she had been concealing her enthusiasm and dedication. This may have arisen from bad advice she received years earlier. As she told it:

> I don't know why I haven't been sharing my passion at work. It may be because a manager once told me that the way to get ahead in corporate publishing is to "keep your head down." At the time, I thought that was good, practical advice. It was not. It was a formula for mediocrity. And, most importantly, it is not me.

My friend's realization was right. Keeping your head down is feckless and self-defeating. And it is poor ethics: people who keep their heads down never learn; they rarely take responsibility; and they make others carry the load for them. That is not the success (or paycheck) I want.

Getting noticed and taking responsibility are more likely, in the long run, to place you in the stream of recognition and good luck. If you step up to responsibility there may be times when you are saddled with blame. And there may be occasions where blame is unfairly pinned on you. But even this can serve to remind you of a lucky practice: *taking proper credit when it is given*. I once sat in a meeting where a publicist was complimented for scoring an important media hit. "I didn't really do anything . . . ," he began. The company's president turned to him and whispered: "*Take credit*. You'll get blame when you don't deserve it, too."

4. Prepared Minds Win

In 1854, pioneering scientist and germ theorist Louis Pasteur (1822–1895) said in a lecture at the University of Lille in Northern France: "In the fields of observation chance favors only the prepared mind."

Preparation heightens all fortuitous chance-factors around you; it ensures that you will be in the proper mental state to notice, receive, and benefit from opportunities.

You should know and be reasonably versed in every aspect of your field, even as you focus on a niche or specialty within it. Be aware of current technology and developments. Above all, be an absolute expert within your area of focus. Practice your craft like a martial artist repeatedly runs a routine to the point where it becomes part of his or her innate self.

Motivational writer Dale Carnegie (1888–1955) began his career as a teacher of public speaking. A former actor, Carnegie grasped that public speaking was a vital skill for business success in the years following World War I. When preparing for a talk or pitch, Carnegie observed that you should amass so much material that you discard ninety percent of it when speaking. The very fact of your preparation gives you the confidence and power to speak without notes and to deliver a relaxed, enthusiastic, and freestyle performance.

Carnegie's formula is a recipe for good outcomes in all areas of life. Ardent preparation makes you persuasive. Your actions are natural and effortless. You can pivot. You gain childlike exuberance. And, as Pasteur alluded, things have a way of reaching you that would otherwise go undetected.

5. Sobriety Is Lucky

A New York City prosecutor once told me: "If you want to avoid violence, keep away from places where large amounts of alcohol are served." He saw a repeat connection between booze and accidents or violence. A majority of cases that crossed his desk, he said, occurred at clubs, sporting events, picnics, or parties where lots of alcohol was consumed.

I enjoy booze and weed and I am far from puritanical on this question. Very far. But it is self-evident that either going clean or taking an extended break improves productivity, dependability, safety, and earning power.

Sometimes the simplest and most impactful thing that you can do to heighten your abilities and avail yourself of opportunities is to get sober, even if for a fixed time. The best part: it is among the few life choices completely in your hands.

6. Persistence Beats Odds

I once knew a seasoned editor at one of New York's largest publishing houses. In truth, he was one of the least talented people I have ever met. His every utterance seemed predicated on consensus opinion. He conceived (and often encumbered) book titles by stringing together lists of stock, often media-trendy phrases. His ideas centered on copycatting whatever worked somewhere else. Yet for years I witnessed him survive in a fairly competitive atmosphere. Why? I believe the answer is *persistence*. If you stick with something long enough and manage to avoid the swing of the thresher, you inevitably experience runs of good luck. And bad luck—more on which in a moment.

In the case of this person, a few of the books he published were hits just because of the odds of the Wheel of Fortune, as explored earlier. Life is a continual ebb and flow. Consider: If a mediocre person benefits, or at least survives, through the dice roll of chance *imagine how much more a truly talented person stands to gain by sticking with a task or effort.*

If persistence possesses hidden power, this is among it: runs of luck, whether good or bad, always reverse. *And in work situations people are likelier to recognize you for the good runs versus the bad.* One success outweighs several failures. That may be irrational but it is how many workplaces and careers function.

Hence, it behooves you to stick with things. Or at least those for which you are well suited and personally enjoy. The Wheel of Fortune will inevitably turn your way. Your gains—especially as a prepared person—outweigh what you lose when the opposite occurs.

7. Failure Is Lucky

This is not some treacly sentiment. I can identify numerous times when a seeming failure proved lucky for either one of two reasons:

A) It protected me from a job, relationship, or course of action for which I was unsuited or which would have placed me in an environment on the precipice of bad luck. I twice lost job bids and felt hurt—but the outcomes proved personally fortunate. One was at a once-hot political magazine *George*, whose celebrity editor—and a hugely nice person—John F. Kennedy, Jr., died in a 1999 airplane crash, plunging the monthly into disorder and failure. (John had personally offered me the job but colleagues foot dragged.) Another time was to head a publishing house that had recently been acquired by an inexperienced buyer who proceeded to gut and nearly wreck the place.

B) Other times failure or setback lit a fire within me by highlighting my own weaknesses and missteps, which drove me to more intelligent striving and long-term realization of cherished aims. This is similar to events in the sci-fi classic (and I think the best science-fiction movie ever made), *The Matrix*, in the which the Oracle tells

Neo that he is not "the One." He is—but must hone his mettle and demonstrate his selflessness to reach that point.

Too much success, too soon, is often self-destructive. I witnessed a talented author get catapulted to sudden notability. Perhaps unprepared, flawed in some deeper way, or both, his success made him insufferable to nearly everyone around him; he took advantage of his status; disrespected people and commitments; and soon grew sufficiently self-satisfied so that his work suffered. Struggle served him better than arrival.

Peaking at a young age, which is a different kind of success, can also prove disadvantageous. In addition to issues of emotional preparation, this is because your run of luck arrives early, almost inevitably reverses, and you spend years ahead trying to regain past glories. At one point in my publishing career, I noticed that nearly every writer I worked with who produced books of depth and posterity was already in middle age. They worked all the harder—and extended their runs of luck—because they never took success for granted. I did not publish my first book, *Occult America*, until age forty-three.

8. '*No*' Is Not Always Final

An enterprising publisher I admire was trying to reach a colleague to get together. But the other party ignored him or put him off. Finally, they did meet—and connected well. My friend asked his once-hesitant companion why he had resisted seeing him.

"Well," the other man said, "you're someone who has a reputation of not taking no for an answer." In other words, he considered my friend pushy and was unsure he wanted to form a relationship. My friend responded pensively: "You're right. I don't take no for an answer. But it's because conditions can change and then the answer changes."

Always remember: *Conditions can change and then the answer changes.*

This does not mean being a pest or badgering people—much less sticking around people who do not appreciate or get you, which is distinctly unlucky. It means keeping open lines of communication and maintaining sound relationships so you can reapproach someone.

Essayist Elbert Hubbard (1856–1915) wrote in his "Credo" in 1912: "I believe that when I part with you I must do it in such a way that when you see me again you will be glad—and so will I."

Conditions in business and other facets of life change or reverse constantly. If you have the capacity to reconnect with people, and the presence of mind to do so, you can benefit from those changes. A music-industry executive once told me: "Be a pest, but be a *nice* pest."

I know a successful movie producer who has a talent for not taking no. He is unerringly friendly to nearly everyone. He offends no one and knows when to back off—temporarily. Hence, he is always ready to revisit plans, pitches, and opportunities.

When conditions shift in your favor, and someone replaces a *no* with a *yes*, accept your good luck gladly—and never bring up his or her previous refusals.

9. Never Conflate Enthusiasm with Optimism

Ralph Waldo Emerson (1803–1882) famously wrote in his 1841 essay "Circles": "Nothing great was ever achieved without enthusiasm." Absent enthusiasm, every task is menial. But never confuse enthusiasm with blind optimism. Indeed, enthusiasm coupled with watchful wariness forms a potent combination.

I know a lucky minority of people who continually check and recheck their work. They do so well past the point where another person would stop. When unexpected glitches occur—and they *always* occur—they catch them before harm is done.

You will never regret giving in to that creeping feeling that *something* may be off. Assuming the worst and rechecking or *resaving* your work will, at one time or another, rescue an important assignment, presentation, legal matter, or exam. Luck favors the pessimistic enthusiast.

10. Humiliate No One

When you insult or disrespect someone you will forget it a lot sooner than he or she will. In fact, when you really humiliate someone—in a meeting, on social media, or at an event—that person literally never forgets. Emotions form memories.

And human nature holds that most people will, at an unexpected moment, strike back if given the opportunity. Life has hidden tendrils of connection.

The same holds true in supposedly private emails, DMs, or texts. Rid yourself of the notion that anything is truly private. Confidential communications are shared all the time. And all of us have had—or will have—the experience of mistakenly hitting "reply all," or copying the wrong party, maybe even the party being discussed.

I know at least three people whose jobs were lost due to such innocent errors. Before you hit send, ask yourself if you've written anything that would embarrass or harm you if it got read in public. A boss once told her staff never to include anything in an email that they would not want read aloud in a courtroom while seated on the witness stand.

When posting on social media, the temptation to be snarky and sarcastic is omnipresent. Distance or anonymity are disinhibiting. Always remember that online comments are forever. Anonymity may afford some protection but I have my doubts. And, believe me, when you insult someone online that person remembers it—always. The injured party may circle back at an unexpected moment.

An entrepreneur once told me, "When you have the opportunity to be a smartass—don't." It could save your job and peace of mind. There are other good reasons too, such as invisible shame and damage to self-respect.

11. Recognize Others

Rather than merely avoiding offense, you should actively buildup people—sincerely and when properly due. Get in the habit of thanking people and recognizing their contribution to a project. Do so in cold, hard cash when the occasion calls for it.

Saying thank you is not just a matter of courtesy and ethics, although it is both. By recognizing other people, privately and publicly, you allow them to feel that they benefit from your success and you give them a stake in its continuance.

In 1896, philosopher William James (1842–1910) wrote in a letter to students: "The deepest principle of Human Nature is the craving to be appreciated." People hunger to be seen. Never underestimate the power of simple recognition.

The opposite is also true. If you fail to recognize people, they won't necessarily hinder your work but they will feel apathy (if not antipathy) toward your needs. I have been thanked innumerable times and truly appreciated it. But, in full disclosure, I more keenly recall when I have *not* been appropriately thanked. It is a fissure of human nature that we are more likely to recall expectations unfulfilled than fulfilled. It might involve some primal need for safety.

In any case, it should always be remembered that "invisible helpers" appear based on whether we have thanked and recognized them. Recognizing people is homage to the gods of luck.

In matters of money, you can and should additionally remunerate valued people. But even if you cannot, or have reasons for not doing so, you can accrue similar benefit by *paying them quickly*. I cannot fully emphasize the goodwill engendered when you pay a contractor, employee, freelancer, or helper quickly—preferably upon completion of a task. That is how you pay a barber or stylist. Why not a freelancer? Quick pay often means as much or more than the fee itself.

I know a publisher who pays people by electronic transfer 24 to 48 hours after delivery of a project. Recent to this writing, an artist for whom I wrote a catalogue essay kept me plugged into the payment process, not forcing me to chase the money but alerting me about when his contract was arriving and the funds could be distributed. These kinds of practices breed tremendous loyalty. They are also good ethics. The dividends are invaluable.

12. Help 'Fate' Find You, or Show Up

Are you reliable? A large part of what makes someone reliable is the simple but vital act of showing up and doing so on time. You have no idea how fully other people notice and judge you by this.

In today's culture, people back out of commitments, whether family, social, or work-related for nearly any reason. The need to run an errand is not a sufficient excuse. Busyness is not a sufficient excuse (at least not usually). Nor is feeling a bit under the weather. We as a culture are, I believe, too self-coddling. We deem things urgent that are merely passing. As philosopher Jacob Needleman (1934–2022) told me: "The only real emergency is a medical emergency."

One night I was speaking with a group of successful news photographers. These were people who had distinguished themselves in the hard-knuckled and rapidly paced world of photojournalism. Many of them knew each other from when they were younger and working as interns at *Time* magazine in New York. As the night went on, they started trading "war stories." To laughter all around, one recounted when he was tasked with transporting important film from news coverage across town. (These were the early digital days.) On the way he got into a car accident, which was not grave but was serious enough so that an ambulance was called and paramedics removed him from his car. Asked how he was feeling, he told them haltingly that he needed to get this film across town.

The group of photojournalists laughed at what seemed an absurd mismatch of priorities. The speaker himself was good-natured about it and, since no one was hurt, it *was* the kind of story that one could look back on and laugh.

But consider how few people demonstrate that quality of dedication. (As it happens, the film *did* arrive by deadline.) Certainly, you could say that he went too far or displayed an unhealthy onesidedness. But is that really so? Wouldn't you want your surgeon, nurse, pilot, or caregiver to demonstrate that kind of dedication? His example highlights the character of those who distinguish themselves. Every photographer who sat in on our discussion had a similar attitude or story.

13. Act Quickly

"Time dissipates energy," a successful literary agent once told me. When presented with a good chance—act on it. Slowness dampens or negates opportunities.

Quick and decisive action should not be confused with impulsiveness. If you are following the rules here you will not fall victim to blind impulse. You will have sufficient information about yourself and your surroundings so that you can intelligently and quickly act when the Wheel of Fortune stops where you are standing.

Intuition arises, at least partly, from amassing and storing a huge amount of information, so that when opportunity beckons the prepared person has "data banks" on which to rely.

Jacob Needleman once asked me: "What do you do when someone offers you a gift?" I looked at him blankly. "You accept it!" he replied. When something good comes your way—an offer, a job, a collaboration—never dither.

If it is the wrong opportunity, handle it with quick and courteous refusal. The unluckiest thing you can do is demonstrate halfheartedness, delay, or silence. No worthy employer or colleague respects that. He or she wants to know that your dedication matches their own. When chance arrives, *act*.

In sum, I offer *Thirteen Aphorisms of Good Luck:*

1. Good luck is not happy accident. It is more often a roster of habits and techniques cultivated to maximize desirable events.
2. Watch for fruitful collaborations. Valuable chemistry is irreplaceable. In areas of your life where it already exists, honor, cultivate, and maintain it. Good chemistry is at the root of good luck. The reverse is also true.
3. Luck reaches those who are seen. Act with dignity and decorum but ensure that people are aware of your work, passions, and contributions.
4. Luck favors the prepared mind. You can seize chances only when you detect them. The practiced eye notices things no one else does.
5. The decision to quit drinking and drugs—even if for a fixed time—is one of the most powerful you can make. Sobriety increases effectiveness, output, and opportunities. It is one of the few decisions placed wholly in your hands.
6. Runs of luck always reverse. A fertile period replaces a fallow one. And back again. In workplaces, successes are often

remembered more than failures. Hence, persistence beats odds. (This is not true in games of chance.)

7. Failure or setback may rescue you from contact with the wrong people and circumstances. It can also stoke your urge toward self-refinement.

8. "Conditions can change and then the answer changes." Watch for chances to revisit missed possibilities—and keep your relational ledger clean so that you can revisit them.

9. Never confuse enthusiasm with optimism. Check and recheck your work. Mishaps will be averted. Entire projects are saved by pessimistic enthusiasm.

10. Any time you humiliate someone you lay a hidden timebomb. People rarely forget and sometimes avenge humiliations. (Plus, it's better not to be a dick.)

11. Thanking and recognizing people—publicly, privately, and, when appropriate, financially—grants them a shared stake in your success. They may assist you at subtle and important moments. Neglecting this invites others to feel apathy (if not antipathy) toward your efforts.

12. Luck shines only upon those it can reach. Show up. Keep commitments. Be in the flow of life.

13. Opportunities dissipate. When they arrive, act quickly and decisively. If you are prepared, this is not impulsivity. Decisiveness is lucky.

CHAPTER FOURTEEN

Is the Wish Enough?

As noted throughout this book, seekers must, in order to truly be seekers, move beyond inherited decisions and templates. We require our own experiments and results, including failures. Those of us who care about magick in any of its varieties owe the spiritual culture—and ourselves—a supportable hypothesis of *how magick works*. We must be equally willing to discard cherished hypotheses or ideals if they prove wanting.

To elucidate how magick works, or at least my personal theory of it, I offer in this concluding chapter articles of experimentation, as well integration of magick with ideas from quantum and computational mechanics, which are in turn converging with psi research, mind causation, and models of interdimensionality. I venture that *warranted realization of our innate extra-physicality* is sufficient for the act of selecting or revising an event or outcome. In matters of magick, *the wish may be enough.*

I begin by quoting twentieth-century mystic Neville Goddard from a 1948 series of lectures in Los Angeles: "Scientists will one day explain why there is a serial universe. But in practice, how you use this serial universe to change the future is more important."

As though responding to Neville's dictum, Google on December 9, 2024, issued this statement about a trial-run of its quantum-computing processer Willow*:

> Willow's performance on this benchmark is astonishing: It performed a computation in under five minutes that would take one of today's fastest supercomputers 10^{25} or 10 septillion years. If you want to write it out, it's 10,000,000,000,000,000,000,000,000 years. This mind-boggling number exceeds known timescales in physics and vastly exceeds the age of the universe. It lends credence to the notion that quantum computation occurs in many parallel universes, in line with the idea that we live in a multiverse, a prediction first made by David Deutsch.**

In elegance, intellect, and prescience, I consider Neville the most penetrating voice to emerge from New Thought. It was not until years after his 1948 statement that quantum physicists began discussing the "many-worlds" theory, postulated in 1957 by physicist Hugh Everett III (1930–1982). This is the inceptive model on which Google's statement rests. Everett was attempting to make sense of extraordinary findings documented for about three decades in quantum mechanics. For example, scientists demonstrate, through interference patterns, that a subatomic particle occupies a "wave state" or

---

* In quantum computing, qubits or quantum bits of data simultaneously exist as 0 and 1 in a state of superposition, enabling radically, almost miraculously, faster computations.

** *The Fabric of Reality: The Science of Parallel Universes—and Its Implications* (Viking, 1997)

state of superposition—that is, an infinite number of places—until an observer or automatized device takes a measurement: only when measurement is taken does the particle collapse, so to speak, from a wave state into a localized state. At that point it occupies a definite, identifiable place. Before measurement, however, the particle *exists only in potential.*

I am using language that sometimes raises objections. A critic wrote me: "The 'wave state' you describe is a wave function, which is descriptive of the particles' energy. That wave function, when squared mathematically gives you a probability of its spatial distribution. So, the wave function is a square root of a probability distribution." Yes and no. As my colleague Dean Radin points out, the "wave function is not about probabilities. It's much stranger than that. It's the square root of probability, which some distinguish from probability by calling what the wave function represents a 'possibility.'" In any case, the wave function describes a state as much as a formula

Now, I have just about squeezed all of quantum physics into a matchbox. I think it is an accurate description, but obviously I am reducing huge complexities into general terms. I believe, however, that here and elsewhere I am faithfully representing the collective data of the last ninety-plus years of particle experiments, as well as emerging experiments on larger objects, such as hydrogen molecules, proteins, and buckyballs, which are groups of sixty carbon atoms in the shape of a soccer ball. We are seeing that on the atomic and subatomic scale matter does not behave as we are conditioned to expect.

About twenty years prior to this writing, it became fashionable for New Agers and laypeople, like me, to put quantum theory at the back of cherished spiritual principles. It became equally fashionable for professional skeptics and mainstream journalists to pushback, crying *B.S.* and *sophistry*. That position, while still heard, has quieted. Not because skeptics have grown more pensive or attenuated to media-speak, but because the proposition of mind-over-matter, strange as it may seem, now resounds in debates on theoretical physics in mainline journals and magazines.*

In 2009, I attended a presentation on the "quantum measurement problem" delivered by parapsychologist Radin before an audience of scientists, social thinkers, and scholars of religion. I asked him to address the 800-pound gorilla in the room: If observation and perspective alter material on a micro level, in the world of waves and particles, might that say something about the legitimacy of the New Thought or mind-power thesis? "It's not complete bullshit," Radin replied. "There may be an inkling of something to it." Another physicist and longtime military researcher was also present. "As the resident skeptic," he said, "I concur."

Our understanding of matter in our macro world generally comes from measuring things through our five senses and experiencing them as singularities. There is one table. It is solid and definable. It is not occupying an infinite number of spaces. But contemporary quantum physicists have theorized that we may not normally see or experience superposition phenomena because of what is called *information leakage*.

This means we gain or lose data based on fineness of measurement. When you measure things with exquisitely well-tuned instruments, like a microscope, you see more of what is going on, i.e., actual reality. But when you pan the camera back, so to speak, your measurements coarsen and you see less of what is actually happening. To cite the most basic example, to all ordinary appear-

---

* E.g., see "Even Physicists Don't Understand Quantum Mechanics" by Sean Carroll, *New York Times*, September 7, 2019.

ances, a table is solid. The floor beneath your feet is solid. Where you are sitting is solid. But measuring through atomic-scale microscopes, we realize that as you go deeper and deeper, space appears within these objects. Particles make up the atom and still greater space appears. We do not experience that; we experience solidity. But no one questions that space prevails among particles composing an atom.

Furthermore, we possess decades of data demonstrating that when subatomic particles are directed at a target system, such as a double slit, they appear in infinite places at once until a measurement is made; *only then does locality exist*. But we fail to see this unless we are measuring things with comparative exactitude. Hence, what I am describing seems unreal based on lived experience—but it is actual.

In any event, my supposition is: if particles appear in an infinite number of places at once until a measurement is taken; and if, as we know from studying the behavior and mechanics of subatomic particles, there exists an infinitude of possibilities; and if we know, as we have since the inception of Einstein's theories, that time is relative, then it is possible to reason—and almost necessary to reason—that linearity itself, by which we organize our lives, is *illusory*.

Linearity is a *requisite* device for five-sensory beings to navigate life; but it does not stand up objectively. Apropos of our earlier exploration of retrocausality, linearity is conceptual: a subjective interpretation of what is going on and a tool of measurement. It is not reflected in Einstein's theory of special relativity, which demonstrates that time slows for an object approaching the speed of light. The individual traveling in a metaphorical spaceship at or near lightspeed experiences time slowing, not from their perspective but in comparison to those not at near lightspeed. This is no mere thought exercise: astronauts in our era, although they are obviously approaching nowhere near that velocity, experience minute effects of time reduction. Nor is linearity reflected in quantum mechanics, where particles appear in an infinitude of places. Linearity is *not* replicated when measurement of a particle serves to localize the appearance or existence of the object.

This begins to clarify why Einstein famously wrote in a letter of March 1955: "People like us, who believe in physics, know that the distinction between past, present, and future is only a stubbornly persistent illusion."*

If we pursue this line of thought further—and here Everett's many-worlds theory returns into play—the very decision to take a measurement (or not take one) not only localizes a particle, but creates a past, present, and future for that particle. Hence, an observer's decision to log a measurement creates a *multidimensional reality* for the particle.

There exists debate over whether a *device* represents a method of measurement distinct from an *observer*, as well as whether the "collapse" from wave to particle results from an observer's individual psyche or "transpersonal mind behaving according to natural laws," as observed by Bernardo Kastrup, Henry P. Stapp, and Menas C. Kafatos in a May 29, 2018, *Scientific American* article, "Coming to Grips with the Implications of Quantum Mechanics." This *transpersonal mind*, the writers continue, "comprises but far transcends any individual psyche," a description similar to the Hermetic concept of *Nous*, sometimes considered an Overmind. The authors compellingly argue that even if a device is used for measurement—and thus localization—perception and intent, either of the individual, the meta-mind, or both, remains the determining force. (For those who think I am exaggerating the implications of quantum mechanics,

---

* "Fear of Nazis and Unpublished Work: Hebrew University Unveils 110 Albert Einstein Manuscripts" by Ofer Aderet, *Haaretz*, March 6, 2019

read any of the pertinent articles referenced in this chapter—you will find, I believe, that I am being conservative.)

Multidimensional reality is implied in the famous thought-experiment called Schrödinger's Cat. Twentieth-century physicist Erwin Schrödinger (1887–1961) grew frustrated with the evident absurdity of quantum theory, which showed objects simultaneously appearing in more than one place at a time. Such an outlook, he felt, violated all commonly observed physical laws. In 1935, Schrödinger sought to highlight this predicament through a purposely absurdist thought experiment, which he intended to compel quantum physicists to follow their data to its ultimate degree.

Schrödinger reasoned that quantum data dictates that a sentient being, such as a cat, can be simultaneously alive and dead. Here is a variant of the Schrödinger's Cat experiment: a cat is placed into one of a pair of boxes. Along with the cat is a collar fitted with a device which, if exposed to an atom, releases a deadly poison. An observer then fires an atom at the boxes. The observer subsequently uses some form of measurement to check on which box the atom is in: the empty one, or the one with the cat and the poisoning device. When the observer goes to check, the wave function of the atom (the state in which it exists in both boxes) collapses into a particle function (the state in which it is localized to one box). Once the observer takes his measurement, convention says that the cat will be discovered to be dead or alive. But Schrödinger reasoned that quantum physics describes an outcome in which the cat is *both* dead and alive. This is because the atom, in its wave function, was, at one time, in either box, and either outcome is real.

Of course, all lived experience tells us that if the atom went into the empty box, the cat is alive; and if it went into the box with the cat and the poisoning device, the cat is dead. But Schrödinger, aiming to highlight the frustrations of quantum theory, argued that if the observations of quantum-mechanics experiments are right, you must allow for each outcome.

To take it even further, many-worlds theorists in the 1950s posited that if an observer waited some significant length of time—say, eight hours—before checking on the dead-alive cat, he would discover one cat that was dead for eight hours and another that was alive for eight hours (and now hungry). In this line of reasoning, observation effectively established the localized atom, the dead cat, and the living cat—and *also established the past*, or in other words, created a history for both a dead cat and a living one. Both outcomes are true.

So, whatever a particle is doing, the very fact that an observer elected to take a measurement at that time, place, moment, and juncture creates a past, present, and future—an infinitude of outcomes. A divergent set of outcomes would exist if that measurement were never taken. A divergent set of outcomes would also exist if that measurement were taken one second later, or five minutes later, or tomorrow. And what is tomorrow? When particles exist in superposition until somebody takes a measurement, there is no such thing as tomorrow, other than subjectively.

Consider too: the cat, from its perspective, is local; the observer, from its perspective, is local—but both, in fact, are in a wave state or superposition. We can speak of them as concrete, singular beings only from their personal perspective. From the quantum perspective, they are infinite. Expanding on this idea, research physician Robert Lanza, adjunct professor at Wake Forest University School of Medicine, argues that death itself is ultimately a mental phenomenon: we "die" only insofar as an observer perceives demise; the consciousness of the "deceased" branches off into one of Everett's many worlds[*]. (This begs the question of *who*

---

[*] "The Impossibility of Being Dead," *Psychology Today*, November 11, 2020

experiences these effects if there is no such thing as "one" person/life.)

And what, finally, are our five senses but technology by which we measure things? Are our five senses anything other than biological technology, not necessarily different in intake from a camera, photometer, digital recorder, or microscope? So, it is possible that within reality—within the extra-linear, super-positioned infinitude of possibilities in which we are taking measurements—we experience things based upon perspective. This is why in considering mind causation I use the term *select* versus manifest.

Here we return to Neville Goddard. His instinct was, I believe, correct in the schema just considered. Neville taught that you effectively take a measurement by employing the visualizing forces and feeling states of your imagination. You are taking a measurement within the infinitude of possible outcomes. Measurement localizes or actualizes the thing itself. In the 1948 lectures quoted earlier, Neville further noted:

> Man can prove the existence of a dimensionally larger world by simply focusing his attention on an invisible state and imagining that he sees and feels it. If he remains concentrated in this state, his present environment will pass away, and he will awaken in a dimensionally larger world where the object of his contemplation will be seen as a concrete objective reality.
>
> I feel intuitively that, were he to abstract his thoughts from this dimensionally larger world and retreat still farther within his mind, he would again bring about an externalization of time. He would discover that, every time he retreats into his inner mind and brings about an externalization of time, space becomes dimen-

sionally larger. And he would therefore conclude that both time and space are serial, and that the drama of life is but the climbing of a multitudinous dimensional time block.

Again, note how foresightful Neville's ideas and language proved of the many-worlds theory. The confoundingly brilliant Aleister Crowley made a statement related to Neville's. Writing in the introduction to his 1904 phenomenally received text *The Book of the Law*—published in a general edition in 1938—Crowley observed:

> Each of us has thus an universe of his own, but it is the same universe for each one as soon as it includes all possible experience. This implies the extension of consciousness to include all other consciousnesses. In our present stage, the object that you see is never the same as the one that I see; we infer that it is the same because your experience tallies with mine on so many points that the actual differences of our observation are negligible . . . Yet all the time neither of us can know anything . . . at all beyond the total impression made on our respective minds.

Neville's formula is simplicity itself: *an assumption, if persisted in, hardens into fact*. But the assumption must be persuasive; it must be convincing. That is why emotions and feeling states have to come into play. Neville observed that you can use hypnagogia—the state of cognizant pre-sleep or drowsy relaxation—to help facilitate this process.

Hypnagogia naturally occurs twice daily: just prior to and following sleep. It is a period of hallucinatory sentience during which you are nonetheless capable of controlling attention; moreover, your rational defenses are lowered. This is "prime time" to visualize a desired end. Hypnagogia is also a period of heightened ESP-related activity, as considered in Appendix A: Wild Talents.

Another way of using Neville's approach is entering an inner state of theatrical or childlike make-believe. Not childish but child*like:* a state of internal wonder and pretending. Children excel at this. We grow embarrassed about this quality as we age, but Neville spoke ingenuously about walking the streets of Manhattan imagining that he was in the treelined lanes of his native Barbados, boarding a ship to some desired destination, or in a location where he wished to be.

He would say: "Unfoldment will come. You will see." Again, he argued that an assumption, though false, if persisted in, hardens into fact. He further advised, "Assume the state of the wish fulfilled. Live from the end." Remember, the teacher reminded, you are not in a state of *wanting;* you are in a state of *having received.* Your aim is occupying the emotional and mental condition that you would experience following fulfillment.

Of course, you must also continue to go about your life in this world of Caesar, currency, and commerce—fulfilling your obligations and remaining accountable. You must cooperate with the world. You must complete the normative tasks life requires. The crisis of the New Age is inability of an outsized number of adherents to fully abide this. In my observation, until someone demonstrates accountability, competency, and agency in outer life, the spiritual path is a diversion, possibly a disastrous one.

Should you accept this challenge, how long will it take to witness your desired changes in outer life? When will tactile existence conform to your internal focus, your act of living "from the end" of your ideal? The question of time intervals is deeply fraught. With all the stress life throws at us, it is difficult to adopt a feeling state and reasonably stick with it for hours, days, or weeks. Psychological barriers and stress sometimes make it impossible.

Neville noted that there could fall a substantial time interval between your visioning and experiencing the wished-for thing. He pointed out that the gestation period of a human life is nine months. The gestation period of a horse is eleven months. The gestation period of a lamb is five months. The gestation period of a chick is twenty-one days. There will almost always fall some time interval. You will find that depth of passion comports with naturalness of persistence. Sometimes it will seem more a matter of the aim holding you than you it, which portends well. This is why clarity of aim and self-honesty are essential: we follow emotions, acknowledged or not.

Johann Wolfgang von Goethe made an interesting observation in this vein. We all know the expression, "Be careful what you wish for; you just might get it." It is rooted in Goethe. Taking a leaf from the philosopher and dramatist's play *Faust* (c.1772–1775), Ralph Waldo Emerson noted this dynamic in his 1860 essay "Fate," which led to the popular adage. Emerson wrote:

> And the moral is that what we seek we shall find; what we flee from flees from us; as Goethe said, "what we wish for in youth, comes in heaps on us in old age," too often cursed with the granting of our prayer: and hence the high caution, that, since we are sure of having what we wish, we must beware to ask only for high things.

We are warned to act with perspective, if any is possible: what we wish for when young will visit us in waves when old.

Goethe's observation relates to Neville's remarks about perceived passage of time and gestation between thought and actualization. Many people can reasonably object that they suffer all kinds of unfulfilled wishes. But testing the truth of this observation requires peeling back the layers of your mind and probing formative images and fantasies from when you were very young. What is the earliest positive dream lodged in your long-term memory, maybe from age three or four? What fantasies occupied your earliest recollective years? Children lead intense fantasy lives even at ages four or five. If you take Goethe's counsel, you may be surprised—barring extreme countervailing events—to discover symmetry between what you are living out today and concepts you harbored when very young.

In any case, Neville advised against thinking in terms of, "It will happen this way" or "I'll do something to make it happen." His attitude was that the event will unfold in its own natural manner, similar to what was explored regarding sigil work and "established lines." Your job is not to draw the map. It is to live from the destination.

I must, finally, add a word about suffering, both personally and globally. New Thought has proven inadequate in addressing matters of implacable tragedy and catastrophe, a topic on which I have written widely.*

My contention is that even if awareness, or the elusive term consciousness, is the ultimate arbiter of existence, we still experience many different laws and forces within the physical framework we know. I once said we *live* under many different laws and forces; I am not sure that is exactly right. We *experience* diffuse laws and forces, and these experiences are hard-baked into us. Hence, it stands to reason that even if emotive thought, perspective, and awareness determine what reality is concretized into experience, there exist myriad, if not necessarily ultimate, laws and possibilities playing out simultaneously and also wielding impact. There are physical param-

---

* E.g., see "The Revelation of Joesph Murphy," Medium, April 20, 2023.

eters, whether of a fixed or perceived nature, which sway experience within our framework. There may be other frameworks in which our psyches are freer. There may be frameworks in which we experience fewer laws and forces that seem to disrupt continuity between intent and experience.

I believe that Neville will be remembered—and is already seen—for having created the most persuasive mystical analog to quantum physics. When I started writing about Neville in 2005—the first journalistic coverage of his life since the 1940s—he was a figure of obscurity, even among most New Thoughters. Today, Neville's voice and work net millions of results in search engines. At a 2022 tech conference, I was floored by the number of programmers and engineers (not the usual suspects) who approached me to talk about him.

As noted, Neville espoused a variant of the many-worlds theory long before the popularization of quantum physics. Indeed, he evinced a series of remarkable instincts in the 1940s that have since been tantalizingly, if indirectly, reiterated by quantum theorists—most of whom have not (yet) heard his name. It would not surprise me if, within a generation, some physics students begin reading Neville as a philosophical adjunct to their work. That may seem a stretch, but remember that many of today's senior cohort of physicists, people in positions of academic and grant-making authority, were inspired by *Star Trek*, Arthur C. Clarke, and *Zen and the Art of Motorcycle Maintenance*. There is visibly greater openness in the field today to matters of perspective, interdimensionality, and perceptual causation.*

---

* Perpetual debate surrounds the question of causation versus correlation. Strictly speaking, physics deals in the former but since we do not know the macro-nature (or even micro-nature) of reality, this uncertainty must be sustained. At some point, the causation-correlation question may be superseded by another set of possibilities.

As suggested, you can use different techniques in connection with Neville's ideas, including those of your own devising: I encourage you to try them and see what happens. I now wish to take matters one more step. Based on all we have just considered, I think it reasonable to venture, as proposed at the start of this chapter, that *the wish itself* may be sufficient to set in motion the selective dynamics I describe.

If time is nonlinear, and if all events exist as potentialities, I can sympathize with a principle quoted earlier from Japanese essayist and novelist Yukio Mishima in his 1968 manifesto *Sun and Steel*: "Anything that comes into our minds for even the briefest of moments, exists."

In my 2014 history of the positive-mind movement, *One Simple Idea*, I called the opening chapter, "To Wish Upon a Star." I was referencing events from adolescence:

> In the late 1970s, my family made an ill-fated move from our bungalow-sized home in Queens to a bigger house on Long Island. It was a place we could never quite afford. After moving in, my father lost his job and we took to warming the house with kerosene heaters and wearing secondhand clothing. One night, I overheard my mother saying that we might qualify for food stamps. When the financial strains drove my parents to divorce, we were in danger of losing our home. Walking back from a friend's house at night, I used to wish upon stars, just like in the nursery rhyme. Since any disaster seemed possible, any solution seemed plausible.

I wished upon stars. A desperate, late-childhood indulgence inherited from folklore reprocessed through entertainment—or something more? At a crossroads in my search, I decided to consider or at least determinedly approach the question.

Throughout this book I have argued that reaching a clarified ideal of what you want in life—and realizing that to which your life is dedicated—is vital to practicing magick and activating the fullest qualities of your psyche. Mental-emotive focus is a precondition for mind causation or selection. This mirrors natural law as well as the nature of measurement.

Hence, can a well-focused and passionately felt wish, the only kind deserving the name, enact selectivity—or magick? In pursuing this question, I studied a pair of innovative papers from Harvard Medical School's program on placebo research. In 2010, researchers from Harvard's Program in Placebo Studies and the Therapeutic Encounter (PiPS) issued a landmark paper, "Placebos without Deception."* Clinicians divided eighty sufferers of Irritable Bowel Syndrome (IBS) into two study groups: forty-three into a no-treatment group and thirty-seven into an "honest placebo" group. Subjects in the latter received a transparently administered placebo. "The placebo pills were truthfully described as inert or inactive pills, like sugar pills, without any medication in it," researchers wrote. "Additionally, patients were told that 'placebo pills, something like sugar pills, have been shown in rigorous clinical testing to produce significant mind-body self-healing processes.'"

Among subjects in the active group, 59% reported sustained and lasting relief compared with 35% in the control group, which is statistically highly significant. Amid a swirl of media coverage, the researchers—to their credit—resisted interpreting or speculating over the results. But the outcome suggests that *belief in the facility of the placebo effect* is itself sufficient to trigger a therapeutic response. Under right conditions, the decoy proves superfluous.

---

* "Placebos without Deception: A Randomized Controlled Trial in Irritable Bowel Syndrome" by Ted J. Kaptchuk, et al., *PLoSONE*, December 2010, Volume 5, Issue 12

In 2016, PiPS and collaborating researchers published a second paper on the transparent placebo, this time among ninety-seven sufferers of lower-back pain in Portugal.* Once more, the subjects, seventy-six of whom completed the trial, were divided into two groups: a no-treatment or control group and a group administered a transparently inert substance with the understanding that a placebo response was being tested for.

"There was," researchers wrote, "a clinically significant 30% reduction in both usual and maximum pain in the placebo group compared to reductions of 9% and 16% in usual and maximum pain, respectively, in the continued usual treatment group." Moreover, "honest placebo" subjects reported a 29% reduction in "pain-related disability" compared to near-zero in the control group.

We hold clear evidence that therapeutic benefit is triggered without the benevolent deception generally relied upon in placebo trials. The success of the transparent placebo experiments heightens my interest in whether we can enact the creative agencies of the psyche, without attempting to dramatize, picturize, ritualize, or otherwise ceremonially summon an idealized outcome. I ask us to consider whether *warranted belief* in psychical or mental-emotive agency is alone sufficient to tap selective energies of self.

I am not advocating a departure from magick, the very subject of this book. To do so would mean damning the ground beneath my feet. Rather, I am suggesting, apropos of earlier suppositions by figures ranging from Arthur Schopenhauer to Jack Parsons, that at the core of magick lies a greater truth about the human condition, one that allows us to take more seriously the Psalmist's melancholic injunction "ye are gods." I believe that as we as a human community grow increasingly aware of our interdimensional existence—an

---

* "Open-label placebo treatment in chronic low back pain: a randomized controlled trial" by Cláudia Carvalho, et al., *Pain*, December 2016, Volume 157, Number 12

awareness justified by psychical research, neuroplasticity, quantum mechanics and computing, placebo studies, interdimensional modeling, and today's deepening UFO query (which itself encompasses the question of interdimensionality)—we may discover, as our Victorian counterparts did of the subconscious mind, that there exists a *faculty of selection* couched in the psyche as an under-recognized but ever-operative, ever-potent facet of human existence.

Your defined, impassioned, and acknowledged wish *may be enough*. It may, at least, open humanity to the *simplicity* of magick, for which Jack wished. Try.

EPILOGUE

Letter to a Prisoner

January 10, 2025

Dear Mike,

Thank you for your letter of November 12 and your birthday wishes.

You cover a lot of interesting ground in your note. In hopes this reply proves useful, I will share an element of my recent search. As you noted, I am unsentimental about wishes: I believe they must be clear, blunt, and unflinchingly self-honest. I also believe in reciprocal ethics.

In my mid-thirties, I discovered the work of spiritual philosopher G.I. Gurdjieff to which I dedicated about eight years of group effort. I treasure the experience daily. The question of what one *wants* from the work was always a hot-button issue for me. I am clear about what I want; one can read it in *Daydream Believer* or elsewhere. My search is pretty public for the sake of exchanging transparently with readers.

I have lately revisited a passage from *In Search of the Miraculous*, P.D. Ouspensky's invaluable record of his time with Gurdjieff. In it, the teacher asks a circle of students to state their personal aims and what they desire from the work. The answers are fairly ordinary: world peace, to know the future, immortality, to be a real Christian, and so forth. In short, Gurdjieff replies:

> Of the desires expressed the one which is most right is the desire to be *master of oneself*, because without this nothing else is possible. And in comparison with this desire all other desires are simply childish dreams, desires of which a man could make no use even if they were granted to him.

For many years, I resisted his formulation. It did not stir my passions. It seemed too far away. (The more involved one becomes with the work, the further and further it seems, almost to the point of impossibility. Only those who have been stripped of fantasies about self can understand that.)

I used to, and in some ways still do, pose an exercise to others and myself. Let's say you encounter the proverbial genie in a lamp. He offers you one—and just one—wish. Your wish will be granted, but only if you are entirely self-honest about what you want. If you are not, you will lose everything. What is it?

I despise treacly responses and set up this question to get down to the emotional skin-and-bone of things. I often say that life strikes a tough bargain with us: we are granted the one thing we want above all else, whether we admit it to ourselves. People object: I have so many needs and obligations; how can I boil it all down to one thing? I say that one well-selected aim can cover a lot of bases: so choose carefully.

Lately, I have been newly posing this genie question to myself. I find that I am starting to sound a little bit like my interlocutors. I have many bases to cover and I want to ensure that no one I love (of whom there are few) gets left behind. Hence, I am thinking anew about Gurdjieff's demand. Is being "master of oneself" possible? Probably not. But this aim fulfilled would allow someone to actually place hands on the levers granted us—and find his or her way in the world, something impossible for someone controlled and contorted entirely by external influences, i.e., all but a very few of us, if any.

I share this by way of exchange. I am happy to send you a copy of this book if you like.

Wishing you all good things,
Mitch

APPENDIX A

*Wild Talents: Why ESP Is Real**

> *"All around are wild talents, and it occurs to nobody to try to cultivate them..."*
> —CHARLES FORT, *WILD TALENTS*, 1932

I believe that our culture is poised for an epochal change in how we understand and accept the core findings of parapsychology—that is, acceptance of the empiricism of the extraphysical. Rejectionism tends to harden on the brink of seismic change, and we are seeing pockets of that as well. But the outcome of the present moment is, I believe, the acknowledgment that we possess indelible evidence of an extraphysical component to life.

Formal scientific scrutiny of anomalous phenomena marked its starting point in 1882, when the Society for Psychical Research

---

* This essay originally appeared under the title "The Parapsychology Revolution" in the Winter 2023 issue of *Quest* magazine, published by the Theosophical Society in America.

(SPR) was founded in London by scientists including F.W.H. Myers (who coined the term *telepathy* for mind-to-mind communication) and pioneering psychologist and philosopher William James.

At its inception, parapsychology sought to test mediumistic phenomena under controlled conditions. The early SPR worked with rigor to hold spirit mediums to proof. Researchers such as the strong-willed Richard Hodgson and James himself ventured to the séance table intent on safeguarding against fraud and documenting claimed phenomena, including physical mediumship, after-death communication, and clairvoyance or what is today called channeling. They probed unexplained cases, exposed frauds, and created historical controversies that have lingered until today. But they were working largely within the lace-curtained settings of Victorian parlors. On the whole, SPR researchers were not functioning in clinical environments, so-called white coat lab settings. The American chapter of the SPR, meanwhile, was stymied by factional disputes between members more interested in the after-death survival thesis and those committed to the more conservative direction of documenting mental phenomena.

I do not intend to leave the impression that lab-based study of psychical phenomena was absent. In the 1880s, Nobel laureate and SPR president Charles Richet, one of France's most highly regarded biologists, studied telepathy with subjects under hypnosis. Richet also introduced the use of statistical analysis in ESP card tests, presaging today's near-universal use of statistics throughout the psychological and social sciences. In the early 1920s, French engineer René Warcollier conducted a series of experiments on long-distance telepathy. Sigmund Freud himself pondered the possibilities of telepathy, sometimes delaying publication of key statements posthumously to avoid professional fallout. This was the case with Freud's "Psychoanalysis and Telepathy," his earliest paper on the topic written in 1921—but withheld from publication until

1941, two years after his death. (This was likely at the urging of his English biographer Ernest Jones, who found the topic professionally compromising.)

The paranormal burgeoned into an acknowledged, if hotly debated, academic field thanks largely to ESP researcher J.B. Rhine (1895–1980) and his wife and intellectual partner Louisa Rhine (1891–1983). In the late 1920s and early '30s, the Rhines established the research program that became the Parapsychology Laboratory at Duke University in Durham, North Carolina, which made paradigmatic advances in the scientific study of ESP.

The Rhines trained as statisticians and botanists at the University of Chicago, where both received doctorates (a considerable rarity for a woman then). In Chicago in 1922, they were inspired by a talk on Spiritualism by English author Arthur Conan Doyle. With his eyes on greater horizons, J.B. soon grew restless in his chosen career. "It would be unpardonable for the scientific world today to overlook evidences of the supernormal in our world," he told what must have been a mildly surprised audience of scientific agriculturalists at the University of West Virginia.

The Rhines began casting around, venturing to Columbia University and Harvard seeking opportunities to combine their scientific training with their metaphysical interests. Initial progress proved fitful. As often occurs in life, just before they gave up their immense efforts, an extraordinary opportunity appeared. In 1930, with the support of Duke's first president, William Preston Few, the new chairman of Duke's psychology department, William McDougall, made J.B. Rhine a formal part of the campus.

Although the founding of Duke's Parapsychology Laboratory is often dated to that year, the program was not christened the Parapsychology Laboratory until 1935, where it remained until 1965. Today the Rhine Research Center continues as an independent lab off campus. It proved a watershed episode in which parapsychology was formally folded into an academic structure and study of the psychical became a profession.

At Duke, J.B. Rhine did not quite originate but popularized the phrase *extrasensory perception*, or ESP, which soon became a household term. The work begun at Duke's Parapsychology Lab in the early 1930s has continued among different researchers, labs, and universities to the present day. The effort is to provide impeccably documented evidence that human beings participate in some form of existence that exceeds cognition, motor skill, and commonly observed biological functions—that we participate in trackable, replicable patterns of extra-physicality that permit us, at least sometimes, to communicate and receive information in a manner that surpasses generally acknowledged sensory experience and means of data conveyance. This field of exchange occurs independently of time, space, or mass.

We have also accumulated a body of statistical evidence for psychokinesis (i.e., mind over matter) and precognition or what is sometimes called retrocausality, in which events in the future affect the present. For several years, Dean Radin, chief scientist at the Institute of Noetic Sciences (IONS) in Northern California, has performed and replicated experiments in precognition in which subjects display bodily stressors, such as pupil dilation or increased heart rate, seconds *before* being shown distressing or emotionally triggering imagery.

These are fleeting references to a handful of recent findings from modern parapsychology. I am going to make a statement, and I am then going to argue for it: *we possess heavily scrutinized, replicable statistical evidence for an extraphysical component of the human psyche*. For decades, this evidence has appeared in—and been reproduced for—traditional, academically based journals, often juried by scientists without sympathy for its findings. This evidence has been procured and replicated under rigorous clinical conditions. It demonstrates that the individual possesses or participates in a facet of existence that surpasses what is known to us biologically, psychologically, sensorily, and technologically. In short: ESP exists.

The search for greater dimensions of life is as old as humanity itself. But what is new and revolutionary is *the advent of science as a method of protocols to identify processes that affirm primordial humanity's basic instinct for the extraphysical.* As noted, this places our generation before a remarkable precipice. It is one that we have not yet been able to cross.

The precipice is the philosophy called materialism, by which Western life has organized itself for nearly 300 years. Philosophical materialism holds that matter creates itself, and that your mind is strictly an epiphenomenon of your brain. Furthermore, thoughts are a localized function of gray matter which, like bubbles in a glass of carbonated water, are gone once the water is gone. And that is the extent of the psyche.

That philosophy is obsolete. Firstly, an enormous amount of data has amassed verifying both the perceptual basis of reality and the extraphysical—gathered through the same methodology that materialism purports to defend. Secondly, we face the progressing realization that materialism is simply a position, a theory, an ideology, of which science is independent.

This does not mean that materialism will fade gently. Its outlook—that matter evinces no calculable reality beyond classical mechanics and that all contrary evidence or implications are false because they contradict its founding premise—will retain influence for decades. The materialist perspective is concretized within key parts of our culture and media. Many opinion-shaping personalities hold to it with conviction.

What evidence exists for my claims of science affirming the infinite? Here I return to Duke's Parapsychology Laboratory in the early 1930s. Rhine's innovation as a researcher was developing clear, repeatable, and unimpeachable methods, with rigor and without drama or speculation, for testing and statistically mapping evidence for anomalous communication and conveyance. To attempt this, Rhine initially created a series of card-guessing tests that involved a deck called Zener cards designed by psychologist Karl E. Zener. Zener cards are a five-suit deck, generally with twenty-five cards in a pack, with symbols that are easily and immediately recognizable: circle, square, cross, wavy lines, and five-pointed star. After a deck is shuffled, subjects are asked to attempt blind hits on what symbol will turn up.

Probability dictates that if you are operating from random chance over large spreads, you are going to hit 20 percent, or one out of five. But Rhine discovered, across tens and eventually hundreds of thousands of rigorously safeguarded trials (by 1940, the database included nearly a million trials) that certain individuals, rather than scoring 20 percent, would score 25 percent, 26 percent, 27 percent, sometimes 28 percent (and in select cases a great deal higher).

At the time, social scientists commonly withheld negative sets of data on the questionable grounds that something was flawed with the methodology. Rhine reversed this practice early on at his lab and helped lead the overall social sciences to do so. All of the data were reported. Nothing was withheld in the file drawer. No negative sets were excluded.

In Rhine's work, every precaution was taken against corruption, withholding, or pollution of data, which was also opened to other researchers (and non-research-based critics) for replication, vetting, and review. In a letter of March 15, 1960, to mathematician and foundation executive Warren Weaver, Rhine spoke of the extra lengths to which the parapsychologist ought to go: "Even though the methodology and standards of evidence may compare favorably with other advances of natural science, they have to be superior in parapsychology because of its novelty; and conceivably, too, by making them still better, everything may be gained in overcoming the natural resistance involved."

The "natural resistance" or partisanship around such findings can be so intense—and sometimes purposefully obfuscating—that lay seekers may come away with the mistaken impression that Rhine's work, or that of more recent parapsychologists, has proven unrepeatable or compromised.

Parapsychologist Charles Honorton (1946–92) sought to analyze critical challenges to Rhine's figures in the years following their publication. He found that "61 percent of the independent replications of the Duke work were statistically significant. This is 60 times the proportion of significant studies we would expect if the significant results were due to chance or error."

Rhine's experiments have proven so bulletproof that even close to fifty years later, his most resistant critics were still attempting to explain them by fantastical (and often feckless) fraud theories, including a prominent English skeptic's nearly vaudevillian supposition that one of the test subjects repeatedly crawled through a ceiling space to peek at cards through a trapdoor over the lab. At such excesses, rationalists fail the test that Enlightenment philosopher David Hume (1711–1772) set for validation of miracles: counterclaims must be less likely than reported phenomena. In any case, Rhine's methods and results have never been upended.

For all that, Rhine may have proved too idealistic regarding what it took to overcome "natural resistance." Mainstream media sources engage in pushback and even disingenuousness against data from parapsychology. A prime example appears in how polemical skeptics today ride herd over articles on parapsychology on the most-read reference source in history, Wikipedia. As of this writing, Wikipedia's article on Zener cards states in its opening, "The original series of experiments have been discredited and replication has proven elusive." This statement is unsourced, something that would get red-flagged on most of the encyclopedia's articles.

How does this occur on the world's go-to reference source? Dean Radin of IONS, described to me the problem of an ad hoc group calling itself "Guerilla Skeptics" policing Wiki entries on parapsychology: "While there are lots of anonymous trolls that have worked hard to trash any Wikipedia pages related to psi, including bios of parapsychologists, this group of extreme skeptics is proudly open that they are rewriting history . . . any attempt to edit those pages, even fixing individual words, is blocked or reverted almost instantly."

Even if parapsychology as a field had ended with Rhine's initial Duke trials, we would possess evidence of paranormal mechanics in human existence. Those basic (though painstakingly structured) card experiments, those few percentage points of deviation tracked across tens of thousands of trials (90,000 in the database by the 1934 publication of *Extra-Sensory Perception*), demonstrate an anomalous transfer of information in a laboratory setting and an extraphysical (call it metaphysical), non-Newtonian exchange of information.

But things did not end there. In the decades ahead, extraordinary waves of diversified experiments occurred in the U.S. and other nations growing from the efforts of the scientists at Duke's Parapsychology Laboratory. These efforts demonstrated, again and again, anomalous mental phenomena, including precognition, retrocausality, telepathy, and psychokinesis (PK). Rhine's lab began studying PK in 1934, an effort that continued until 1941, after which many lab members were summoned to the war effort. During their nine years of investigation, researchers conducted tens of thousands of runs in which individuals would attempt to affect throws of random sets of dice. Devices were soon employed to toss the dice in such a way that ensured randomness, which ought to demonstrate no pattern whatsoever. Again, similar statistical results to the Zener card experiments appeared: among certain individuals, across hundreds of thousands of throws, with every conceivable safeguard, peer review, methodological transparency, and reportage of every set, there appeared a deviation of several percentage points, suggesting a physical effect arising from mental intention.

We have now logged generations of experiments designed to test the effects to which I am referring. Today's parapsychologists believe, I think with justification, that the basic, foundational science for psychical ability has already been laid. Although parapsychology remains controversial, the field has already moved on from basic testing for ESP, a matter that was more or less settled in the 1940s.

Recent researchers are concerned with questions including telepathy (mind-to-mind communication); precognition (the ability to foresee or be affected by things that, within our model of the mind, have not yet occurred); retrocausality (the effect of future events on current perceptions or abilities); a biological basis for psi (including biologist Rupert Sheldrake's morphic-field theories); spontaneous psi events, such as premonitions or crisis realizations; dream telepathy; a "global consciousness" effect during periods of mass emotional reaction; and the practice of remote viewing or clairvoyance. The field also investigates other important areas, including out-of-body experiences, near-death experiences, deathbed visions, after-death survival, and reincarnation.

The scientific study of reincarnation was pioneered as an academic field by the remarkable research psychiatrist Ian Stevenson (1918-2007), who founded the Division of Perceptual Studies at the University of Virginia. For five decades, this conservative researcher "traveled six continents, accumulating more than 2,500 cases of young children who recounted details of previous lives, which he meticulously verified with witnesses, hospital records, autopsy reports, death certificates, and photographs," eulogized the *Journal of Near-Death Studies* in Spring 2007.

One of the most important figures in psychical research died of heart failure in 1992 at the tragically young age of forty-six. I mentioned him earlier: his name is Charles Honorton. Honorton's passing was a tremendous loss for the field, nearly equivalent to losing Einstein at the dawn of his relativity theories.

It is critical to understand what Honorton accomplished. In the late 1960s and '70s, he engaged in direct research into dreams and ESP at the innovative Division of Parapsychology and Psychophysics at Maimonides Medical Center in Brooklyn. Honorton proceeded to assemble possibly the most significant body of data we possess in the parapsychology field. It was through a long-running series of experiments designed with colleagues in the 1970s and '80s known as *ganzfeld experiments*. *Ganzfeld* is German for *whole* or *open field*. Honorton had an instinct for the conditions under which ESP or telepathy—mind-to-mind communication—might be heightened, which formed the basis of his studies.

Honorton noted that the classic Rhine experiments were largely focused on subjects believed to have a predilection for ESP. Rhine believed that ESP may be detectable throughout the human population but was readily testable through figures who possess innate abilities. He did not consider ESP something for which you could train or that was necessarily intrinsic to everyone. Rather, he focused on what he considered naturally gifted individuals, who made prime subjects.

Honorton took a different tack. He wondered whether psychical abilities are, in fact, general throughout the population—but perhaps the psychical signal, so to speak, gets jammed or the psyche's circuitry gets overloaded due to excessive stimuli in daily life.

Honorton pondered what it might reveal to test for ESP among subjects who are placed into conditions of relaxed, comfortable sensory deprivation. He ventured that you may be able to spike the ESP effect if you place a subject into sensory-deprived conditions without noise or bright light—for example, seating the person in a comfortable recliner in a dimly lit, noise-proof room or chamber, fitted with eyeshades, and wearing headphones that emit white noise. These conditions induce the state called *hypnagogia*, a kind of waking hypnosis.

In fact, you enter into the hypnagogic state twice daily: just before you drift to sleep at night and just as you are coming to in the morning. It is a deeply relaxed, motionless state in which you might experience hallucinatory or morphing images, aural hallucinations, tactile sensations of weightlessness, or even bodily paralysis. Yet you remain functionally awake: you are self-aware and able to direct cognition. The morning state is sometimes called *hypnopompia* (a term coined by psi research pioneer F.W.H. Myers). Hypnagogia and hypnopompia are similar with some differences; for example, hallucinations occur somewhat more commonly during the nighttime state.

Since this state is an apparently inviting period for self-suggestion—the mind is supple, the body relaxed, and the psyche unclouded by stimuli—Honorton pondered whether these conditions might facilitate heightened psychical activity. To test for telepathy, he placed one subject—called the receiver—into the relaxed conditions of sensory deprivation I have described, while a second subject—called the sender—is seated outside the sensory deprivation tank or in another space. In the classical ganzfeld experiments, the sender attempts to "transmit" a preselected image to the receiver. After the sending period ends, the receiver then chooses among four different images (one target image and three decoys) to identify what was sent.

Like the Zener cards, there is a randomly selected target on each successive trial and, in this case, a one in four or 25 percent chance of guessing right. In meta-analyzed data, subjects on average surpassed the 25 percent guess rate. Depending on the analytic model, the most stringently produced experiments demonstrated an overall hit rate of between 32 percent and 35 percent. Since the mid-1970s, this data has, in varying forms, been replicated by dozens of scientists across different labs in different nations, often under increasingly refined conditions. The ganzfeld experiments not only documented a significant psi effect but also suggested that a detectable ESP or telepathic effect may be more generally distributed among the population. The protocols themselves suggested conditions under which psi phenomena are most likely to appear.

Given its significance, the ganzfeld database attracted intense scrutiny. In a historic first, which has never really been repeated, Honorton in 1986 collaborated on a paper with a prominent psi skeptic, Ray Hyman, a professor of psychology at the University of Oregon. After trading written disputes over the validity of parapsychological experiments, the interlocutors decided to collaborate on a joint study for the *Journal of Parapsychology*, analyzing the data, highlighting areas of agreement and dispute, and recommending protocols for future experiments. In an arena where arguments often devolve into rhetoric, it proved a signature moment.

"Instead of continuing with another round of our debate on the psi ganzfeld experiments," they wrote, "we decided to collaborate on a joint communiqué. The Honorton-Hyman debate emphasized the differences in our positions, many of these being technical in nature. But during a recent discussion, we realized that we possessed similar viewpoints on many issues concerning parapsychological research. This communiqué, then, emphasizes these points of agreement."

In a joint statement—one that ought to serve as a general guardrail in our era of digital attack speech—Honorton and Hyman wrote: "Both critics and parapsychologists want parapsychological research to be conducted according to the best possible standards. The critic can contribute to this need only if his criticisms are informed, relevant, and responsible."

Beyond laying down general principles and research protocols, the collaborators conducted a joint meta-analysis of key ganzfeld experiments up to that moment.* "The data base analyzed by Hyman and Honorton," wrote UC Irvine statistician Jessica Utts, "consisted of results taken from 34 reports written by a total of 47 authors. Honorton counted 42 separate experiments described in the reports, of which 28 reported enough information to determine the number of direct hits achieved. Twenty three of the studies (55%) were classified by Honorton as having achieved statistical significance." The success rate was similar to Honorton's findings in his 1978 meta-analysis.

Notably, the psychical researcher and the skeptic wrote in their abstract: "We agree that there is an overall significant effect in this data base that cannot be reasonably explained by selective reporting or multiple analysis." And further: "Although we probably still differ on the magnitude of the biases contributed by multiple testing, retrospective experiments, and the file-drawer problem, we agree that the overall significance observed in these studies cannot reasonably be explained by these selective factors. Something beyond selective reporting or inflated significance levels seems to be producing the nonchance outcomes. Moreover, we agree that the significant outcomes have been produced by a number of different investigators."

In sum, here was a key psychical researcher and a leading skeptic (Hyman was among the few skeptics who conducted his own research) disagreeing over the general nature of the ESP thesis—a reasonable disagreement—but affirming that the most important psychical data of the period proved unpolluted and that the methodology of the studies in their sample reflected significant improvement from the dawn of the experiments in the early to mid-1970s. But the

---

* A meta-analysis is a cumulative study of different but similar experiments to test pooled data for statistical significance.

key data, they wrote, was free from substantial error, corruption, or selective reporting. Hyman agreed that a statistically significant effect appears in the data and justifies further research. That's all. No concession of belief in ESP. Nor was any needed. Just an informed critique by a parapsychologist and a career-long skeptic, both with significant credentials, concluding that the data and practices are normative and a statistically significant anomaly appears.

It is tragic, both in terms of human pathos and intellectual advancement, that Honorton died six years after that paper was published. He was one of the only parapsychologists able to reach across the nearly unbridgeable partisan divide to a professional skeptic and create progress in dialogue and research. That process has never been repeated. Indeed, as of this writing, Wikipedia's article on the ganzfeld experiments introduces them as a "pseudoscientific technique," without sourcing.

It is worth asking why this chasm has remained so wide. Wonderful strides have occurred in parapsychology, but the advances are not what they could be. Statistician Jessica Utts has noted that during the more than 110 years since the founding of the Society for Psychical Research, "the total human and financial resources devoted to parapsychology since 1882 is at best equivalent to the expenditures devoted to fewer than two months of research in conventional psychology in the United States."

For comparison, the American Psychological Association reports that in 2017, $2 billion of the United States' $66.5 billion in federal research funding went to psychological research.

Think of it: the field of parapsychology has, since its inception worldwide, been funded in adjusted dollars at a rate of less than two months of traditional psychological experiments in the U.S. (experiments which, like much of the work in the social sciences, are routinely overturned to reflect changes or corrections in methodology). That is less than $333,500,000, or a little more than the cost of four fighter jets. This figure compares with trillions that have been spent worldwide during the same period on physics or medical research.

This funding situation reflects, in part, the success of the most vociferous skeptics in disabling the legitimacy of parapsychological data. Most academic researchers steer clear, fearing damage to their reputation and ability to get other projects funded.

Even in this atmosphere, however, some scientists prevail against the tide. A historic episode occurred in 2011, which marked the publication of a paper called "Feeling the Future" by well-known research psychologist Daryl J. Bem of Cornell University. For about ten years, Bem conducted a series of nine experiments involving more than 1,000 participants into precognition or "time reversing" of widely established cognitive or psychological effects, such as memorization of a list or responding to negative or erotic stimuli flashed as images on a screen. Bem's discoveries demonstrated the capacity of cognition across boundaries of linear time.

Bem, like other researchers including Dean Radin, identified factors that seem to correlate with precognition, such as the body's response to arousing or disturbing imagery. As Bem wrote of previous experiments: "Most of the pictures were emotionally neutral, but a highly arousing negative or erotic image was displayed on randomly selected trials. As expected, strong emotional arousal occurred when these images appeared on the screen, but the remarkable finding is that the increased arousal was observed to occur a few seconds before the picture appeared, before the computer had even selected the picture to be displayed."

In one of Bem's trials, subjects were asked to "guess" at erotic images alternated with benign images. "Across all 100 sessions," he wrote, "participants correctly identified the future position of the erotic pictures significantly more frequently than the 50% hit rate expected by chance: 53.1% . . . In contrast, their hit rate on the nonerotic pictures did not differ significantly from chance: 49.8% . . . This was true across all types of nonerotic pictures: neutral pictures, 49.6%; negative pictures, 51.3%; positive pictures, 49.4%; and romantic but nonerotic pictures, 50.2%."

The response to either arousing or disturbing imagery is suggestive of the *emotional stakes* required for the presence of a psi effect. Stakes must exist, and strong emotions must be in play. Passion is critical. In *New Frontiers of the Mind*, Rhine emphasized the role of spontaneity, confidence, comity, novelty, curiosity, and lack of fatigue. (And, as it happens, caffeine.)

But Bem's horizons extended further. In the most innovative element of his nine-part study, he set out to discover whether subjects displayed *improved recall* of lists of words that were to be practice-memorized *in the future*. In Bem's words, "whether rehearsing a set of words makes them easier to recall—even if the rehearsal takes place after the recall test is given."

Participants were first shown a set of words and given a free recall test of those words. They were then given a set of practice exercises on a randomly selected subset of those words. The psi hypothesis was that the practice exercises would retroactively facilitate the recall of those words, and, hence, participants would recall more of the to-be-practiced words than the unpracticed words.

Bem found a statistically significant improvement of recall on the lists of words studied in the near future: "The results show that practicing a set of words after the recall test does, in fact, reach back in time to facilitate the recall of those words." In short, future memorization heightened current recall.

Unsurprisingly, Bem's 2011 paper met with tremendous controversy. Within a year of Bem's publication, a trio of professional skeptics published a rejoinder. Playing off of Bem's "Feeling the Future," their paper sported the media-friendly title, "Failing the Future." The experimenters reran one of Bem's experiments. They concluded, "All three replication attempts failed to produce significant effects . . . and thus do not support the existence of psychic ability."

But the authors omitted a critical detail from their own database. By deadline, they possessed two independent studies that validated Bem's results. They made no mention of these studies, despite their own ground rules for doing so. Bem wrote in his response: "By the deadline, six studies attempting to replicate the Retroactive Recall effect had been completed, including the three failed replications reported by Ritchie et al. and two other replications, *both of which successfully reproduced my original findings at statistically significant levels* . . . Even though both successful studies were pre-registered on Wiseman's registry and their results presumably known to Ritchie et al., they fail to mention them in this article" (emphasis added).

Although there unquestionably exists a significant crisis of replicability and data manipulation—not to mention fraud—in the sciences, no one has tied any of this to Bem or his methods. As of July 2020, Bem's experiments (including the original trials) proved confirmatory in a meta-analysis encompassing 90 experiments in 33 laboratories in 14 countries, "greatly exceeding" the standard for "'decisive evidence' in support of the experimental hypothesis," as Bem and his coauthors wrote in the abstract of their follow-up paper.

I believe that I am highlighting only the glacial tip of how parapsychological data is misreported within much of mainstream news media and large swaths of academia. The question returns: *why?* I have difficulty understanding human nature, which is, finally, the crux of the matter. After a certain point of tautological criticism of nearly a century of academic ESP research, it becomes difficult to avoid using a strong word that I prefer not to use and that I do not use lightly: *suppression*. Not of any centrally organized sort, but of a *cultural sort* in which prevailing findings run so counter to materialist assumptions that critics—who ironically perceive themselves as arbiters of rationality—assume an "at any cost" stance to dispel contrary data. Winning becomes more important than proving. It is the antithesis of science. This is the irony to which professional skepticism has brought us.

This kind of practice—in which self-perceived rationalists do injustice to truth in pursuit of what they consider a *defense of rationalism*—has run riot throughout the professional skeptics' field. Cambridge biologist Rupert Sheldrake, in addition to his own research into psi phenomena, has proven determined and intrepid in responding to serial problems among professional skeptics and the toll they have taken in reference media and journalism. Sheldrake was named one of the top 100 Global Thought Leaders of the year by Switzerland's prestigious Duttweiler Institute. Yet today on Wikipedia he is called a purveyor of "pseudoscience" for his theories of biological resonance and psi.

I have already mentioned earlier that the social and natural sciences are experiencing a credibility gap. One study has suggested that fraud rates in biomedical and psychology research are probably at a respective 9 percent and 10 percent.

I consider it defensible to state that parapsychology today may be among the *few exceptions* to common fraud in the social sciences. When I posted about the matter in late 2021 on social media, parapsychology journalist Craig Weiler put it this way:

> Because parapsychology doesn't convey any honors from successful research, either through social acknowledgment or an improvement in professional status, there is little motivation for cheating. Successful studies also have to run the skeptical gauntlet. So, little incentive... Just a personal observation, the field seems to attract uncorruptible people. The people who take it seriously and publicly, have to have a generally reduced fear level and be willing to fight for the importance of truth. That doesn't describe your average cheater.

Indeed, it is infinitely more important to me as an advocate of parapsychology research that we *get it right* versus win a debate. I would rather lose ground a hundred times over than proffer an argument that is strictly rhetorical or tactical in nature or that misrepresents key findings when a debate goes against me. That is why I am so flummoxed (perhaps naively) when I encounter self-described skeptics who use deceptive or slippery methods in the interest of promulgating intellectual soundness.

The point is not to win but to search—to honor the basic human question of what lies around the next hill. Our society needs greater academic and intellectual leeway in this area so that parapsychologists need not fear damage to career or reputation. As noted, psi research is inexpensive. Because the skeptics have proven so successful, however, most parapsychologists today must secure independent funding. Anyone who has written grant proposals knows that that process can be the equivalent of a job in itself. But the men and women who populate parapsychology today carry out this labor while also conducting their research and often holding academic or clinical positions to pay the bills. What's more, they often endure professional insults and calumny.

I recognize that skeptics fear a wave of irrationality will be unleashed on the world if headlines start announcing, "Harvard Study Says ESP Is Real." Consequently, they strive against that day (although in various forms it has already come and gone), just as in an exchange with Sigmund Freud, his English disciple Ernest Jones protested that acknowledging telepathy "would mean admitting the essential claim of the occultists that mental processes can be independent of the human body."

The issues I am describing have easily cost us more than a generation of progress in parapsychology. We are at least thirty or forty years behind where we ought to be, dated from when the professional skeptical apparatus began to ramp up in the mid-1970s. One real challenge for parapsychology—and addressing this is, I think, necessary to the field's next leap forward—is to arrive at a *theory of conveyance*. I believe the field needs a persuasive theoretical model that pulls together the effects and posits how information is transferred in a manner unbound by time, space, distance, linearity, and common sensory experience. Researchers have made preliminary steps in this direction. Advances are overdue.

In 1960, Warren Weaver, a highly regarded mathematical engineer and grant-making science foundation executive, uttered a semi-famous lament about ESP research at a panel discussion at Dartmouth College: "I find this whole field [parapsychology] intellectually a very painful one. And I find it painful essentially for the following reasons: I cannot reject the evidence and I cannot accept the conclusions." Weaver caught hell for his statement; some colleagues questioned whether his judgment had slipped; a few others (including Dartmouth's president) privately thanked him for broaching the topic.

Weaver had toured Rhine's labs in early 1960. On February 22, he privately wrote Rhine to raise several issues. Near the top of his seven-page, singled-spaced letter, Weaver made this point: "For if you could make substantial progress in analyzing, explaining, and controlling, then the problem of *acceptance* would be largely solved." Rhine had long labored to demonstrate *effect*, Weaver wrote, but he now needed to describe *mechanics*. His letter continued:

> But for three main reasons—or at least so it seems to me—the problem of acceptance remains. First, these phenomena are so strange, so outside the normal framework of scientific understanding, that they are inherently very difficult to accept. Second, the attempts to analyze, understand, and control have not been, as yet, very successful or convincing. And third, unreasonable and stubborn as it doubtless appears to you, very many scientists are

not convinced by the evidence which you consider is more than sufficient to establish the reality of the psi phenomena.

Rhine replied:

The three main reasons you give in your analysis are recognizably correct. Had you been inclined at this point to go a step further into the intellectual background for these reasons, this might have been the point to draw upon the judgments of some of the philosophers and other commentators who have dealt with the problem of acceptance. There is an increasingly candid recognition of the difficulty as an essentially metaphysical one. Psi phenomena appear to challenge the assumption of a physicalistic universe.

Rhine was reluctant to draw theoretical conclusions from his findings. As his daughter, Sally Rhine Feather, wrote in a private communication to me: "I have never known him to have gone very far in this direction... But he was always so cautious at going beyond the data and had this aversion to philosophers who did so—except for the implications of the nonphysical nature of psi on which he actually speculated extremely broadly at times." She went on to quote from his book *New World of the Mind*: "It will be the task of biophysics and psychophysics to find out if there are unknown, imperceptible, extraphysical influences in nature that function in life and mind, influences which can interact with detectable physical processes."

In his response to Weaver, Rhine was referencing commonly accepted physical laws at the time. For psychical researchers today, studies in quantum theory, retrocausality, extra-dimensionality, neuroplasticity, string theory, and "morphic fields" that enable communication at the cellular level (the innovation of Rupert Sheldrake) suggest a set of physical laws that surpass the known and may serve as a kind of macroverse within which familiar mechanics are experienced. It was already clear in Rhine's era that extrasensory transmission could not be explained through a "mental radio" model, since, according to Rhine's tests and those of others, ESP is unaffected by time, distance, or physical barriers.

This returns us to the question: If the psi effect is real, *how does it work?* How does mentality exceed the obvious boundaries of sensory transmission?

Perhaps science overvalues theory. Nonetheless, I believe that it falls to each generation to venture a theory of phenomena in which it professes deep interest. That theory can ignite a debate—it can be thrown out and replaced, it can be modified—but I do not believe that researchers and motivated lay inquirers (like me) can eschew the task. For this reason, I attempted a theory of mind causation in the closing chapter of my 2018 book *The Miracle Club* entitled, "Why It Works."

Consider this: when you say the word *precognition*, it strikes many people as fantastical, as though we are entering crystal-ball territory. Why the incredulity? We already know, and have known for generations, that *linear time as we experience it is an illusion.* Einstein's theories of relativity, and experiments that have affirmed them, establish that time slows down in conditions of extreme velocity—at or approaching lightspeed—and in conditions of extreme gravity, like black holes. The individual traveling in a metaphorical spaceship at or near lightspeed experiences time slowing (not from their perspective but in comparison to those not at that speed), and this is not a mere thought exercise. Space travelers in our era, although they are obviously not approaching anywhere near that velocity, experience minute effects of time reduction.

In short, linear time is a *necessary illusion* for five-sensory beings to get through life. Time is not an absolute. What's more, ninety years of work in quantum physics leads us to conclude that we face an infinitude of concurrent realities—not in possibility but in actuality—one of which we will localize or experience within our framework based upon perspective or when we look.

To switch tacks, string theory posits that all of reality is interconnected by vast networks of vibrating strings. Everything, from the tiniest particle to entire universes to other dimensions, is linked by these undulating strings. Hence something that occurs within another dimension not only affects what happens in the reality of the dimension that we occupy but signals an infinitude of events playing out in these other fields of existence, as in ours.

We may even crisscross into these concurrent realities, occupying lives that are infinite in terms of the psyche and variable in dimensional occupancy. Experiencing data or events from other dimensions may also be extrapolated to UFO encounters or other anomalous phenomena.

Perhaps an individual, either because he or she is uniquely sensitive at a given moment or experiences a reduction of sensory data while retaining awareness (as in the ganzfeld experiments), is capable of accessing information—or taking measurements—from other states or dimensions that exist along the theorized bands of strings. We call these measurements precognition, telepathy, ESP, or psychokinesis, the last of which may be a form of pre-awareness or movement or both. But maybe that is simply *what finer measurement looks like*. It is possible that measurement not only informs but also (at least in certain cases) actualizes, localizes, and determines. *Measurement selects.* Perhaps if we gleaned what was actually going on, or exercised fuller capacities of sensation, the experience would prove overwhelming. We would be overcome with data. Hence we may *need* a linear sense of time and a limited field of information in order to *navigate experience*.

And yet: given that we understand spacetime as flexible, is it really so strange, so violative of our current body of knowledge, that there exist *quantifiable exceptions to ordinary sensory experience*? As we document these exceptions, trace their arc, and replicate the conditions under which they occur, perhaps we approach what poet and mystic William Blake foresaw in 1790 in *The Marriage of Heaven and Hell*: "If the doors of perception were cleansed every thing would appear to man as it is: Infinite." And thus ineffable.

In closing, I posit Seven Laws of Parapsychology:
1. Information exchange occurs outside common sensory experience or known technology.
2. This exchange occurs beyond boundaries of mass, space, or linearity.
3. Actions taken in the perceived future are backwardly causative in the perceived present—or retrocausal.
4. Retrocausality is governed by quantum measurement not by the "arrow of time" or second law of thermodynamics.
5. Hypnagogia or sensory deprivation heightens extrasensory exchange.
6. The aforementioned effects are replicable throughout the population though variable by individual.
7. The aforementioned effects are non-violative of special relativity or quantum mechanics notwithstanding contradictions between both.

APPENDIX B

The 30-Day Mental Challenge

American philosopher William James (1842–1910) yearned to find a practical spirituality, one that produced concrete improvements in happiness.

The Harvard physician grew encouraged, especially in his final years, by his personal experiments with New Thought, which in his 1902 *The Varieties of Religious Experience* he called "the religion of healthy-mindedness." I challenge today's seekers to continue James's search for a testable, workable spiritual system. Will you attempt a 30-day experiment that puts positive-mind metaphysics to the test?

The experiment is based on a passage from a 1931 book, *Body, Mind, and Spirit* by Elwood Worcester and Samuel McComb. The authors, both Episcopal ministers, in 1906 founded the Emmanuel Movement, a respected healing ministry popular in the early twentieth century. The Emmanuel Movement was named for Emmanuel Church in Boston's Back Bay. Worcester and McComb, joint pastors of the church, drew together ministers, physicians, psychologists, and patients to study and apply the regenerative abilities of the mind. They collaborated with mainstream medical authorities, the most remarkable of which was

Harvard physician and scientist Richard C. Cabot (1868–1939), who acted as Emmanuel's chief

medical adviser. Cabot aimed to wed the possibilities of mind-power to scientific rationalism, and to devise a mental therapeutics that could win allies among medical authorities.

In *Body, Mind, and Spirit,* a prominent scientist, who the authors did not name, told a small audience how he radically improved his life through a one-month thought experiment. I have condensed his testimony:

> *Up to my fiftieth year I was unhappy, ineffective, and obscure. I had read some New Thought literature and some statements of William James on directing one's attention to what is good and useful and ignoring the rest. Such ideas seemed like bunk—but feeling that life was intolerable I determined to subject them to a month-long test.*
>
> *During this time, I resolved to impose definite restrictions on my thoughts. In thinking of the past, I would dwell only on its pleasing incidents. In thinking of the present, I would direct attention to its desirable elements. In thinking of the future, I would regard every worthy and possible ambition as within reach.*
>
> *I threw myself into this experiment. I was soon surprised to feel happy and contented. But the outward changes astonished me more. I deeply craved the recognition of certain eminent men. The foremost of these wrote me, out of the blue, inviting me to become his assistant. All my books were published. My colleagues grew helpful and cooperative.*
>
> *It seems that I stumbled upon a* path of life, *and set forces working for me which were previously working against me.*

Let's repeat this experiment together: 1) Choose your start date, 2) write out the full italicized, quoted passage above by hand (never underestimate the value of that), and 3) add: "I dedicate myself on this day of _____ to focus on all that is nourishing, advancing, and promising for thirty days (signed) _____"

That's it.

I suggest writing this passage on an index card and on the reverse creating a grid in which you mark off each of your thirty days. I advise rereading the scientist's testimony each morning and each time you mark off a day, as well as whenever it feels necessary. You may want to carry your statement with you during the day.

Whenever you find yourself sliding into old habits of thought, do not worry; simply steer back to the experiment. You do not need to start over. Just carry on.

APPENDIX C

The Kybalion *Without Tears*

Understanding a Controversial Occult Classic

A little book of "Hermetic Philosophy" from 1908 called *The Kybalion* has recently polarized online opinion. Defenders of the "true way," if ever there was such a thing, damn the slender work of popular metaphysics as fraudulent, plagiarized, or "crap."

The facts are both simpler and subtler. Locating them requires less in the way of caffeinated language and more in the way of game investigation. Understanding occultism in the first part of the twentieth century and our own means reckoning with the popular or dramatized literature consumed by many seekers, including *The Kybalion*. Such an approach may open new doors—even for the critic. I know because I was one.

Like many readers, I once considered *The Kybalion* little more than a novelty of early twentieth-century occultism, which, in part, it is. Fancifully attributed to "Three Initiates," *The Kybalion* calls itself a commentary on a remote, hidden Hermetic work of the same name whose aphorisms are only quoted. The title phrase has no known antecedent but is probably a Hellenized version of Kabbalah. Based on sales data and manifold editions, the diminutive volume is easily among the most widely read occult works of the past century.

When I discovered the book nearly twenty years ago, I regarded it as a faux-antique work of New Thought or mind-power philosophy, costumed in pseudo-Hermetic garb, and offering a handful of serviceable but not greatly significant ideas of practical spirituality. I confidently announced all this one day to philosopher Jacob Needleman (1934–2022) who had collaborated laboriously on a privately printed translation of classical Hermetic tracts. He got a gleam and in his eye and replied, "There are some good ideas in that little book."

Years of deeper reading into traditional Hermeticism and a return to *The Kybalion* validated Needleman's statement. My early judgment was wrong. The "little book" has earned its posterity.

Although some of *The Kybalion*'s reference points and formulations are plainly modern, the tract is defensible as an authentic if dramatized retention of certain classical Hermetic themes. Indeed, the book serves as something close to what it claims to be: a "Great Reconciler" of metaphysical, transcendental, and New Thought philosophies, at least as practiced in the twentieth and twenty-first centuries.

Before saying more about the value I find in *The Kybalion*, let me address the question of authorship. The identity of "Three Initiates" has long been a source of contention; this can distract from the book's significance.

The Kybalion was written and published by New Thought philosopher William Walker Atkinson (1862–1932), a remarkably energetic Chicago publisher, writer, lawyer, and spiritual seeker. I identified Atkinson's sole authorship in my 2009 *Occult America*;

I wasn't the first. I also issued an edition that year that identified Atkinson's hand, more on which below.

Atkinson was among the most incisive New Thought voices of the twentieth century. He ran an innovative esoteric publishing house called the Yogi Publication Society from Chicago's Masonic Temple Building. His company issued a wide-ranging catalogue of highly recognizable, compact blue hardcovers from the publisher's offices in the twenty-one-story skyscraper, which housed Masonic meeting rooms at the top. It was built in 1892 and demolished in 1939.

For years, Web 2.0 buzzed with debate over the personas of the Three Initiates. Most documentary and contextual evidence supports that it was Atkinson writing alone. Atkinson acknowledged sole authorship in an entry in *Who's Who in America* in 1912.

American occultist Paul Foster Case is sometimes identified as one of the Three Initiates, and he appears to have told as much to some of his colleagues.* But Case was just twenty-four when the book appeared in 1908, also at a time that he had just arrived in Atkinson's hometown of Chicago, so I consider the collaboration unlikely, although it's possible that they corresponded about some of the book's concepts.

It should also be noted that in traditional literature, Hermes Trismegistus addresses himself to three disciples: Tat, Ammon, and Asclepius, which may have been a source of inspiration for William Walker Atkinson's byline (or possibly his own use of a tripartite byline). Atkinson wrote prolifically under many pseudonyms. Three Initiates has proven his most enduringly popular but he also used names including Yogi Ramacharaka, Theron Q. Dumont, and the somewhat strained Magus Incognito. Atkinson was a prodigious

---

* See *Paul Foster Case: His Life and Works* by Paul A. Clark (OHM, 2013).

writer and aficionado of New Thought and the mind-power metaphysics that were sweeping the Western world and have since become deeply entrenched in American spiritual life. His work exposed tens of thousands of early twentieth-century readers to esoteric spiritual and psychological ideas, which they might not otherwise have had wide opportunities to encounter. He wrote at least thirteen books under the byline Yogi Ramacharaka alone.

Some observers tag these works ersatz Vedism, novelty yoga, and phony Swamism. And there is, of course, truth in that verdict. Yet it is also true that this enterprising man introduced many people to variants of Vedic and yogic ideas, which would not explode across the American scene until the mid-to-late 1960s. Traditional gurus, such as Swami Vivekananda (1863–1902), had visited America prior to Atkinson's calico adaptations. But his popular work, like Madame H.P. Blavatsky's, helped prime Americans for the wave of spiritual teaching from the East that was soon to come, especially with relaxed immigration laws instituted in 1965.

When Maharishi Mahesh Yogi (1917–2008), for example, traveled to the U.S. in 1959 to teach Transcendental Meditation—an authentic technique from Vedic tradition—large swaths of the public, and certainly those within the metaphysical culture, were able to receive and understand what Maharishi and others who followed were offering. Never underestimate the power of novelty to open doors, whet appetites, and prime interest.

More important than *The Kybalion*'s dramatic framing is how the book highlights ideas about mind, matter, and thought creativity, some of which demonstrate resonance with philosophical Hermetica. *The Kybalion* is not merely, or at least not only, modern New Thought clothed in antique conceit; rather, the book connects readers, however tenuously, to late-ancient Hermetic themes of *correspondence, development of psyche, scale of creation,* and *an all-creative Overmind.*

Although Atkinson relied on several sources—including the work of accomplished occult writer Anna Kingsford (1846–1888)*—he was probably drawing upon the seminal Hermetic translation, *Thrice-Greatest Hermes* by G.R.S. Mead, which appeared two years before his dramatization.

Mead was a scholar of ancient mysticism and one-time secretary to Madame Blavatsky, a figure whom Atkinson revered. (The influence of her 1888 opus *The Secret Doctrine* is evident at several points in Atkinson's work.) Mead's 1906 translation of the Hermetica, while turgidly worded in late-Victorian prose, and sometimes almost purposely written as if to assume an antique affect, was then one of the few sources of Hermetic ideas in English.

With a skilled and discerning eye, Atkinson identified and distilled insights that paralleled the sturdiest aspects of New Thought, a field in which the writer-publisher was steeped. Atkinson used his considerable curatorial abilities to produce a marriage of ancient and modern psychological insights.

Atkinson focused primarily on the veritable Hermetic principle that *Mind is the Great Creator.* According to Hermetic literature, a supreme Mind, or *Nous*, uses as its vehicle a threefold process consisting of: 1) subordinate mind (*demiurgos–nous*), 2) word (*logos*), and 3) spirit (*anthropos*), concepts that echo, albeit distantly, in Atkinson's work.

The Kybalion is structured around "Seven Hermetic Principles," which correspond to the Hermetic concept of "seven rulers" of nature. Man, we are told in book I of the *Corpus Hermeticum*, "had in himself all the energy of the rulers, who marveled at him, and each gave him a share of his own nature."**

---

* Credit is due historian Mary K. Greer for this insight. Important documentary forensics have also been contributed by scholars Philip Deslippe (*The Kybalion: The Definitive Edition*, TarcherPerigee, 2011) and Richard Smoley (*The Kybalion: Centenary Edition*, TarcherPerigee, 2018). I published both latter works.

** *Hermetica: The Greek Corpus Hermeticum and the Latin Asclepius in a New English Translation* with Notes and Introduction by Brian P. Copenhaver (Cambridge University Press, 1992)

Atkinson is particularly supple in adapting the Hermetic conception of *gender*, in which the masculine (conscious mind, in Atkinson's terms, and original man in the Hermetica) impregnates the feminine (subconscious mind to Atkinson, and nature in the Hermetica), to create the physical world. Further still—and this is vital to the book's usefulness—*The Kybalion* ably ventures a theory of *mind causality*. The book explains why, from its metaphysical premises, our minds appear to possess formative, creative abilities; and yet, even as we evince powers of causation, we are also subject to limits of physicality, mortality, and daily mechanics.

As noted in Atkinson's chapter "'The All' in All," the individual may wield traits of a higher causative Force — but that does not make the individual synonymous with that Force. Man, the book counsels, may accomplish a great deal within given parameters, including transcendence of commonly presumed limitations, influence over the minds of others, and co-creation of certain circumstances; but the book reminds the idealist that we bump against physical parameters even as we are granted the capacity, within proscribed framing, to imitate the Power that set those parameters. In classical Hermeticism, there exists possibility of rising through the seven spheres of creation, based on the ancient conception of the seven planets, to grow increasingly free of restrictions placed on human creative capacity.

Atkinson also offers compelling philosophical definitions of concepts of *rhythm, polarity, paradox, compensation*, and aforementioned "Mental Gender," or the notion that nonbinary traits occupy every mind and combine to create. In a sense, the philosophy found in *The Kybalion* is a modern application of Hermeticism, Neoplatonism, Transcendentalism, and New Thought. The book further attempts, however fitfully, to correspond its ideas to the early twentieth-century's nascent insights into quantum mechanics and the "new physics," which gained currency in the decades following its publication.

In this sense, the author exaggerates only slightly when he writes: "We do not come expounding a new philosophy, but rather furnishing the outlines of a great world-old teaching which will make clear the teachings of others—which will serve as a Great Reconciler of differing theories, and opposing doctrines."

The overall spirit of *The Kybalion* can be traced to book XI of the *Corpus Hermeticum*—the Renaissance-era translation that brought Hermeticism into modern awareness—in which Hermes is told by Supreme Mind that through the uses of imagination he can discover the workings of Higher Creation: "If you do not make yourself equal to God you cannot understand Him. Like is understood by like."*

Hermes is told to use his mind to travel all places, to unite opposites, to know all things, to transcend time and distance: "Become eternity and thus you will understand God. Suppose nothing to be impossible for yourself."

Hermeticism, at least as it has reached us, teaches that we are granted a Divine birthright of boundless creativity and expansion through the imagination or psyche. This teaching is central to Hermetic philosophy and its modern adaptation in *The Kybalion*.

In closing, I must note that my interest in the book is not impersonal. In 2022, I hosted, cowrote, and produced a feature documentary about the book directed by Emmy-nominee Ronni Thomas and shot on location in Egypt. The movie premiered as the #3 documentary on iTunes, of which I am proud. In whatever form or byway it takes, Atkinson's minor masterpiece is not going away. Nor are its ideas.

---

* This quote and the next are from *The Way of Hermes: New Translations of The Corpus Hermeticum and The Definitions of Hermes Trismegistus to Asclepius* by Clement Salaman, Dorine van Oyen, William D. Wharton, Jean-Pierre Mahe (Inner Traditions, 2000).

INDEX

A
Abel, 116
abracadabra, 26
Abraham, 41
Abrahamic tradition, 39, 42, 59, 61, 64
 as Judaism-Christianity-Islam, 67, 107, *see also these specific religions*
 magick within, 25
Abrams, J. J., 128
Abraxas, 26
acting quickly, 216–217
Adam, 115–116
Adorno, Theodor W., "Theses Against Occultism," 150–151
Agrippa, Cornelius, *Three Books of Occult Philosophy*, 16–17, 38, 39–40
Aiwass, 50
alchemy, 24, 27, 32, 40, 84
 sex transmutation (Hill), 51, 81–89, 175
alcohol, 208–209
Alexander the Great, 59
Alien Encounters (Discovery/HBO/Max series), 128, 129, 140–141, 183
Alliette, Jean-Baptiste, 47
al-Majriti, Maslama ibn Ahmad, 38
American Association for the Advancement of Science (AAAS), 163–164
American Psychological Association, 254
anarchic magick, 94, 129–135
 deity worship and petition in, 129–131
 departure from rulebooks, 133–135
 highly involved spells in, 129–131

anarchic magick (*cont.*)
  personal experiences with, 126, 127–129
  spontaneous spells and rituals in, 125–131
animal magnetism (Mesmer), 45, 51, 81, 82, 94
animism, 58
anonymity, 213–214
Aquino, Michael, 117
Aristotle/Aristotelianism, 42, 101
as above, so below (Hermeticism), 31–33, 36–37, 69–70, 74, 103, 131–132, 177
Association for Research and Enlightenment (A.R.E.), 57, 58
astral light (Lévi), 51, 81–83
astrology, 30–31, 38, 47
Atkinson, William Walker
  bylines of, 271–272
  The Kybalion, 42, 204, 269–275
Attrell, Dan, 38
authenticity, 182–186
Aykryd, Dan, 128, 182–183

B

Baby Girl (2024 movie), 76–77
backwards causation, *see* precognition/retrocausality
Baker, Phil, 99
Bakunin, Mikhail, 135
Balthasar, Cardinal Hans Urs von, 37
Baphomet (serpent), 83, 84
Barrett, Paul M., *Glock*, 133–134
Barton, Blanche, *The Secret Life of a Satanist*, 173
Beatitudes, 62
beginner's mind, 133–134
behavioral rules for fostering luck, 204–218
  acting quickly, 216–217, 218
  changing conditions and, 211–212, 218
  cultivating chemistry, 206, 217
  enthusiasm vs. optimism and, 212–213, 218
  failure and setbacks and, 210–211, 218
  getting noticed, 206–207, 217
  humiliation and, 213–214, 218
  learning to be lucky, 205–206, 217
  persistence and, 209–210, 217–218
  prepared minds and, 208, 217
  recognizing others, 214–215, 218
  showing up, 215–216, 218
  sobriety and, 208–209, 217
being yourself, 182–184
Bem, Daryl J., 151–157, 255–257
Benedict XVI, Pope, 37, 83
Bernays, Edward, 171, 179
Besant, Annie, 48, 179
  Thought Forms (with Leadbeater), 36
Better Call Saul (TV series), 162
Bhagavad Gita, 62
Biblical passages
  Deuteronomy 6:4-9, 24

Deuteronomy 11:13-21, 24
Genesis 1:27, 32
Genesis 3, 115–116
Genesis 41:43, 25
Isaiah 28:15, 122–123
John 1:1, 28
Psalm 82, 80
black
   black cats as sacred, 203
   mourning and, 202–203
Blake, William, 110
   The Marriage of Heaven and Hell, 115, 133, 264
Blavatsky, Madame H. P., 42, 272
   as cofounder of the Theosophical Society, 19, 48–49, 61
   "The Ensouled Violin"/ *Nightmare Tales*, 120
   as occultist, 39
   The Secret Doctrine, 39, 108, 273
   self-creation and, 118
Blofeld, John, 29
Bradley, Ed, 121–122, 189
Bristol, Claude M., *TNT*, 179
broom, jumping the, 201
Bruni, Frank, 119
Bruno, Giordano, 43
Budai (chubby Buddha statues), 22
Budde, Karl, 115
Buddhism, 24, 36, 48–49, 58–59, 62, 64, 67, 99–100, 107, 134, 162
bullying, 73–74, 152, 191, 192–193

Bulwer-Lytton, Edward, 51, 81, 94
Burroughs, William S.
   Ah Pook Is Here, 99–100
   Naked Lunch, 100
   orgones, 88
   The Third Mind (with Gysin), 51, 100–101, 103–104
Byron, Lord, 110
   Cain, 56, 116

C

Cabot, Richard C., 266
Cagliostro, Alessandro, 43–44
Cain, 56, 116
Cameron, Marjorie, 11
Carlisle, Belinda, 158
Carnegie, Dale, 208
Carroll, Peter J., 93
   Liber Null & Psychonaut, 53, 94
Casaubon, Isaac, 41
Case, Paul Foster, 271
Castaneda, Carlos, 52–53, 174–175, 178–179, 205–206
Castel, Jacqueline, 128, 183
caste systems, 64–66, 65–66, 109, 177, 179
Catholicism, 24, 25
   backlash against occultism and, 42–43
   Freemasonry and, 44
   Hermeticism and, 36–38
   Inquisition and, 43–44
   Paulines/Daughters of St. Paul, 83
   Protestantism vs., 40–41, 42–43

Catholicism (*cont.*)
   Vatican and exorcism, 17–18
   see also Biblical passages;
     Christianity
causation
   backwards, *see* precognition/
     retrocausality
   thoughts as causative, 171, *see
     also* New Thought
Cavendish, Richard
   The Black Arts/The Magical Arts,
     78–80
   Man, Myth & Magic, 80
Cayce, Edgar, 57–58
ceremonial magick, 11–14,
   48–49, 98, 117–118
   sigil/chaos magick vs., 51–52
chaos/sigil magick, 53
   ceremonial magick vs., 51–52
   chaos theory and, 52, 94–95,
     204
   cut-up magick and, 94, 99–105
   established lines of growth
     (Wattle) and, 97–98, 231
   sigil work and, 93–96, 172,
     173, 231
   Spare and, 172
chaos theory, 52, 94–95, 204
children
   bullying and, 191
   early experiences and sexuality,
     76–77
   exposing infants to mirrors, 198
   importance of earliest
     memories, 16
   make-believe and, 229, 231,
     233
   in reincarnation studies, 249
   social media and, 18–19
Chinmoy, Sri, 39
Christianity
   Beatitudes, 62
   Christ/Jesus Christ and, 24, 27,
     31, 41, 58, 113, 199, 204
   Constantine and, 34, 53, 59
   Kabbalah and, 46–48
   Protestantism, 25, 40–43
   see also Biblical passages;
     Catholicism
Churchill, Winston, 147–148, 149
Church of Satan, 117
Clarke, Arthur C., 232
Clement, Pope, 204
Clement XII, Pope, 44
Conan Doyle, Arthur, 243
conditioned idealism (Spare), 92
confidential communications,
   213–214
confirmation bias, 15n
Confucianism, 58
consciousness theory, 29–30, 93,
   150, 163–164, 226–227, 228,
   231–232
Constantine, 34, 53, 59
Constantinople, 34, 59
Corpus Hermeticum, 31, 33, 41,
   42, 273, 275
Coué, Émile, *My Method,
   Including American
   Impressions*, 91–92

Court de Gébelin, Antoine, *Le Monde Primitif/The Primitive World*, 47
Covey, Edward, 73–74
Crowley, Aleister, 113
   The Book of the Law, 50, 77–78, 228
   ceremonial magick and, 11–12, 20, 51–52, 117–118
   definition of magick, 20
   Hermetic Order of the Golden Dawn and, 49, 50, 99
   Kabbalah and, 48
   On the Rights of Man *(Liber Oz)*, 11–12
   Thelema (Will), 50, 117–118
   True Self, 50, 78
   True Will, 77, 81, 94, 115
cruelty, 73–74, 111–112, 191, 192–195
Crumb, Robert, 104
curses, 67–69
cut-up magick, 94, 99–105
   applications of, 101–103
   essential ethic of, 103–105
   origins of, 99–100
cycles of nature, 67–68, 130–131, 146–148, 150, 198
Cypher Manuscripts, 49

D

Dartmouth College, 260
Dass, Ram, 145
Davis, Andrew Jackson (Poughkeepsie Seer), 46
DCA (definite chief aim), 127–128, 184–186, 234, 238, 239
death
   covenants with, 122–123
   as a mental phenomenon, 226
   parapsychology/psi research on reincarnation, 249
   Sheol (afterworld) and, 122–123
   supraliminal mind (Myers) and, 87
   wearing black while mourning, 202–203
The Death of Superman (graphic novel), 56
Dee, John, 41, 172
deity worship and petition, 125–135
   in anarchic magick, 129–131
   ethics and emotion as basis of, 23–24
   as fundamental to spirituality, 14–16
   grimoires (spell books) in, 13–14, 17, 26, 38, 40, 53
   New York Public Library Prometheus figures and, 134–135
   "spirit binding" and, 17, 40
   worship as self-expansion, 131–132
de Molay, Jacques, 204
demons/daemons
   exorcism and demonic possession, 17–18
   as term, 16–17

Deutsch, L. D., *Time, Myth, and Matter*, 163
Dhammapada, 62
Diana (god), 183
dice throws, 248–249
D'Intino, Antonio, 128
Diotima (prophetess), 84–85
Dirnberger, Jake, *The Pocket Austin Osman Spare*, 93
disincarnate entities
  demons/daemons, 16–17
  jinn/genie, 17
DisInfo Con (2015), 93
Ditko, Steve, 104
Dos Passos, John, *U.S.A.*, 100
Douglass, Frederick, 73–74, 193
dream research, 250
drugs, 52–53, 78, 178–179, 208–209
Duke University, Parapsychology Laboratory/Rhine Research Center, 243–249, 260–262
Dutweiler Institute, 258
Dylan, Bob, 121–122, 189

E

Einstein, Albert
  linearity as illusion and, 152, 262
  relativity theories, 163, 167, 223–224, 250, 262
  second law of thermodynamics, 162, 163
Eisner, Will, 104
Eliot, T. S.
  The Hollow Men, 58
  The Waste Land, 100, 101
Elizabeth I, Queen, 41
Ellegua (Eshu), 121, 122
The Emerald Tablet/Table, 32, 37
Emerson, Ralph Waldo, 60, 77
  "Circles," 212
  "Compensation," 67
  The Conduct of Life, 195–196
  "Fate," 230
  "Power," 195–196
  "Self-Reliance," 132–133, 135
Emmanuel Movement, 265–266
emotions
  empathy and, 56–57
  parapsychology and, 154
  as source of ethics, 23–24
empathy
  in deity worship and petition, 23
  as ethics, 55–57
  fine emotions and, 56–57
  honest discussions and, 195
  as magnetic center (Gurdjieff), 57
Enlightenment, 26–27, 43, 60, 247
Enochian (language), 172
enthusiasm, optimism vs., 212–213
entropy, 162, 166
equinoxes, 131
Eriksen, Leif, 126
Eros, 84–85
Erotic Crystallization Inertia (ECI), 77, 173–175
Escolà-Gascón, Álex, 18
Eshu (Ellegua), 121, 122

esotericism, 18, 18n, 20, 26, 29, 31, 36, 40
   Freemasonry, 43–45, 47, 50
   see also Hermeticism
ESP (extrasensory perception), 128, 157, 243, 244–246, 249, 250, 253–254, 259–262, see also parapsychology/psi research
established lines of growth (Wattle), 97–98, 231
ethics and magick, 55–80
   curses and, 67–69
   cycle of preparation and payment, 67–69
   emotions as source of ethics, 23–24
   empathy in, 55–57
   gaslighting and, 193–194
   karma (cosmic reciprocity) and, 65–67, 75, 110–111, 161–162, 180
   Pirkei Avot or *Ethics of the Fathers* (Talmudic text), 57, 62, 142
   power and, 55, 69–73, 79
   precursory ethics, 62–66
   self-honesty and, 76–77
   see also religions *and specific religions*
Euripides, 60
Evans, David, *Tommy Johnson*, 120–121
Eve, 56, 115–116
Everard, John, 42
Everett, Hugh, III, 220–221, 224, 226–227, 228, 232
Ewen, Stuart, 171
exorcism, 17–18
The Exorcist (1973 movie), 18, 127

F

failure
   as learning experience, 210–211
   as protective, 210
   too much success, too soon vs., 211
Faithfull, Marianne, 52
Farr, Florence, 49
Faust, Johann Georg, 120
Faust legend, 16, 58, 79, 119–120, 230–231
Feather, Sally Rhine, 261
Ferdinand II, 42–43
Few, William Preston, 243
Feyerabend, Paul, 62, 118
Feynman, Richard, 166–167, 168–169
Flowers, Stephen E., *Lords of the Left-Hand Path*, 172
forgiveness, 111, 160
Fort, Charles, 241
Fortune, Dion, 49
Fox, Kate and Margaret, 45–46
Frankenstein (Shelley), 35, 80
Frankfurt School, 150–151
Franklin, Benjamin, 44–45
Freemasonry, 43–45, 47, 50
   Grand Lodge of England, 44
   Illuminati, 44
Freud, Sigmund, 242–243, 259

G

Gandhi, Mahatma, 179–180, 183
ganzfeld experiments, 250–254, 263
Garden of Eden/Paradise, 56, 115–116
Gardner, Gerald, 113
  Witchcraft Today, 52
gaslighting, 193–194
gender, in Hermeticism, 274
genii/jinn/genies, 17, 86–87
genius, 86–87
George (magazine), 210
Glock Gaston, 133–134
Gnostic sects, 25–26
Goddard, Neville
  gestation time between thought and action, 229, 230–231
  hypnagogia and, 228–229
  imagination as God and, 112
  lectures, 111–112, 165–169, 220, 227–228
  lefthand path of attainment and, 111–112
  make-believe and, 229–230
  mystical analog to quantum physics and, 227–233
  New Thought and, 14, 220
  popularity of, 112
  pruning shears of revision and, 159–160, 161
  retrocausation and, 165–166, 168
  time passage and, 230–231
Goethe, Johann Wolfgang von, *Faust*, 16, 79, 119–120, 230–231

Goetia/The Lesser Key of Solomon (spell book), 13–14
Goldi, Anna, 43
Google Willow (quantum-computing processor), 220–221
gossip, 194–195
graphic novels, 23, 56
Great Recession, 190
Greene, Heather, *Lights, Camera, Witchcraft*, 114
Greene, Robert, *The 48 Laws of Power*, 184
Greer, Michael, *Doctrine and Ritual* (with Mikituk), 82–83
grimoires (spell books)
  contemporary, 53
  Goetia/The Lesser Key of Solomon (spell book), 13–14
  Liber Medicinalis (Samonicus), 26
  Picatrix/The Goal of the Sage, 38
  "spirit binding" and, 17, 40
Gurdjieff, G. I., 13, 42, 57, 65, 67, 237–239
Gysin, Brion, *The Third Mind* (with Burroughs), 51, 100–101, 103–104

H

Hanegraaff, Wouter J., 31
Hanley, Spencer, 156–158
happiness, 57, 64, 77, 175, 192, 205–206
Harrington, Michael, *Socialism*, 113

Hartmann, Franz, *Magic*, 108
Harvard Medical School, Program in Placebo Studies and the Therapeutic Encounter (PiPS), 234–235
Hemon, Aleksandar, 104
Heraclitus, 94–95
Hercules (god), 183
Hermes (god), 41, 60, 121, 122
Hermes Trismegistus (thrice-greatest Hermes), 60, 271, 273, 275
Hermeticism, 31–34
  as above, so below, 31–33, 36–37, 69–70, 74, 103, 131–132, 177
  Catholicism and, 36–38
  Corpus Hermeticum, 31, 33, 41, 42, 273, 275
  The Emerald Tablet/Table, 32, 37
  Hermetic Order of the Golden Dawn, 49–52, 99
  The Kybalion, 42, 204, 269–275
  The Kybalion (2020 documentary), 102, 275
  like attracting like, 33, 60, 68, 74, 198
  Nous (Overmind), 31, 32, 51, 87, 224–225, 272–274, 275
  Picatrix/The Goal of the Sage and, 38
  Tarot and, 47, 137–138, 144, 146
hieroglyphics, 27–28, 59–60
Hill, Napoleon
  genii/jinn/genies, 86–87
  Infinite Intelligence and, 87
  sex transmutation and, 51, 81–89, 175
  Think and Grow Rich, 84, 104–105, 127, 191–192
Hinduism, 24, 58, 59, 162
history of magick, 21–53
  astrology in, 30–31, 38, 47
  deity worship and petition in, 23–24
  freemasonry in, 43–45, 47, 50
  Hermeticism in, 31–34, 36–37, 38, 41–42, 47
  Neanderthal and early hominid spirituality in, 21–23
  occultism and backlash in, 16–17, 38–50
  religions in, 24–30, 34–38, 40–44, 53
  Rosicrucianism in, 40–41, 44, 50
  sigil/chaos magick in, 51–52
  Tarot in, 36–37, 47
  Theosophy in, 19, 48–49
Hitler, Adolf, 51
Hodgson, Richard, 242
Homer, 60
hominid spirituality, 21–23
homosexuality, 63
honesty
  frankness about your aim, 184–186
  gaslighting vs., 193–194
Honorton, Charles, 247, 250–254
hoodoo, 45, 73–74, 121, 197, 201
Horowitz, Mitch
  awards and honors, 126–127

Horowitz, Mitch (*cont.*)
  in *Beyond: UFOs and the Unknown* (2024 MGM docuseries), 128
  correspondence with prison inmates, 112–113, 237–239
  Daydream Believer (2022), 101–103, 237–238
  Extraordinary Evidence: ESP Is Real (podcast), 128
  family background, 191, 233
  as host of *Alien Encounters* (Discovery/HBO/Max series), 128, 129, 140–141, 183
  The Kybalion (2020 documentary), 102, 275
  Mind as Builder (2017), 57–58
  The Miracle Club (2018), 262
  Modern Occultism (2023), 103–104
  in *My Animal* (2023 movie), 128, 183
  Occult America (2009), 211, 270–271
  One Simple Idea (2014), 233
  on *The Proof Is Out There* (History Channel series), 128–129
  as Romantic Satanist, 57–58
  Science of Mind article on Neville Goddard (2005), 112
  TarcherPenguin imprint and, 190
  Theosophical Society in America course on magick (2022), 19–20
  on *The Unbelievable* (History Channel series), 128, 182–183
  in V/H/S/BEYOND 2024 installment, 128, 183
horror movie genre, 18
horseshoes, 200–201
hospitality, to strangers, 96
Howard, Vernon, 195
Howe, Irving, *The American Newness*, 151
Hubbard, Elbert, "Credo," 212
Hubbard, L. Ron, 11
Hume, David, 164, 247
humiliating others, avoiding, 213–214
Hyman, Ray, 252–254
hypnogogia, 228–229, 251
hypnopompia, 251

I

I Ching *(Book of Changes)*, 28–30
  Tarot and, 139, 142–143, 144–145
  time and, 150
Igrath (autumnal equinox), 131
Illuminati, 44
India
  caste system, 65–66, 177, 179
  nonviolent political change in, 179–180
  social and religious cultures of, 180
  Theosophical Society relocation to (1878), 19, 48, 179–180
  unlucky thirteen and, 203

Institute of Noetic Sciences
  (IONS), 153, 244, 248
Introvigne, Massimo, 18
intuition
  harnessing, 217
  in quick and decisive action,
    216–217
Isaacs, Oscar, 132
Islam, 24, 25, 59, 67, 68, 107,
  131–132

J
Jacuzzi, Geneva, 123
Jagger, Mick, 206
James, William, 94, 242
  on being appreciated, 214
  "Is Life Worth Living?," 14–15
  pragmatism, 92
  *The Varieties of Religious
    Experience*, 265
Jansen, Gary, 83
Japan Society (New York City),
  123
Jenkins, Sandy, 73
Jesus Christ/Christ, 24, 27, 31,
  41, 58, 113, 199, 204
Jewish Publication Society (JPS),
  122–123
jinn (genie), as term, 17, 86–87
John Paul II, Pope, 37
Johnson, LeDell, 120–121
Johnson, Robert, 120
Johnson, Tommy, 120–121
Jones, Ernest, 243, 259
Joseph, 25
Journal of Near-Death Studies, 249

Journal of Parapsychology, 252
Journal of Scientific Exploration,
  18
Jowett, Benjamin, 84
Judaism, 24–26, 35, 59, 63, 107
  Hebrew alphabet and Tarot, 47
  Kabbalah and, 25, 35, 40, 45,
    84, 270
  mezuzahs and, 24–25, 63
  Talmudic texts, *Pirkei Avot* or
    Ethics of the Fathers, 57, 62, 142
Judas Iscariot, 203
Judge, William Quan, 48
Julius Caesar, 110
jumping the broom, 201
Jung, Carl, 94, 101, 142, 144–145
Jupiter (god), 34, 129, 200
justice, 161–162
Justinian, 34

K
Kabbalah, 25, 35, 40, 45, 270
  Christian, 46–48
  Crowley and, 48
  Lévi and, 46–48
  rulebook and, 133
  sex transmutation and, 84
Kafatos, Menas C., 224
Kahn, Pir Vilayat Inayat, 68–69,
  75
Kali (goddess), 129
Kandinsky, Wassily, *Concerning
  the Spiritual in Art*, 36
karma (cosmic reciprocity),
  65–67, 75, 110–111, 161–162,
  180

Kastrup, Bernardo, 224
Kaufmann, Walter, 66
Kennedy, John F., Jr., 210
Khan, Hazrat Inayat, 75
Khan, Pir Vilayat Inaya, 68–69, 75
Kia (Spare), 51, 81, 92–93, 94
Kidman, Nicole, 76–77
Kingsford, Anna, 273
K M T *(Kemet),* 27–28
Knight, Michael Muhammed, 131–132
Knights Templar, 204
know thyself, 69–70, 74
Krishnamurti, Jiddu, 135, 179
The Kybalion, 42, 204, 269–275
The Kybalion (2020 documentary), 102, 275

L
Labouré, Catherine, 83
ladders, walking under, 199
Langer, Ellen, 175–176
Lanza, Robert, 226
Lao Tzu, 60
Last Supper, 199, 203
LaVey, Anton, 171–174
  Balance Factor and, 172
  Church of Satan, 117, 171
  The Cloven Hoof (newsletter), 186–187
  The Devil's Notebook, 96, 173
  Erotic Crystallization Inertia (ECI), 77, 173–175
  pragmatic magic and, 172
  ritual or ceremony and, 172–173
  The Satanic Bible, 172

law of cycles, 146–147
Leadbeater, Charles, 48
  Thought Forms (with Besant), 36
Lee, Spike, 132
lefthand path of attainment, 107–124
  "dark side"/Satanism and, 109–110, 113–117
  Flowers and, 172
  nature of, 107–108, 109
  reverse pentagram and, 39, 40, 102, 108, 114
  risk and, 118–119
  as self-driven, 107
  vamachara (lefthanded attainment), 39, 108
Leonardo da Vinci, "The Last Supper," 199
Lévi, Eliphas (Alphonse-Louis Constant), 46–50, 51, 81–84
  astral light and, 51, 81–83
  The Doctrine and Ritual of High Magick, 46–47, 108, 189–190
  Kabbalah and, 46–48
  sexuality-thought-will and, 83–84
light of nature (Paracelsus), 51
light of speculative thought (Schopenhauer), 33, 51, 81–82, 94, 103
like attracting like (occultism), 33, 60, 68, 74, 198
Lilith (vernal equinox), 131
Lincoln, Abraham, 46
Lincoln, Mary Todd, 46

linearity
  as illusion, 143, 149–151, 152, 165–169, 176, 223–227, 233, 262–263
  see also precognition/retrocausality
Loew of Prague, Rabbi, 35
Loki (god), 203
Lucifer (light-bringer), 56, 82–83, 109, 118
luck, 197–218
  behavioral rules for fostering, 204–218
  charms and talismans of magick, 197
  omens of good and bad luck, 197–204
  Thirteen Aphorisms of Good Luck, 217–218

M

magick
  as causative ritual, 13
  Crowley and, 11–12, 20, 51–52, 117–118
  ethics and, *see* ethics and magick
  greater truth about human condition and, 235–236
  history of, *see* history of magick
  human "wish box" relationship with, 71–73
  interdimensional existence and, 235–236
  Eliphas Lévi and, 46–50, 51, 81–84
  Parsons and, 11–12, 13
  psyche and, 12–14
  as term, 11, 13, 20, 61
  Theosophical Society in America course (2022), 19–20
  warranted belief and, 12–13, 235, *see also* parapsychology/psi research
magickal primitivism, 23
Mahalath (winter solstice), 131
Maharishi Mahesh Yogi, 272
Maier, Michael, *Lusus Serius,* 138
Maimonides Medical Center (Brooklyn), Division of Parapsychology and Pschophysics, 250–252
Malcolm X (1992 movie), 132
Marcus Aurelius, *Meditations,* 62
Marlowe, Christopher, *Doctor Faustus,* 58, 119–120
marriage
  "jumping the broom," 201
  see also relationships
Marx, Karl, 42
materialism, 104, 118, 245
Mathers, Moina, 49
Mathers, S. I. MacGregor, 49
The Matrix (1999 movie), 210–211
Matthews, Luke J., 18
Mayan Long-Count calendar, 150
McComb, Samuel, *Body, Mind, and Spirit* (with Worcester), 265–266

McDougall, William, 243
McKenna, Terence, 29–30, 145
McMartin Preschool (California), 114
Mead, G. R. S., 42
Thrice-Great Hermes, 273
Meditations on the Tarot, 36, 37
mediums/mediumship, 46, 61, 242
Mellet, Comte de, 47
mental-emotive focus, 234–235
Mercury (god), 34, 38, 121, 130, 183
Mesmer, Franz Anton, 46
  animal magnetism, 45, 51, 81, 82, 94
Meyer, Peter J., 29–30
mezuzahs, 24–25, 63
Michael (archangel), 40
Miguel, 13–14
Mikituk, Anthony, *Doctrine and Ritual* (with Greer), 82–83
Milton, John, 56
  Paradise Lost, 110, 119
Minerva (goddess), 34, 53, 129
Miraculous Medal (1830), 83
mirror, breaking a, 198
Mishima, Yukio, *Sun and Steel*, 34, 233
Moore, Alan, 104
Mormonism, 24–25, 26
Morrison, Grant, 93
Moses, 24, 41
Moses de Leon, Rabbi, 35
A Most Violent Year (2014 movie), 132

mourning process, 202–203
Muhammad, 24, 69
Murphy, Joseph, 13–14
Murray, Margaret, 52
Museum of the Moving Image (Astoria, Queens), 127
music, 120–122, 206
My Animal (2023 movie), 128, 183
Myers, Frederic W. H., 241–242, 251
  Human Personality and Its Survival of Bodily Death, 87

N

Naamah (summer solstice), 131
Neanderthal spirituality, 21–22
Needleman Jacob, 215, 217, 270
Nehru, Jawaharlal, 179–180, 183
Neoplatonism, 34, 37, 274
New Age culture
  crisis of, 229
  exorcism and, 17–18
  Satanism and, 117
  "white magic," 78, 108
New Thought
  The Kybalion (2020 documentary), 102, 275
  The Kybalion and, 42, 204, 269–275
  Murphy and, 13–14
  Wattles and, 97–98, 231
  see also Goddard, Neville
Newton, Isaac, 32, 157
New York Public Library, Prometheus figures, 134–135

New York Times, 104, 119
Nietzsche, Friedrich, 77
   Beyond Good and Evil, 66, 79, 161–162
Noah, Daniel, 128
Nobel Prize, 78, 166–167, 168, 242
nonattachment ideal, 64, 108, 176–177
"No," responding to, 211–212
Norumbega Tower (Charles River, Massachusetts), 126–127
Nous (Overmind), 31, 32, 51, 87, 224–225, 272–274, 275

O

Objectivism (Rand), 117, 118
objectification, 61, 66
occultism, 16–17, 38–50
   backlash against, 42–44
   critics of, 150–151
   defense of, 116–119
   Eastern traditions vs., 58–59
   emergence of, 60–61
   esotericism vs., 18n
   as term, 48, 61
   viewed as sound approach, 150–151
   see also Hermeticism
Olcott, Henry Steel, 48, 61
omens of luck, 197–204
   black cats, 203
   breaking a mirror, 198
   horseshoes, 200–201
   jumping the broom, 201
   knocking on wood, 198–199
   opening an umbrella indoors, 200
   rabbit's foot, 197, 201–202
   sneezing, 200
   spilling salt, 199
   thirteen, 203–204
   walking under a ladder, 199
   wearing black while mourning, 202–203
   wrong side of the bed, 202
optimism, enthusiasm vs., 212–213
orgone (sexual energy), 88
Ouspensky, P. D., *In Search of the Miraculous,* 238
Ovalle, María Alejandra, 18

P

Paganini, Niccolò, 120
Pan (god), 34, 183
Paracelsus, 51
parapsychology/psi research, 13, 110–111, 151–157, 241–264
   areas of study in, 242, –243, 248, 249, 261–262
   Bem and, 151–157, 255–257
   bridge between causative nature of the psyche and, 154
   critics and skeptics, 247–248, 252–255, 256–260
   Duke University Parapsychology Laboratory/Rhine Research Center, 243–249, 260–262
   ESP (extrasensory perception), 128, 157, 243, 244–246, 249, 250, 253–254, 259–262

parapsychology/psi research (*cont.*)
  ganzfeld experiments, 250–254, 263
  Honorton and, 247, 250–254
  Hyman and, 252–254
  hypnogogia and, 228–229, 251
  inception of field, 241–242, 254
  lack of funding for, 254–255, 259
  Maimonides Medical Center (Brooklyn) Division of Parapsychology and Pschophysics, 250–252
  need for theory of conveyance, 260–262
  psi effect and, 154, 155, 249, 252, 256, 262
  Rhine and, 56, 94, 95, 154, 243–244, 245–249, 256, 260–262
  séances and, 242
  Seven Laws of Parapsychology, 264
  Sheldrake and, 249, 258, 261
  telepathy and, 242–243, 248–251, 259–263
  thought causation and, 154
  transformation to academic science, 56
  University of Virginia, Division of Perceptual Studies, 249
  Weaver and, 260–262
  Zener cards in, 246–249, 251
  see also precognition/retrocausality
Parsons, Jack
  ceremonial magick and, 11–12, 13
  Crowley and, 11–12
  death (1952), 11
  "On Magick," 12
passion
  emotional stakes in precognition studies, 256
  enthusiasm vs. optimism, 212–213, 218
  getting noticed, 206–207
Pasteur, Louis, 208
Peace of Westphalia (1648), 43
pentagram, reverse, 39, 40, 102, 108, 114
Pentland, Lord John, 65–66
Perry, Jim, 128
persistence
  importance of, 209–210, 217–218
  responding to "no" and, 211–212
Philip IV, King, 204
Picatrix/The Goal of the Sage, 38
Pirkei Avot or *Ethics of the Fathers* (Talmudic text), 57, 62, 142
Pirsig, Robert, *Zen and the Art of Motorcycle Maintenance*, 232
Place, Robert M., *The Tarot*, 139–141
placebo research, 234–235
Plato, 60
  Symposium, 84
Plutarch, 110
Pol Pot, 113
polytheism, 34, 58
Porreca, David, 38
P-Orridge, Genesis, 104

Powell, Colin, 181–182
power
   being "in the know" and, 195
   components of, 195–196
   concentration as, 69–73
   ethics and, 55, 69–73, 79
   laws of, 184
   to limit relationships, 194
   of persistence, 209–210
precognition/retrocausality, 154–169, 244
   backwards movement in time, 162–164
   Bem and, 151–157, 255–257
   evidence for, 152, 153, 156–158, 166–167, 168
   Feynman and, 166–167, 168–169
   Goddard and, 165–166, 168
   linearity as illusion and, 149–151, 152, 262–263
   Quantum Retrocausation III (QRC-III), 163–164
   Retroactive Recall effect, 255–257
   30-Day Mental Challenge, 157, 265–267
preparation, importance of, 208
prisons/incarcerated population
   author correspondence with inmates, 112–113, 237–239
   prison ministries and, 57–58
   Theosophy and, 19–20
Proclus, 34, 60
Prometheus (god), 134–135
Protestantism, 25, 40–43
pseudoepigrapha (false writings), 40
pseudoskepticism, 151–152
psi research, *see* parapsychology/psi research
psyche
   bridge between ceremony and, 13–14
   deity worship and, 15–16
   magick and, 12–14
psychedelics, 52–53
psychics, 57, 95
psychokinesis (PK), 248
Ptolemy, Claudius, *Tetrabiblos* ("Four Books"), 30, 31
Ptolemy V, 59
public speaking, 208
Purdue, Eric, 17
Putin, Vladimir, 114
Pythagoreanism, 34
Pythagorus, 60

Q

quantum computing, 157, 220–221
Quantum Retrocausation III (QRC-III), 163–164
quantum theory, 162–164, 220–227
   information leakage and, 222–223
   linearity as illusion, 143, 149–151, 176, 223–227, 233, 262–263
   "many worlds" theory (Everett) in, 220–221, 224, 226–227, 228, 232

quantum theory (*cont.*)
  multidimensional reality and, 224–228, 235–236
  quantum measurement problem, 222–223, 227–228, 263–264
  Schrödinger's Cat thought experiment and, 160, 225–227
  spiritual theories and, 221–233
  transpersonal mind and, 224–225
  wave state of superposition in, 220–221, 225–227
  see also Einstein, Albert; precognition/retrocausality
quick and decisive action, 216–217
Quinn, D. Michael, *Early Mormonism and the Magic World View*, 26

R
rabbit's foot, 197, 201–202
Radin, Dean, 23, 56, 153, 221, 222, 244, 248, 255
Rand, Ayn, Objectivism, 117, 118
Randi, James, 151–152
recognition, importance of giving, 214–215
Regardie, Israel, 49
Reich, Wilhelm, 88
reincarnation, 249
relationships
  chemistry in collaboration, 206
  cruelty and, 73–74, 111–112, 192–195
  gossip and, 194–195
  jumping the broom in marriage ceremonies, 201
  as key to fortune, 148
  love and intimacy and fulfillment in, 96–98
  power to limit number of, 194
  recognizing and thanking others, 214–215
reliability, 215–216
religions, 24–30, 34–38, 40–44
  Abrahamic tradition, 25, 39, 42, 59, 64, 67, 107
  Eastern traditions, 30, 33, 36, 39, 42, 58–59, 62, 64, 65–66, 107–108, 146, 176, 195
  In God We Trust and, 53
  in the history of magick, 24–30, 34–38, 40–44, 53
  miraculous claims and, 24
  nature of religious models, 118–119
  polytheism and, 34, 58
  as product of human hands, 177
  religious history and, 60–61
  Theosophy and universality of, 61–62, 63
respect, humiliating others vs, 213–214
retrocausality, *see* precognition/retrocausality
reverberation, 160
reverse pentagram, 39, 40, 102, 108, 114
Rhine, J. B., 94, 95

Duke University Parapsychology Laboratory/Rhine Research Center, 243–249, 260–262
Extra-Sensory Perception, 154, 248
New Frontiers of the Mind, 154, 256
New World of the Mind, 261
transformation of psi studies into academic science, 56, 154
Rhine, Louisa, 243
Richet, Charles, 242
risk
  lefthand path of attainment and, 118–119
  Satanism and, 117, 118–119
Ritchie, Stuart J., 257
Romantic Satanism, *see* Satanism
Roosevelt, Franklin D., 197, 202, 203–204
Rosetta Stone, 59
Rosicrucianism, 40–41, 44, 50
Ruska, Julius, 32

S
sacred triangle, 199
salt, spilling, 199
Samonicus, Serenus, 26
Sanders, Bernie, 113
Satan, 55–56
Satanic Temple, 117
Satanism, 55–58, 109–117
  "dark side" and, 109–110, 113–117
  defense of occult or metaphysical practices and, 116–119
  lefthand path of attainment and, 109–110, 113–117
  music and, 120–122
  pact with *Sheol* (afterworld) and, 122–123
  prejudice against, 117
  Putin and, 114
  redefining, 115–116
  risks of following, 117, 118–119
  Romantic poets and writers and, 55–56, 110, 115–116, 119, 132–133
  Satanic Panic and, 114, 117
  soul selling and, 119–123
  as term, 61
  see also LaVey, Anton
Saturn (god), 38
Scholem, Gershom, *Major Trends In Jewish Mysticism,* 48
Schopenhauer, Arthur
  light of speculative thought, 33, 51, 81–82, 94, 103
  On Will in Nature, 81–82
Schrödinger, Erwin
  linearity as illusion and, 152
  Schrödinger's Cat thought experiment, 160, 225–227
Schwaller de Lubicz, R. A., 150, 151
Science of Mind magazine, 112
Scientific American, 224
Scientology, 11
séances, 45, 46, 242

Secret Transmissions (online 'zine), 129–130
Sefer Yetzirah (Book of Formation), 35
self-creation, 117, 118
self-expression, 109, 177
self-honesty, 76–77
self-image, 176, 180–184
self-knowledge, 69–70, 74, 182–184
self-possession, 181–182
self-worth, 177
Senusret I, 25
Set (god), 129
sexuality
  Baby Girl (2024 movie) and, 76–77
  childhood experiences and, 76–77
  as creative urge, 85–88
  Erotic Crystallization Inertia (ECI, LaVey), 77, 173–175
  erotic images in precognition studies, 255–256
  homosexuality prohibitions, 63
  LaVey and, 77, 172–175
  sex transmutation (Hill), 51, 81–89, 175
  sigil work and, 93–98, 175
  total environments (LaVey) and, 171–173
Shadad (Destroyer), 24
Shaddai (Almighty), 24
shamanism, 52, 107
Sheehan, Daniel, 163–164
Sheldrake, Rupert, 249, 258, 261

Shelley, Mary, 80
Shelley, Percy Bysshe, 110
Sheol (afterworld), 122–123
Shintoism, 58
siddhis (attainments in Sanskrit), 24, 39
sigil magick, *see* chaos/sigil magick
silence, 189–196
  around magickal operations, 189–193
  opinions of others and, 190, 191–192
  seeking validation vs., 190–191
Singer, Isaac Bashevis, 78–79
Sinnett, A. P., 48
60 Minutes, 121–122, 189
Smith, Joseph, 26
Smith, Lucy Mack, 26
Smith, Pamela Colman, 139, 141, 144
sneezing, 200
sobriety, 208–209
social cohesion, 63–64
social media, 18–19, 68, 141–142, 194, 207, 213–214, 258
Society for Psychical Research (SPR), 241–242, 254
Socrates, 84–85
Solomon, King, 40
solstices, 131
soul selling, 119–123
Spann, Leslie, 184–186
Spare, Austin Osman, 91–96
  The Book of Pleasure (Self Love), 94
  The Formulae of Zos Vel Thanatos, 92, 95

Kia, 51, 81, 92–93, 94
  sigil work and, 53, 91, 92–96, 99
  Zos, 51, 92–95
SpectreVision, 128
spell work
  in anarchic magick, 125–131
  author participation in, 129–130, 133–134
  fear surrounding, 75
  see also grimoires (spell books)
"spirit binding," 17, 40
spirit raps, 45–46
Spiritualism, 46, 243
spirituality, 21–22
spontaneity of action, *see* anarchic magick
Sri Chinmoy movement (1931–2007), 39
Stalker (1979 movie), 70–73
Stapp, Henry P., 224
Star Trek (2009 movie), 232
Stevens, Matthew Levi, 103
Stevenson, Ian, 249
string theory, 118, 261, 263
Strugatsky, Arkady and Boris, *Roadside Picnic*, 70–73
Strummer, Joe, 206
subconscious mind, 14, 45, 87, 236, 274
Suckley, Margaret, 202
suffering, 67–68, 231–232
Sufism, 68–69, 75
Sun Tzu, 60
Superman, 23, 56
superstitions, 197–200, 202–203
Swedenborg, Emanuel, 44–45

T

Talmudic texts, *Pirkei Avot* or *Ethics of the Fathers*, 57, 62, 142
Tantra
  sex transmutation and, 84
  varmachara (lefthanded attainment), 39, 108
Taoism, 58, 62, 84, 92–93, 107, 150, 195
Tao Te Ching, 62, 150
Tarkovsky, Andrei, 70–73
Tarot, 137–148
  carte de trionfi, 137
  effectiveness of, 141–148
  Florentine Tarot, 144
  Grand Etteila Tarot, 47, 138–139
  Hermeticism and, 47, 137–138, 144, 146
  history of, 47, 137–141
  I Ching and, 139, 142–143, 144–145
  imagery of, 137–141, 144
  linearity as illusion and, 143
  Marseilles Tarot, 137, 138–139, 144
  Meditations on the Tarot, 36, 37
  Sola Busca Tarot, 139
  three-card method, 139–141
  Wheel of Fortune, 144, 146–148, 209–210, 216
Tartini, Giuseppe, 120
telepathy, 242–243, 248–251, 259–263
Temple of Set, 117
Tequfot (equinoxes and solstices), 131

Terayama, Shuji, *Duke Bluebeard's Castle*, 123–124
Thelema (Will), 50, 117–118
The Theosophist (journal), 120
Theosophy/Theosophical Society
  founding (1875), 19, 48–49, 61
  Hermetic Order of the Golden Dawn and, 49–52, 99
  members of, 36, 48–49
  relocation to India (1878), 19, 48, 179–180
  Theosophical Society in America course on magick (2022), 19–20
  universality of religion and, 61–62, 63
Think and Grow Rich (Hill), 84, 104–105, 127, 191–192
thirteen, fear of, 203–204
30 Day Mental Challenge, 157, 265–267
Thirty Years' War (1618–1648), 42–43
Thomas, Ronni, 128, 275
Tibetan Buddhism, 36, 99–100
time, linearity as illusion and, 143, 149–151, 176, 223, 233, 262–263
Timewave Zero (calendar), 29–30
Tithonus (Trojan prince), 80
Tolstoy, Leo, *War and Peace*, 149–150
Tomberg, Valentin, 36–37
total environments, 171–187
  Castaneda and, 174–175
  dress/costumery and, 176, 179–182
  Erotic Crystallization Inertia (ECI) and, 77, 173–175
  LaVey and, 171–174
  nature of, 171–172, 174
  priorities of others and, 186–187
  purposeful, intentional image in, 179–180
  self-image and, 176, 180–184
Transcendentalism, 146, 270, 274
Transcendental Meditation (TM), 24, 272
transpersonal mind, 224–225
Tree of Knowledge of Good and Evil, 115–116
Tree of Life, 115–116
triangle, sacred, 199
Trithemius, Johannes, 40
True Self (Crowley), 50, 78
True Will (Crowley), 77, 81, 94, 115
Trump, Donald, 52, 119
Trussell, Duncan, 118
Tull, Jethro, *Hymn 43*, 58
Tully, Grace, *F.D.R. My Boss*, 203–204

U

UFO encounters, 128, 134, 236, 263
umbrella, opening indoors, 200
Underhill, Evelyn, 49
University of Oregon, 252
University of San Diego (USD), 163–164

University of Virginia, Division of Perceptual Studies, 249
Utts, Jessica, 253, 254

V
Valiente, Doreen, Wiccan Rede, 113
vamachara (lefthanded attainment), 39, 108
Vanden Broeck, André, *Al-Kemi*, 150, 151
Vedic tradition, 19, 24, 30, 48–49, 64–67, 107–108, 202, 272
   karma (cosmic reciprocity) in, 65–67, 75, 110–111, 161–162, 180
Venus figurines, 22
virtual reality, 171–172
Vivekananda, Swami, 272
Vodou, 45, 121
voice quality, 181
Voodoo, 121
Vril (Bulwer-Lytton), 51, 81, 94

W
Wachtler, Aidan, 53
Waite, Arthur Edward, 49, 139
Warcollier, René, 242
Wattles, Wallace D.
   established lines of growth, 97–98, 231
   The Science of Getting Rich, 97
Weaver, Warren, 246, 260–262
Weiler, Craig, 258
Westermann, Claus, 115

Wheel of Fortune, 144, 146–148, 209–210, 216
White, Gordon, 53
Wicca, 52, 113
Wikipedia, 247–248, 254
Wilhelm, Richard, 29, 144–145
Willow (Google), 220–221
witchcraft
   cats as witch companions, 203
   modern, 52–53
   spilling salt and, 199
   Wicca and, 52, 113
   Witch Craze and, 43
   witch trials, 203
Wood, Elijah, 128
wood, knocking on, 198–199
Worcester, Elwood, *Body, Mind, and Spirit* (with McComb), 265–266
written communication
   anonymity and, 213–214
   confidential forms of, 213
   social media, 18–19, 68, 141–142, 194, 207, 213–214, 258

Y
Yeats, W. B., 49
Yogi Publication Society, 271

Z
Zener, Karl E., 246
Zener cards, 246–249, 251
Zeus (god), 60, 153–154
Zohar (Book of Splendor), 35
Zos (physical man or energy manifest), 51, 92–95

ABOUT THE AUTHOR

MITCH HOROWITZ is a historian of alternative spirituality and one of today's most literate voices of esoterica, mysticism, and the occult. Mitch is the PEN Award-winning author of books including *Occult America, One Simple Idea, The Miracle Club, Daydream Believer, Uncertain Places, Modern Occultism,* and *Happy Warriors. The Washington Post* says Mitch "treats esoteric ideas and movements with an even-handed intellectual studiousness that is too often lost in today's raised-voice discussions." *Filmmaker Magazine* calls him "a genius at distilling down esoteric concepts." Mitch hosts Discovery/HBO Max's *Alien Encounters: Fact or Fiction*, SpectreVision's podcast, *Extraordinary Evidence: ESP Is Real*, and plays himself in Shudder's *V/H/S/BEYOND*, a Critics Choice Award nominee. A former vice president at Penguin Random House, Mitch has written on alternative spirituality for *The New York Times*, *The Wall Street Journal*, *The Washington Post*, *Time*, *Politico*, and appeared widely in national media. Mitch's writing has called attention to the worldwide problem of violence against accused witches, helping draw notice to the human-rights element of the issue. Mitch's work has been translated into French, German, Arabic, Hebrew, Chinese, Italian, Spanish, Korean, Japanese, and Portuguese. He is censored in China.

www.ingramcontent.com/pod-product-compliance
Lightning Source LLC
Chambersburg PA
CBHW071954070526
44583CB00015B/1184